Religion and
Popular Culture
Second Edition

D1571027

Religion and Popular Culture

Rescripting the Sacred

SECOND EDITION

RICHARD W. SANTANA *and*
GREGORY ERICKSON

McFarland & Company, Inc., Publishers
Jefferson, North Carolina

LIBRARY OF CONGRESS CATALOGUING-IN-PUBLICATION DATA

Names: Santana, Richard W., author. | Erickson, Gregory, author.
Title: Religion and popular culture : rescripting the sacred / Richard W.
    Santana and Gregory Erickson.
Description: Second edition. | Jefferson, North Carolina : McFarland &
    Company, Inc., Publishers, 2016. | Includes bibliographical references
    and index.
Identifiers: LCCN 2016039318 | ISBN 9781476663319 (softcover : acid free
    paper) ∞
Subjects: LCSH: Religion and culture—United States. | Popular culture—
    Religious aspects. | United States—Religion.
Classification: LCC BL2525 .S258 2016 | DDC 201/.70973—dc23
LC record available at https://lccn.loc.gov/2016039318

BRITISH LIBRARY CATALOGUING DATA ARE AVAILABLE

ISBN (print) 978-1-4766-6331-9
ISBN (ebook) 978-1-4766-2708-3

Front cover image of Jesus Christ © 2016 CSA-Printstock/iStock

Printed in the United States of America

McFarland & Company, Inc., Publishers
    Box 611, Jefferson, North Carolina 28640
    www.mcfarlandpub.com

Table of Contents

Acknowledgments

This book is the result of many engaged discussions, considered thought and, on at least two occasions, moments of epiphanic outbursts while floating in a pond in upstate New York. No book comes to print without the help and support of many who give of themselves to improve the project. We would like to thank all who have been a part of this process, for their help, advice, and encouragement. Specifically we would like to thank the Rochester Institute of Technology for its generous support through the Paul and Francena Miller Faculty Fellowship, which afforded Richard time to bring this work to fruition, and New York University's Gallatin School of Individualized Study, which offered Greg financial and intellectual support. We would also like to thank the organizers and members of the Popular Culture Association/American Culture Association conferences, where many of our ideas were first exposed to public scrutiny. We would also like to thank all of the students we have had over the years for helping keep us engaged with new texts of popular culture. Greg's students in his yearly Religion and Popular Culture offered invaluable insight and advice for the second edition.

On a more personal note, we'd like to thank Tanya Radford, Jennifer Lemberg, Colleigh Stein, Tess Brewer, Melissa Bloom, and Craig Bernardini who privileged our text with their careful editorial eyes. We would like to thank our families for their support and forbearance while we worked on this rather lengthy project. We would like to thank Danese Santana and Angelina Tallaj for the love, emotional, corporeal, and spiritual support they have given us and for putting up with our protracted and distracted gaze once again as we took on a second edition.

A version of Chapter 2 appeared in *The Cooperstown Symposium on Baseball and American Culture, 2000* © 2001 State University of New York, College at Oneonta, by permission of McFarland & Company, Inc., Box 611, Jefferson NC 28640. www.mcfarlandpub.com.

Preface to the
Second Edition

The first edition of this book, written in the opening years of the twenty-first century and published in 2008, was conceived in a time when one still occasionally had to apologize for writing seriously about popular culture. Political and social events of those years also deeply influenced our ideas at the time: the attacks of 9/11, the decision to go to war in Iraq, the George W. Bush presidency, and the antagonistic rhetoric of the "new atheists." In many of the texts and figures we chose to examine—*Buffy the Vampire Slayer*, Mel Gibson's *Passion of the Christ*, Madonna, Billy Graham—we almost self-consciously pointed to a bridging of the twentieth and twenty first centuries. The book was, in retrospect, often a way of looking both backward and forward. 2016 still finds us hesitatingly trying to understand our new century. In this second edition we have tried to maintain much of that sense by only lightly editing some of the sections from the previous edition.

On the other hand, we have extensively revised and updated other sections, trying to bring in texts, practices, and ideologies that seem to have emerged much more forcefully in the years since the first edition. Many events of the last eight to ten years have made a second edition necessary—the economic crash and the election of Barack Obama; the iPhone, Spotify, Twitter, and Netflix streaming; the movements of Occupy and Black Lives Matter; the massacres in Paris, Brussels, San Bernardino, and Newtown; the debates over guns, healthcare, climate change, transgender rights, and gay marriage; the continuing movement of younger generations away from traditional religious identification and toward categories of "none" and the SBNR (spiritual but not religious); the rise of the Tea Party, Islamophobia, and Donald Trump. Obviously, our book cannot attempt to offer coverage of all these trends and events, but we have tried to weave many of them into our analysis of the ways that popular culture and popular religion continue to influence and co-create each other.

1

One of the more obvious changes in recent years has been a rise of interest in publishing books like this one. In 2007 ours was one of the few books on the market to take a scholarly yet accessible approach to the intersection of popular culture and popular religion. More recently a number of books have been published that address the subject seriously: *Religion and Popular Culture a Cultural Studies Approach*; *Understanding Religion and Popular Culture*; *The Routledge Companion to Religion and Popular Culture*, as well as a number of books on individual subjects such as religion and hip hop, religion and video games, and religion and *Doctor Who*. Most of these books, however, are either edited collections or textbooks. Our book was and still is a book with a thesis: while statistically Americans revere the Bible and its words perhaps more than any culture in history, the actual biblical text goes largely unread and that popular culture is involved in a complex and significant process of rescripting the sacred texts around which popular religion has traditionally organized itself. Our emphasis continues to be on the popular "rescriptions" within what remains a textually obsessed country. The fact that advancing digital technology forces us to rethink the definition of "text" or "scripture" will be a through line in this story.

While our thesis remains the same, there are two new areas of emphasis that have emerged in this edition. The first is to give more attention to the tension between material and digital. The concept of what is "real" is ancient within theology and religious practice and is one we touch on in our first edition, but one we more deeply analyze here. Thinking about "rescripting" involves defining what "scripture" is, and, in an age when much scriptural engagement happens through technologically mediated practices like streaming and downloading text and images rather than owning, holding, and reading Bibles, Torahs, and Qur'ans, involves a larger ideological shift than most people are aware, a shift that must be negotiated and understood through popular culture.

The second shift is a move to more often think in terms of "lived religion," or, in other words, to focus on what people *do* as much or more than what they *believe*. Although this represents a shift within the academic study of religion, it also, we think, represents a change in the way that the general public thinks about being religious. Although the United States is still a strongly religious and overwhelmingly Christian country, there is also a much more fluid definition among many over what constitutes being "religious"; practices such as yoga, veganism, soul cycle, and adult coloring books have blurred the idea of religious practice. In the same way that religion turns more to practice—the idea of lived religion—popular culture has turned to the participant. Although we will retain our focus on the idea of scriptural re-imaginings, we will also look more closely at the role of fans, players, and practices in that process.

The final shift we want to point to in this book is perhaps the most difficult for us to articulate and that is how *we* have changed. When we wrote the first edition, we were graduate students moving into the job market. As we wrote the revised sections in this second edition, it became clear that our relationship to popular culture had changed. As we met to work on these revisions—in Richard's house in upstate New York, Greg's apartment in Brooklyn, or at hotels, libraries, and coffee shops in Syracuse, Washington, D.C., and Seattle—the ways in which we have stayed the same and changed became more obvious. We are now older, steadily employed, and with a decade of teaching and administrating behind us. While we are still working academics and fans of popular culture, we have to admit a deeper gap in experiencing and writing about topics that are more commonly in the domain of the young. But, this is part of the sense of looking both ways; where we once drew inspiration from our graduate school training and professors, we are now more likely to get ideas from our students. Whether we are talking about participatory online culture or zombie lore in *The Walking Dead*, our students have become a way for us to keep looking forward.

Textual Note

Throughout this text we have chosen not to capitalize pronouns related to God or Jesus except within quotations where they were originally capitalized. In citations of the Bible we have used either the King James Version or the New Standard Revised Version and we identify as (KJV) and (NSRV) respectively in the text.

CHAPTER 1

Popular Culture
and Popular Religion
in America

"Where is God?" he cried. "Well, I will tell you. We have murdered him—you and I."—Friedrich Nietzsche

> NIETZSCHE: *God is dead*
> GOD: *Nietzsche is dead.*
> —American bumper sticker

Word, word and World

For American Jews, Christians, and Muslims (not to mention constitutional literalists) sacred texts are often assumed to be perfect copies of heavenly originals. But, as scholars of the book know, texts are always in flux, both in their content and in the ways they are read. When religious texts moved from scroll to codex, it changed how they were read; now it was possible to flip back and forth between pages, finding connections and repetitions not possible before. Looking at online scripture or even at video games is a way to understand the very literal rescripting that digital technology does to writing scripture and religious practice. The use of Bibles and Qur'ans online and on phone apps will change meaning in ways that print-based thinkers fail to understand. If we are shaped by a religion of the book, what does it mean when there is no material book? And for young readers, raised on digital texts and video games, the idea of an unchanging and linear text that is read the same way we have traditionally read books is no longer how they imagine the place of stories and scripture in the world. These texts are manipulable, searchable, and malleable in ways not previously envisaged. Digital editions and video games provide more flexibility, and, as Rachel Wagner writes "our fascination with fluidity results in a transformation from stories as fixed texts to stories as fictional worlds" (17). As we will explore throughout this book, the power of the written word—and the tension between the idea of its permanence and its potential to be rewritten, erased, or altered—is at the core of American popular culture and religion.

In 2013, Deandre Poole, a professor at Florida Atlantic University, was put on administrative leave stemming from a controversy which arose when he asked students in the class to write the name "Jesus" on a piece of paper and then step on it. The outrage that followed the event—including even the Florida governor—focused on the familiar narrative of college students being taught to scorn religious values. (In actuality the instructor was a self-identified Christian who took the exercise from a Catholic teaching manual.) The point was, the instructor explained, to get students to think about the power of cultural symbols. More important, for our purposes, is how this event is a contemporary dramatization of the centuries old discussion of word and Word. In what ways does a handwritten piece of paper with five letters on it—that you yourself have written—represent anything "sacred"? What did these students and protesters think had been created? And, would it have been different if the instructor had asked them to type it into their phones and then step on their phones?

Popular Apocrypha

"Read it and be enlightened" proclaimed the back of the 2005 paperback edition of The Da Vinci Code, and hundreds of thousands of readers claimed just that experience, while others accused the novel of being satanic or blasphemous and boycotted both the book and the movie version. The novel, a thriller that features Gnostic Christianity and a massive Catholic cover-up of secrets about Christ, inspired countless internet discussions, related books, responses by theologians, official condemnation by influential Catholic and Protestant groups, and Time magazine stories on Mary Magdalene and the conservative Catholic organization Opus Dei. Americans, Christian or not, who previously could not have named the four Gospels, debated the canonicity of Gnostic writings, the role of Mary Magdalene, the power of the church to influence scriptural interpretation, and the ontology of the Holy Grail.

Despite an almost immediate scholarly reaction to discredit many of the novel's pseudo-historical claims, the book truly is, as Timothy Beal writes, "nothing short of a modern-day apocryphal Gospel … that … has emerged as the latest addition to the New Testament apocrypha" ("Romancing the 'Code'"). In other words, the novel and movie, as cultural products, literally take on the functional role of religious texts. *The Da Vinci Code* and the resulting response in books, television documentaries, church protests, web discussions, magazine articles, and sermons is only one in a series of events in which popular culture, religious practice and belief become inextricably connected, forming new ways of thinking, reading, writing, and practicing religion and theology. These events are part of a singularly American way of creating meaning and events that could only have been produced within the paradoxical American religious imagination.

The years between the publication of *The Da Vinci Code* in 2003 and the release of the film version in 2006 were particularly active ones for the intersection of American popular religion and popular culture. Mel Gibson's film, *The Passion of the Christ* (2004), was a massive commercial success and, despite criticism about the appropriateness and accuracy of its images and narrative, changed how Hollywood thought about religiously themed films, and changed how viewers thought about the death of Jesus. Both Catholics and evangelical Protestants flocked to the movie, claiming it offered a "true" representation of the crucifixion and an intensely religious experience. Historian of early Christianity, Bart D. Ehrman, who became a bestselling author in the wave of interest incited by *The Da Vinci Code*, notes that "Mel Gibson, much more than Matthew, Mark, Luke, or John, will affect how people understand Jesus' death, for at least the coming generation" (5). This replacement of biblical text by a work of popular culture and its role in the public consciousness is characteristic of American religious and cultural ideology.

The United States has been accurately described as a "biblical" culture that does not actually read the Bible, but there is no debating the huge impact religiously themed books have played in popular culture and popular religion. In addition to the spectacular success of *The Da Vinci Code*, other bestselling books included the final installments of the end-times fantasy books of *The Left Behind* series in which the figure of Christ finally appears on earth to defeat the anti–Christ, the newly found and translated Gnostic text of the Gospel of Judas, the wildly popular Christian self-help book *The Purpose Driven Life*; these and other books with titles like *What Jesus Meant, The Jesus Papers,* and *Holy Blood, Holy Grail* are no longer relegated to Christian book stores. Debate over Gibson's *Passion* and *The Da Vinci Code* brought previously specialized theological discussions of the last days of Christ and of Gnostic texts into popular discourse on talk radio, the internet, and prime time news, thrusting little known scholars of religion into the public view. In politics, school board debates over teaching "intelligent design" along with evolution, the fight for and against gay and transgender rights, courtroom arguments over the public display of the religious symbols, and reinvigorated legal discussion on abortion have placed theology into the courts and onto the front pages of newspapers and magazines at an unprecedented level. So, although the twentieth century is often characterized as beginning with an explosion of secularism (Freud, Einstein, Darwin, Nietzsche, Lenin), and while the cover of *Time* magazine claimed the death of God in 1966, the first decades of the twenty-first century, at least in the United States, has featured a return of religion that has left scholars scrambling to catch up.

On the other hand, the second decade of the twenty first century saw the apparent rise of a much-discussed generation claiming the importance of religious experience but identifying outside of any official religious designation. This seeming shift has moved the complex task of defining just what religion is outside of the academy and into American Popular culture. Many of the most recent popular texts we will look at, from Kanye West to *South Park*, can be interpreted as expanding definitions of what religion is, where we find it, and what it does.

Some of the most obvious expressions of religion in popular culture in the early twenty-first century were *South Park* episodes (followed of course by the very popular *Book of Mormon* Broadway musical written by South Park creators Trey Parker and Matt Stone). *South Park* continually offered irreverent commentary on current religious events in such episodes as "The Passion of the Jew" (a parody of Mel Gibson's *Passion*), "Red Hot Catholic Love" (the sexual abuse scandals), and "Trapped in the Closet" (Scientology).

The 2009 *South Park* episode "Margaritaville" (13.3) typically provides both religious and political parody in a plot that offers one of their more thought provoking explorations about the deep rooted presence of religious ideology in secular and popular systems as it built on both the *Passion of the Christ* and on the failing economy. The episode begins with the protagonist, Stan, walking into the South Park bank with his father, Randy. Randy's attempt to show his son the importance of saving backfires when the bank announces it has instantly lost Stan's money and then the money of almost everyone in the town. Later, Randy starts to accurately explain to Stan the reasons behind the collapse, but then shifts the blame to a greater power: "mocking the Economy made the Economy very angry." In the next scene, orators in the town's square try to assign the blame (government, Wall Street) but Randy, wearing bed sheets as a robe, announces in Hebrew Bible fashion that South Park has "mocked the Economy. And now the Economy has cast its vengeance upon us all!" In a characteristic *South Park* plot, the whole town comes to view him as a prophet. What results is a semi-biblical culture of wearing bed sheets as clothing and riding llamas for transportation.

While echoing actual phrases heard in the media and in Washington, the episode makes even more explicit the biblical and religious language that was applied to the economy—language of fear, hope, faith, sin, and transcendence. Like evangelicals seeking an older more authentic church and economic conservatives urging austerity, Randy the prophet suggests that the town revert to a more simple time, spending money on only the "bare essentials: Water, bread ... and margaritas, yea." He continues his austerity sermon, mimicking biblical language: "We have become lovers of pleasure rather than lovers of the economy.... No more needless spending. The Economy is our shepherd. We shall not want."

For a *South Park* viewer, the intervention into this scene is both brilliant and predictable, as the plot turns to a young Jew "speaking heresy toward the Economy." This Jesus figure is Stan's young Jewish friend, Kyle. Kyle convinces his friends (now followers) that the economy is not a jealous or vindictive force, but is rather a socially constructed system powered by faith. Speaking more like a twenty first century religious studies scholar than a first century rabbi, Kyle explains that the "Economy is not real, and yet it is real." It is "just an idea," and is "something made up by people" that is "truly meaningless until we put our faith in it. Faith is what makes an economy exist. Without faith, its only plastic cards and paper money." Kyle, radical theologian, argues for the reality of a divine being that is yet created only through human desire, and, like political leaders in the U.S. and around the world, he encourages his followers to just believe in the economy and in the process keep spending.

The *South Park* episode pushes its Christian analogy even further as word spreads that Kyle is the "Economy's only son. Sent to save us." Rejecting this idea, the town council (including a "Roman soldier" just laid off from Little Caesars) decides they need to "kill the Jew." There is a Last Supper scene with Kyle and his friends that resembles Leonardo's Da Vinci's painting as they sit in Whistlin' Willy's pizza parlor. As they hide from Randy and the followers of austerity who disagree with Kyle's views on the Economy, Kyle confesses "I have this strange feeling that one of you is gonna totally betray me." It is his friend Eric Cartman, the Judas in this scene, who plans to betray Kyle in exchange for the new Grand Theft Auto game.

Kyle's final act is, of course, a parody of Christian gift and sacrifice, as he gets a platinum American Express card and pays for everyone's debts, to save people from their sins against the economy and to allow them to spend money. In other words, it is a theological form of "justification," or as a South Park townsperson says, "he paid for our debts so we could spend some more." As Josh Ben-Ami writes, "the collective debt of South Park citizens is Kyle's cross to bear" and when too much credit card swiping causes Kyle to pass out, he is carried to his bed in another echo of an iconic biblical painting. There is much to say about this episode and about the role of *South Park* in the popular theologies many aspects of popular culture, but what is significant for us here is how the episode reveals the theological and biblical roots of our everyday thinking about power, structure, money, and capitalism.

The episode can be read as just parodic, but it, like virtual scripture, points up the ways in which the culture reframes, reshapes and reinterprets the sacred text not from the standpoint of a linear, stable, unchanging signifier, but one that ultimately comprises the relationship believers have with the divine. The analogy of the Economy as a deity (as either the angry Old Testament Yahweh or the personally accessible Jesus) implies a causal relationship between faith and the real. While it feels new (maybe even post modern) to imagine sacred texts as shifting signifiers whose meanings are entangled with all other cultural products, the American religious experience has been traditionally untraditional in its relationships with the sacred.

The Virtual Armor of God

In an apt symbol of the transition from the twentieth to the twenty-first century in American religion, in June of 2005, the 86-year-old Billy Graham, probably the most important American religious figure of the twentieth century and the inheritor of a nineteenth century tradition of folksy charismatic preachers and massive outdoor gatherings, brought his crusade to New York City for one final time, amidst a blitz of production and media only possible in the twenty-first century. A front-page *New York Times* article comparing the climate of the 2005 event to Graham's earlier visits to the city in the 1950s claimed that New York, previously a "famously secular city," was now "drastically changed," with a "vibrant" and "growing population of Evangelical Christians" (Luo). This population was in evidence, as hundreds of thousands of Christians came to Flushing Meadows Park in Queens to see Graham and the surrounding events. Although the aged Graham only spoke a few minutes each evening, the three-day-long spectacle was surrounded by activities both part of and related to the actual crusade. To attend the crusade was to experience American popular religion in all its vibrancy and complexity.

On the morning of the second day of the crusade, several thousand parents and their children came to see, not Billy Graham himself, but a special family and children's presentation. The central component of the family day activities was a dramatic production called *Bibleman Live: A Fight of Faith*. Bibleman, obviously familiar to many children in attendance, is a superhero character marketed exclusively to evangelicals through DVDs and video games. The plot of the live show featured Bibleman and his partner Biblegirl in a battle with satanic enemies, Wacky Protestor and Rapscallion P. Sinister. Wacky and Rapscallion attempt to create the evil "ART," or the Animated Reconstructive Transport which will result in, as Wacky proclaims, an animated world of "no churches, no Bible, no faith and best of all … no God … boo … hiss." In their attempt to save the world from this fate, Bibleman and Biblegirl are aided by their assistant, a hip hop loving DJ figure who feeds them virtual information from the "Biblecave," a high-tech command center which includes a software program that provides the heroes appropriate and useful Bible verses to use in combat situations. The main conflict comes from an attempt at cyber theft, as Wacky tries to download Bible verses from the Biblecave software, rendering the heroes temporarily weaponless and vulnerable.

The production fell somewhere between a high budget Sunday school pageant, a Batman movie, and the *Teenage Mutant Ninja Turtles*. In the climactic battle between the good guys and the bad guys, complete with special effects, electronic swords, flashing lights, and loud music, Bibleman and Biblegirl prevail, aided by the power of biblical texts, and protected by their very literal "helmet of salvation" and "breastplate of righteousness." The use of secular popular culture was the most obvious stylistic and structural feature of the production; it borrowed from film (*Superman, Batman, Star Wars*), used popular music (a "Jesus rap"), and imitated video games. The production was a clear example of popular culture influencing how Americans practice religion.

Marc Peyser, writing in *Newsweek*, characterizes contemporary Christian entertainment, like the Bibleman videos as a "kinder, gentler yet more searching alternative for an audience that has long felt overlooked by the prevailing media and entertainment culture." But, he goes on to say

> as those products have become more successful—and the people in those industries have become savvier—the category has edged closer to the mainstream. Pop music that never mentions the word Jesus. Movies that spend as much time blowing up buildings as saving souls. As with other groups that have created their own subcultures—women, African-Americans, gays and lesbians—Christian entertainment has emerged from its sheltered infancy and has begun to straddle two worlds: the religious one that created it and the secular one it was designed to avoid.

The obvious blend of evangelism, popular media culture, and marketing in *Bibleman Live* was, on the one hand, a simplistic depiction of how the power of God wins out over evil, a not terribly unique—if high budgeted—strategy to convince children that the Christian God is the only path to a safe, happy life. On the other hand, viewed with a critical eye, it communicated a complex and paradoxical message, one that is far from simple and straightforward, and one that is suggestive of the themes we are exploring in this book.

Significantly, the characters in *Bibleman* fight in order to maintain God's superior position over villains who clearly represent elements of secular popular culture and "intellectualism" ("ART"); yet the production is constructed using tools borrowed from popular secular culture—the victory over secular culture in some ways serving to reaffirm it. Although the characters claim to be fighting for God or Jesus (the "greatest superhero of all"), the actual plot seems to privilege not divine personage, but texts, words, and the modes of presenting them. Despite their names, Bibleman and Biblegirl get their power not from reading or understanding the Bible, or even from the existence of the book itself, but by the presence of the words, in this case often presented as virtual objects in cyberspace.

The emphasis on words as objects and forces of power—presented as just slightly more effective weapons than swords—rather than as signifiers, harkens back to a time when language was magic: a medieval epistemology where words have transformative and creative power. Yet in this twenty first century postmodern depiction, there is no theology, just action; no spirituality, just power. This power comes with its own questions. If the emphasis is not on the book, but on the virtual language—power that can be downloaded and infected by viruses—then it suggests the unstable wandering and ephemeral language and God of postmodernism. While the emphasis on a form of cyber-religion was clearly intended to appeal to their younger, more digitally aware audience, what was no doubt unseen by most viewers is that on some levels the performance enacted the absence of God more than the presence.

Although the fundamentalist Christianity out of which the production was created is characterized by a faith in a fundamental text that is unambiguous, commonsense, decidable, and has a clear original intention, the words and images of *Bibleman Live* point to an absence of a solid reality, and even subliminally suggest that words have no relationship to any reality at all. The production becomes an example of Jean Baudrillard's concept of simulacrum—images and symbols with no original—or "an uninterrupted circuit without reference" (*Simulations* 1–36). In *Bibleman Live*, the original is not the Bible, which ironically is portrayed in the production as a literal weapon, but a virtual text based on a video game, a text whose insistence on literality is subverted by its virtual status. *Bibleman Live*, in this context, becomes an expression of the "hyperreal," borrowing its style and content from narratives based on video games with no reality as a referent. This production illustrates a particularly American experience of religion, embodying multiple positions, tensions, and influences; it is both insistently concrete—the word of God becomes armor and a physical force—and wandering and without origin. It is at the same time literal and fundamentalist, yet radically creative, ultimately dangerously, paradoxically unstable and subversive.

The "Return" of God

Our reading of *Bibleman Live* goes beyond what was intended to be portrayed or what may have been consciously perceived by participants and viewers. This kind of analysis, based on theoretical models of postmodernism such as Baudrillard's idea of the simulacrum, finds in statements of faith dark corners of atheism, and sees the necessarily negative side in all claims of positive belief. By the same token we can find in the "godless" texts of popular culture shards of belief and religious ideology. This tension and balance of the positive and negative, real and virtual, theistic and atheistic can be described as "atheological," a position between atheism and theology, between or outside of faith or disbelief. An atheological position recognizes the theological roots of our metaphysical assumption and our cognitive processes at the same time that it attempts to think outside of a classical theology based on a determinate sense of a divine being.

Recent philosophers and cultural theorists have pointed to the ubiquity and inescapability of Christian ways of thinking in the West, even within the disbelief of the twentieth century. For Jean-Luc Nancy, despite rising secularization, "Christianity is inescapable.... Although the de-Christianization of the West is far from being a hollow phrase, the more it takes hold and the more visible it becomes, the more we are bound within the very fabric of Christianity" (115). If, as Nancy says, "*all* our thinking, our very being is Christian through and through" (115), then, although the existence of the Christian God that we have created can be questioned, its theological significance to our thinking cannot.

The worlds of popular religion and popular culture in the United States exist in a rapidly shifting vortex, and call out for new modes of analysis in order to be satisfactorily understood. The technical innovations that have shifted how we construct and think about popular culture have developed in tandem with the "return" of religion, and these parallel developments are neither coincidence nor unrelated. Many theorists have found in our digital and virtual age a renewal of a form of the divine. Mark C. Taylor, for example, who insists throughout his theoretical work that religion is always most interesting where we do not expect it, finds that the traditional transcendent God of classical theology is indeed dead, but also has been recreated in the complexities of modern art, popular culture, and information technology. Taylor finds this "God" in the empty space of installation art and the lights and virtual images of Las Vegas and Times Square.

> In the hot sands of Vegas's silicon lights, the transcendence of the real vanishes, leaving nothing in its wake. In the dark light of this nothingness, it appears that what is *is* what ought to be. When this word of acceptance is actively embraced, the Holy Land ceases to be a distant dream and the Kingdom becomes virtually real [*About Religion* 201].

Taylor's melding of high and low culture, advertising and theology, goes against the grain of much contemporary scholarship that still insists on categories and separation. Hent de Vries writes in his collection of essays, *Religion and Media*, that the renewed prominence of the religious and the proliferation of political theologies it entails, on the one hand, and the equally unanticipated revolution in information technologies, on the other, are analyzed as if we were dealing with two totally independent developments [19].

Building on thinkers like Taylor and de Vries, and rather than continuing to demonstrate how popular culture borrows from religion, or vice versa, we need to re-contextualize and re-conceptualize how we see their interrelationship. A recent book by philosopher Peter Sloterdijk, *You Must Change Your Life* (2013), offers another model. Sloterdijk is not interested in the current battle between belief and non-belief and between competing faiths. Instead he proposes a model of human behavior in which there is no such things as "religion." For him, the category of religion is a modern construction that forces into one category a group of activities that then leave out others. A better way of looking at these various activities, he says, is to think in terms of a continuous and historical set of "practices" or of a "general training consciousness." Although his book aims to show these practices from antiquity to modernity, it is a particularly useful concept in thinking about modern practices and popular texts that push at the limits of what we traditionally have called "religion." Yoga, Soul Cycle, cosplay, meditation, veganism, and beer making could all be seen as examples of what he identifies as a movement from "production" to "practice."

Our analyses will often focus on issues of language as a type of practice, and reflect our belief that the intersection of culture and religion is one defined and created by language. As Susan Mizruchi writes in the introduction to her *Religion and Cultural Studies*, "human thoughts on the nature of the divine are *ex post facto* thoughts about the nature of language itself" (xi). What one chooses to call God reveals as much about one's relationship to creating meaning through language as it does to one's relationship to an idea of the divine. As has often been pointed out, a characteristic that separates American belief from historical Christianity is that most Americans believe that God and Christ love *them*, and love them in a personal way. But what do we mean when we say God loves us? God's love for us is not something Augustine (who asked, "who do I love when I love my God?") could have understood. Even our definition of love would be foreign to Spinoza or Augustine. The concept of love in American culture has been created through popular culture; it is a product of Hollywood films, Hallmark cards, and popular songs. God and love can only be understood in their totality if we think of their context and history as words with unstable meanings and complex histories.

Historical Backgrounds

The twenty first century has seen an increased awareness in both popular culture and academic works in alternative spiritualties, new religious movements, and in non-traditional forms of lived and popular religion. But while this awareness has often been identified as something new, attempts to define American popular religion point to a long history of such ways of thinking. Definitions of American popular religion locate its origins at different times; while some see it "largely as a result of the expanding role of mass media in American culture and their ability to present an array of alternative religious ideas to the public" (Lippy 12), following the media and technological advances of World War II, others see it as merely the most recent phase in movements whose roots go back to the nation's origins. Lippy argues, "by and large those who examine popular religiosity fix their vision on the later twentieth century … popular religiosity is not merely a phenomenon of the modern or postmodern period, but a constant in American culture" (17). Therefore, although most of this book will concentrate on texts from the last 30 years, it is useful to be aware that many of the elements that make up the unique blend of religion and culture in this country are defined by its singular historical development. The more radical elements of American religion that we will be talking about come out of what religious historians term the "Protestant Dissent" of Europe confronting the difficulties and opportunities of a New World. When European Christianity crossed the Atlantic, it was suddenly open to a vast new set of possibilities. As religious historian Jon Butler says, "Old World Christianity had long been sheltered and supported by a complex infrastructure of theology, law, and social process" (36). The New World Christianity, with a new ecclesiastical order unenforced by state law and a new political structure on which to build a mythology, provided the appearance of a blank slate as well as the idea of a chosen people and a chosen land—a combination that was prime for adaptation into new forms, and that led to the creation of new religions, belief systems, mythologies, and supernatural entities.

Although scholars have often attempted to simplify the history of American Christianity and to emphasize its roots in the Puritans, important scholars of American religion such as Butler and Nathan Hatch propose "that we attach less importance to Puritanism as the major force in shaping religion in America and more importance to the religious eclecticism that has long been prominent" (Hatch 2). They focus on multiple strands of influence, the unprecedented plurality that emerged within American Christianity, including the importance of the folk, the popular, and the repressed. For Butler, the story of religion in America from 1700 on is one "so complex and heterogeneous as to baffle observers and adherents alike" (2). Butler expands and complicates not only the historical roots of American belief, but the very definition of religion by including popular practices of magic, astrology, and occultism in his categorization. By showing how these have always been part of American religion, he demonstrates that many seemingly fringe elements of contemporary belief should actually be seen as part of a long and characteristically American tradition.

Hatch's book, *The Democratization of American Christianity*, situates the popular elements of American religious practice as important from the outset. The quote that serves as an epigraph to his book—from an 1844 text by Philip Schaff expresses this idea:

> Tendencies, which had found no political room to unfold themselves in other lands, wrought here without restraint.... Every theological vagabond and peddler may drive here his bungling trade, without passport or license, and sell his false ware at pleasure. What is to come of such confusion is not now to be seen [vii].

What became of "such confusion" is the paradoxical, creative, and unique American popular religion that survives to this day. Hatch was one of the first historians of American religion to stress popular religion as perhaps the major force in shaping the whole of American Christianity. According to Hatch, "the wave of popular religious movements that broke upon the United States in the half century after independence did more to Christianize American society than anything before or since" (3). The various Protestant leaders that Hatch traces "shared an ethic of unrelenting toil, a passion for expansion, a hostility to orthodox belief and style, a zeal for religious reconstruction, and a systematic plan to realize their ideals" (4). This revolutionary sentiment helped define American Christianity as an inherently radical and a contradictory set of religious movements.

In the nineteenth century, these movements "empowered ordinary people by taking their deepest spiritual impulses at face value rather than subjecting them to the scrutiny of orthodox doctrine and the frowns of respectable clergymen," an attitude that resulted in a "ready acceptance to consider dreams and visions as inspired by God" (Hatch 9). This attitude, which continues today, justifies the scripting (or re-scripting) of alternate sacred texts such as the *Book of Mormon* (which proposes a whole additional testament and alternative mythology of Christ's visit to the New World) or the popular prophetic fiction of the *Left Behind* series (based on what began as a little known theory of biblical interpretation in the nineteenth century). As Hatch and others have pointed out, the most important characteristic of these popular nineteenth century movements was a "radical simplification of the gospel" and a "new form of biblical authority calling for common people to interpret the New Testament for themselves" (68–69). In other words, religion developed a simple and absolute center of truth and yet no authoritative center of interpretation. These two contradictory elements produce a formative tension within American religion and perhaps for American culture more broadly. This basic paradox at the hub of American Christianity has produced an almost incomprehensible amount of variation within belief, practice, and ritual, especially within popular religion.

In Hatch's view, "religious populism … remains among the oldest and deepest impulses in American life" (5) and "has less to do with the specifics of polity and governance and more with the incarnation of the church into popular culture" (9). This trend toward the complicating and commingling of the popular and the sacred has continued and grown through the century and a half since the so-called Second Great Awakening. The trends identified by Hatch and Butler have expanded in ways they could not have predicted even a few years ago, and as we move further into the twenty-first century, popular culture and popular religion assume an unprecedented influence.

American Popular Culture and Popular Religion

No single word in this section's title is unproblematic. What do we mean by "popular culture"? By "popular religion"? By "American"? Americans in general are suspicious of definitions and perhaps it is appropriate to start with the concept of experience. American Christianity is an experiential religion; it is not real unless it is felt, an attitude that permeates American culture both sacred and secular. The great heroes of American culture, from Ralph Waldo Emerson to Clint Eastwood, are skeptical of what they do not experience for themselves. This sensibility within American religious thought goes back at least to the eighteenth century, but is perhaps best expressed by William James, whose definition of religion focuses on the "immediate personal experiences": the "feelings, acts, and experiences of individual men in their solitude, so far as they apprehend themselves to stand in relation to whatever they may consider the divine" (Chapter 2). American religion, then, is more about what each individual feels than its European precursors.

What then is "*popular* religion"? For Butler, popular religion means "no less and no more than the religious behavior of laypeople" (4). Yet this simple definition leads to very complex discussions. Peter Williams, an early and influential explicator, defines popular religion through three characteristics. For Williams, popular religion exists apart from or in tension with established religious groups (social structure); is transmitted through channels other than the official seminaries or oral traditions of established religious communities (sociology of knowledge); and generally looks for signs of divine intervention or manifestation in the realm of everyday experience (symbolism, expression, and behavior) (17–18). By focusing more on what American Christians do rather than what they think, as Colleen McDannell points out in *Material Christianity: Religion and Popular Culture in America*, "we cannot help but notice the continual scrambling of the sacred and the profane" (4), a dualistic understanding that is at the root of most accepted definitions of traditional religion.[1] It is in this very separation from traditional religion and this blurring of accepted boundaries that we begin to understand American popular religion. Eric Michael Mazur and Kate McCarthy, editors of *God in the Details: American Religion in Popular Culture*, explain:

> Popular religion, whether it be defined by its extra institutional status, its non-elite practitioners, its immediacy and informality, or the sheer numbers of people it draws, still refers to behavior and ideas recognized by both participant and observer as *religious*, even if the practices are not condoned by the religious elite [13].

Many recent books, for example the 2015 *Routledge Companion to Religion and Popular Culture*, often acknowledge the constructedness of the word "religion" itself, and the dangers of Christian or Western biases in even using the term. Robert Orsi, the most influential thinker in the rise of interest in "lived religion," has written critically about the problems of the term *popular* religion. For our purposes, however, popular religion exists in forms of religious practice that surround us in our everyday lives; they are the ways that ordinary people use religious texts, ideas, narratives, practices, and spaces to make sense and give meaning to their lives, a religion more about bumper stickers than about philosophy and theology and less about the Bible than about religious tracts. On the edges of this definition is the useful formulation of "lived religion" which scholars have found helpful in defining religion more by what people do than what they believe.

In their book, Mazur and McCarthy ask the question, "What constitutes 'culture' (popular or otherwise) and 'religion,' and where do they meet in everyday experience?" (2). They suggest, "the lines between religion and culture blur in contemporary America in ways that leave scholars dizzy" (2). We can see this blurring in the mass media of popular culture and in theoretical approaches to it. In reading and analyzing these phenomena, we want to propose an already merged amalgam of culture and religion; always functioning simultaneously, though not always toward the same goal, and in fact often in conflict. It is part of the purpose of this book to demonstrate ways these two categories blur together, to show that the ultimate questions most Americans still assume belong to the experience of either organized religion or high art are constantly and necessarily being worked out within our popular culture. This circumstance is ultimately not a new development of the postmodern; in fact, the postmodern condition might very well be described as only the awareness that the major categories that surround and give meaning to our lives all flow in and out of each other without clear demarcations of where one ends and the other begins; whereas, the condition itself has always been present.

Paradox Regained

In its composition, American religion lives in contradiction, and it has become commonplace to introduce a work on American religion by pointing to its paradoxes and contradictions.[2] The paradoxes within what is a uniquely American religion were perhaps first explored in an influential book published in 1955 entitled *Protestant, Catholic, Jew*. Commenting on this lack of "authentic Christian (or Jewish) content" in American religion, author, Will Herberg states that "it is this secularism of a religious people, their religiousness in a secularist framework, which constitutes the problem posed by the contemporary religious situation in America" (67). What Herberg was pointing to more than 60 years ago is even truer today, as the secular and the religious—although still often perceived as separate or antagonistic—participate in a relationship that is constantly creating and erasing meaning. This Penelope–like creation and destruction of a web of meaning is at the heart of the American experience, aesthetic and spiritual.

Perhaps the most interesting contradiction in American popular religion for its potential as a force within the space of popular culture and religion is the perception of the Bible and religion as containing stories, concepts, and lessons that are literal, stable and unchanging at the same time that they are always open to new constitutive interpretations. American religious ideology has taken the two Protestant dictums expressed by Luther—the emphasis on the "Bible alone" and on his "priesthood of all believers"—and constructed them into a central paradox that is apparently incompatible. American popular religion insists on the literal—encouraging belief in the supernatural, magical, and demonic as real or probable—while yearning for actual physical contact with the divine, an expressible and understandable divine, and one that is more friend than mystery. Although this may seem to resonate with the superstitions of folk religion, the basis, justification, and structure for this free ranging ideology remains the Bible. It is the existence—if not the actual text—of the Bible to which Americans turn to establish their relationships to theological questions and religious experiences.

While a majority of Americans believe that the Bible *must* be infallible, they do not actually read it. (Poll results consistently show that about 50 percent of Americans believe the Bible must be read literally and is incapable of scientific or historical errors, but an even higher percentage than that cannot name the four Gospels). This absolute faith in the words of a "Book" that is not actively read, a distrust of "intellectual" literary analysis and an encouragement to personal interpretations are nodes that frame the boundary for the radical new revisions, experiences, stories, and even new scriptures and holy figures unique to American religion. The Bible exists as an idea—an origin of truth and a promise of an absolute—but not as an *actual* practiced source of creative popular thought. Instead, ideas and beliefs come from alternate texts such as *Bibleman Live, The Passion of the Christ, Killing Jesus, Noah,* and *The Da Vinci Code* which in turn emulate or become the sacred; the religion of Americans is overwhelmingly textual but not biblical. American popular religion is both literal and literary and anti-intellectual and abiblical. While asserting fixed events and ideas of truth, American religion, because of its insistence on the layperson's power to interpret as s/he sees fit, has been simultaneously open to radical re-conceptions of texts and beliefs. It has, in particular, challenged traditional Western definitions of the idea of sacred, ritual, real presence, biblical, and divine. Out of the literal belief in the Word and a concurrent freedom of re-interpretation emerge new religions, new sacred texts, new supernatural beings and prophets, and new ways of thinking about the human relationship to the world and the unknown.

The conflict between the never-changing absolute of the Bible, and the ever-shifting ideas of what a believer thinks it means is found in two key definitional categories in American popular religion—fundamentalism and pentecostalism—which form directly conflicting religious views and yet work together in forming the tensions that create an ideology and an aesthetic that pervade American religious and popular culture. Often conflated in the media, followers of the two movements, who represent these categories, appear to be in basic conflict: fundamentalists distrust the emphasis on emotion in pentecostalism, and pentecostals find fundamentalism too text-based and not experiential enough. Opposed as these groups appear to be, the tenets of fundamentalism justify the most extreme pentecostal claims and experiences, and the creative energy of pentecostalism pushes fundamentalism towards its most extreme theological interpretations.

Paradoxes and contradictions arising from what appear to be primarily interpretive or theological issues manifest themselves in texts of popular culture and popular religion in ways that are not always obvious. The intersections of popular culture and popular religion can be found everywhere we look. They can be found on Hill Cumorah in Palmyra, New York, where thousands of Mormons annually celebrate the discovery of their sacred tablets with a pageant deeply influenced by the *Star Wars* films,[3] in scholarly journals where professors write about the "ontology of the soul in *Buffy the Vampire Slayer*," and in religious movements such as "spiritual warfare" that are largely inspired by fantasy novels. American religion and popular culture must be studied specifically through their interconnections beyond the influences they have on each other. To talk of influence is to maintain separation, but the symbiotic and agonistic relationship of this juxtaposition is simultaneously in action in ways that are neither completely opposing nor completely separate; it forms a uniquely creative tension. Characteristically American theological tensions find a place in new prophets like Joseph Smith, new experiences such as alien abductions, and new heroic icons such as space-age gunslingers or female vampire slayers. These tensions can also overheat and lead to events of deadly seriousness such as the murders of abortion doctors, the mass suicides of the members of the People's Temple at Jonestown and of the members of Heaven's Gate in California, and the deaths of hundreds of Branch Davidians in Waco, Texas. While these high profile events have been heavily debated, they continue to be largely misunderstood within a larger and more textual cultural context, misunderstandings that have had tragic consequences.

The failure of the government agents who attacked the Branch Davidian compound in Waco—including their own biblical "experts" (just how much does the FBI budget for theologians, anyway?) who were sent in to discuss interpretations of the Book of Revelation—for example, has been attributed to a poor understanding of the mindset of charismatic religious movements and their beliefs (Allitt 214). According to Stuart Wright, "Attorney General Janet Reno and the FBI repeatedly claimed to have consulted with 'cult experts' but refused to identify any of these individuals. At the same time, scholars of new or marginal religious movements complained loudly and in near unison that they were not consulted" (xiv). The government's errors show a miscalculation of the basic polarity and paradox we are describing. Government agents first seemed not to understand a basic premise of American religion when they made an attempt to "prove" theologically to the Davidians that their interpretations were "wrong," which refused them their right of personal interpretation; in a sense, the agents asserted one tenet of the American religious equation, literalism, a belief in a definable right or wrong, while denying the other, the freedom of personal interpretation.

The Branch Davidians were not and are not as marginal in their beliefs as many would like to think. Their apocalyptic expectations place them within the boundaries of the Seventh-Day Adventist Church, a major and rapidly growing denomination, from which they splintered in 1929. The general public, however, influenced by government and media depictions of the group as a "cult," and media misrepresentations of leader David Koresh's view of himself as the Christ, was not sympathetic. Ninety-three percent of the American population blamed the Davidian messianic leader for the deaths, and 73 percent supported the decision to teargas (for seven hours) the men, women, and children of the compound (Wright xv). How is it possible to understand the cultural epistemology that results in this complex event and reaction?

While public opinion was overwhelmingly against the Koresh-led community, it is hard not to see the community itself as a characteristically American institution. They followed the American obsession with fundamental and literal belief, insisting both on their Constitutional right to bear arms and on the inerrancy of biblical prophecy concerning an imminent apocalypse, both views supported by a majority of Americans. They insisted on their right to interpret the Bible on their own terms, and Koresh's biblical interpretations were in the tradition of dispensationalist readings that have been popular since the nineteenth century. Finally, their organization is typically American in its willful individualism and the creation of a new type of prophet, in the mold of a Joseph Smith or a William Miller, a charismatic and creative figure, willing to believe in the truth of what he is saying in the face of extreme opposition.

There is, inherent in the various views of this situation, a typically American stalemate of understanding, and one that we will examine in another (less tragic) situation at the end of this chapter. There was within public opinion an almost universal view that Koresh's prophecies and theology were somehow wrong, a view that creates conflict with the sense that it is wrong to privilege one form of belief over another, and the accepted opinion that the Judeo-Christian Bible offers us a stable ground for ethical judgments. The problems here are obvious. If we assume that the Bible offers an ethical base to our culture and yet assume that we cannot judge another culture's religion and yet universally condemn Koresh's (or others') biblical reading, then the ground from which we base our ethics is taken away. What does it mean when our vision of government, our vision of religion, and our vision of what is ethical clash? Again, we see the double movement of both creating and dissolving the ground of meaning that exists throughout American culture.

Questioning the Author

> Christ on the cross: *"My God, my God, why hast thou forsaken me?"*—Matthew 27:46 (KJV)

> Tigger stuck in a tree: *"Please narrate me down from this tree."* —Walt Disney's *Winnie the Pooh*

The quotations above point to contemporary interpretive issues central to understanding the intersection of popular culture and religion. In both cases it forces us to ask: just who is in charge of the story? In the case of the Bible, is it God, the evangelist, or the reader? In the Walt Disney example, the movie shows Tigger stuck in a tree appealing to the narrator of the movie who is shown reading from the book version of *Winnie the Pooh*. The multifaceted scene again asks the question: where does the author(ity) lie? The juxtaposition of these two moments reveals a way of thinking about and within the ideology of American popular religion. Walt Disney's Tigger, in a truly postmodern moment, acknowledges the author of the original text, the creator of the animated film, the reader and narrator in the film, and questions the authorial decision to place him up in a tree. Jesus on the cross, by questioning father, God, creator, author, and plot, acknowledges and questions the same creative (and destructive) forces.

Tigger and Jesus both appeal to the apparent author(s) of their situation to remove them from danger. In doing so, they foreground the issue of narrative and authority for readers and viewers. Both stories are, in effect, finished already; no one who reads the Gospel of Matthew or watches *Winnie the Pooh* has a version of the text that is unfinished or one in which the final outcome is different (Tigger will always get down from his tree, Christ will always die on his), and most readers and viewers have experienced the text numerous times before, though not necessarily in their original. Yet the questions asked by Tigger and Jesus give the illusion of agency and give the situation a deeper relevance. The juxtaposition of the two stories reveals a desperate desire on our part for an ultimate authority who can reach in and pluck us out of danger; at the same time it reinforces our realization that while all books have authors, every text is simultaneously an unstable "fiction" and ultimately out of the author's control. This space of questioning and self-reflexive reading is part of the skeptical perception of the Bible and *Winnie the Pooh*. It is this triple tension that drives our interpretations in this book.

The questioning by Jesus on the cross could represent a moment of weakness within God, and in this context suggests theorist Slavoj Žižek's characterization of Christianity's essence being in its divine and "fundamental imperfection" (*On Belief* 146). This essence manifests itself when God, through the humanness of Christ, realizes his own dark side and an "impenetrability of God to Himself." It is at this moment that "God the Father Himself stumbles upon the limit of his own omnipotence" (*On Belief* 146), in other words his inability to be a true author; like the narrator in *Winnie the Pooh*, the question itself undermines the omnipotence of the narrator. What we see in this analysis is an aspect of American popular culture, a way of thinking built on American Christian ideas and equally built on a post-existential, post-enlightenment questioning of determinate belief and ideology—it ultimately results in a way of thinking that both proclaims the infinite unchanging power of a text and asserts our rights to question it.

The self-reflexive question of just who is in charge of a text has become a more central plot device in the twenty first century as the rise and ease of digital reproduction has intensified issues of authorship and control. Once the domain of difficult postmodern novels, the narrative device of breaking down the wall between creator and created has moved firmly into texts of popular culture. Fan favorite characters, fictional worlds, and similar plot lines exist simultaneously in competing versions in books, films, TV, pod costs, comic books, and video games, and debates over what is canonical have moved away from primarily academic debates to common fan conversations on websites and blogs. The massively popular book series *A Song of Ice and Fire* and its adaptation in the HBO series *Game of Thrones* and the explosion of film and television based on the Marvel and DC characters are just the most recent examples. Video games based on films, television dramas, and comics or graphic novels have become increasingly popular and have added to complicated discussions over narrative and over the canonicity of texts. A text like *The Walking Dead*, for example, exists as a series of graphic novels, a television show (with a spin off), a talk show, video games, and a digital comic. Like religious stories and rituals that are infused with complex mythologies, liturgies, and back-stories, these games are connected across mediums and fan communities to multiple sources of text, story, and meaning. What makes the current situation more interesting is the increased level of interconnectivity between genres and platform. To play a game, watch a show, or write fan fiction that is part of a larger narrative "universe" is part of what creates what might be called an "interpretive community" and changes the relationship between perceiver and text in a fundamental way. Although the theological ramifications of these newly relocated debates are rarely discussed in mainstream formats, texts of popular culture, no doubt unintentionally, again often negotiate these issues in these very terms.

The ABC fantasy television drama *Once Upon a Time* (2011–present) gives us yet another dramatization of this writer/God/author problem, but now often shifted into a central issue of the plot. The main concept for the initial season is that a bunch of characters from various fairy tales have been transported to the modern day world ("Storybrooke," Maine) and stripped of the memories and identities from their previous lives back in the "enchanted forest." Characters included the Evil Queen, Rumpelstiltskin, and Snow White. The very concept of the show then is about remixing the traditional stores and fairy tales, which, of course, already exist in multiple versions. The only character in the first season that knows the truth is the adopted son of the Evil Queen who has a book of fairy tales that he uses to identify character from the town. The idea of the "book" as a source of true identity is complicated by the framing of the show itself which not only borrows identities from multiple fairy tale traditions, but does so within an essentially Disney universe. The characters of Sleeping Beauty or Peter Pan, in other words, are rooted in the versions presented in the Disney animated versions, and later characters come from Disney movies (*Frozen*), classic films (*Wizard of Oz*), literature (*Frankenstein*), and even mythology (Hades).

The young Henry's book becomes a central object of the show in several ways. It is both a form of scripture—some characters believe and others do not—and it is also a valuable object, one of a kind that can be lost, damaged, hidden, or stolen. One way to see the book is to imagine it as a type of Bible, a signifier of absolute truth. On the other hand, we can see it from other perspectives as an object through which narratives and identities can be questioned. In fact the various devices and narrative concepts of the show allow the book to play all of these roles. In the fourth season, Regina, the evil queen seeks the "Author" of Henry's book so that she can finally have him "rewrite her happy ending." In other words, characters realize that to some extent they are being "written" into a narrative, but with enough agency to perhaps change the writing. Although ultimately the show tends to lean toward "love" and "goodness" as irreducible forces, the actual experience of watching the show forces viewers to question the solidity or possibility of these concepts in a world governed by a book. When the 2016 promo for ABC's reality series *The Bachelorette* quoted the evil queen's wish to "rewrite her happy ending," the level of interconnectivity between reality and fantasy increased even further.

Without ever referencing religion, Christianity, or theological justifications, *Once Upon a Time* explicitly addresses these issues within the main story line. For example, in the episode "Smash the Mirror" (4.8), the Queen associates the book with the good will of a unfair universe when she complains to Snow White "Whenever you need help it just magically shows up—like Henry's book." Snow White tries to explain, "When you do good the universe takes care of you. That's why it showed up," and then offers a theory of soteriology: "Doesn't mean you can't earn forgiveness, a chance at grace. I have to believe that.…You are not all evil, and I'm not all good. Things are not that simple." The Queen though, echoes Tigger in the tree and Christ on the cross in appealing to a dictatorial God/author: "Well, whoever's guiding all this seems to think it is. You're the hero and I'm the villain. Free will be damned. It's all in the book." What is interesting, of course, is the extent to which actual Christian language—damned, grace, forgiveness—is used in this discussion on a network fantasy show.

Rescripting the Sacred

While the playfully postmodern *Once Upon a Time*, exists and extends its narrative on the premise that stories can be continually rewritten, both Tigger and Jesus fail to rewrite their stories. They do, however, question whether such a rewriting might be possible and in doing so change the impact of the story. They create a tension between the idea of the absolutely stable text and the subjective experience of reading and interpreting. America's counter reaction to the 1960s proclamation of the death of God can be seen as a strong shift back to the absolutely stable and literal divine figure that radical theologians and existential philosophers were questioning. Yet popular culture, while borrowing from the imaginative power of this literal belief, also maintains this tension between human (or divine) weakness and supernatural perfection. Our suggestion, then, is that although often unread, the *idea* of the Bible as literal truth that is yet open to personal interpretation provides a paradigm with which Americans read cultural texts and through which Americans frame their religious experience. In other words, even if the actual original text is unknown or unread, there is a sense that words can represent and create magical and actual events; and, that every single person has the authority to interpret, believe, and therefore even create these events. The obvious paradox in this situation is continually negotiated within popular culture and will be our main theme in this book. This tension has become even more dramatic in the twenty first century as sacred texts are read on smart phones, digital notepads, and through apps.

Although we automatically associate the Bible with the beliefs and practices of Christianity, its importance as a central text and object is a relatively recent event. Medieval and Renaissance Catholics based their theology on the church fathers and early Protestants emphasized sermons as central texts. Reportedly Martin Luther, educated as a Catholic monk, did not even see a Bible until his 20s. Yet, although it was not owned, studied, or even read like it would be later, the biblical stories and events were universally known by both the literate and the illiterate. Builders of the medieval cathedrals in Europe constructed catechistic architecture so that the illiterate general public could familiarize themselves with the stories of the Old and New Testament through viewing the sculpture and the stained glass. Renaissance painters attempted to create works that would teach and inspire Christian thought and piety. The stories of the Bible used to provide a background of ideas, tales, and allusions from which to draw both art and everyday communication. Although statistically Americans revere the Bible and its words more than any culture in history, they no longer have this same frame of biblical reference; however, as Kelton Cobb writes in *The Blackwell Guide to Theology and Popular Culture*, "whole generations in the West have had their basic conceptions of the world formed by popular culture" (7). Today's popular culture—television shows, music videos, and film dialogue—give appropriate recognizable resonance and importance to everyday life. A typical American, religious or not, knows little about the intimate relationship between David and Jonathan in the Hebrew Bible, but instantly recognizes the *Seinfeld* phrase "not that there's anything wrong with that" as a reference to homosexuality. In other words, popular culture is involved with a complex and significant process of rescripting the sacred texts around which popular religion has traditionally organized itself. For both the religious and non-religious, popular culture is largely responsible for the passing down of religious interpretation, grappling with existential problems, and providing a common frame of reference, all roles traditionally filled by more established religious institutions and texts.

An early example of a twentieth-century rescription of religious texts was the 1925 novel *The Man Nobody Knows* by Bruce Barton, in which Jesus was re-imagined as an athletic business man. Barton saw his novel as a corrective to contemporary depictions of Jesus as a "pale young man with no muscles and a sad expression" (11). Unlike the Old Testament heroes who Barton admired as masculine leaders, Jesus had become "something for girls—sissified" (12). The Christ that Barton depicts in his book is compared to great American presidents and businessmen, leaders who were stoic, strong, and manly. Although this book has been largely forgotten, when it is discussed today scholars are often interested in how it represented the need of Americans to remake the figure of Jesus into a twentieth-century masculine figure. However, contemporary readers of the book, as Stephen Prothero points out, did not seem aware of Barton's conscious casting of Jesus as a successful capitalist or a manly athlete. Instead, as letters to Barton indicate, what drew millions of readers to the book was how it brought Jesus to life, making him seem "life-like," as reader after reader commented. Readers felt that Barton's Jesus was "real," even going so far as to claim it was the "truest picture of Jesus in existence" (Prothero 104–105), therefore privileging the book over even the Gospels.

Barton's book is a classic twentieth-century American example of how an artifact of popular culture rescripts a sacred text. Another is Warner Sallman's famous painting, *Head of Christ*, which according to Prothero, "became far and away the most common image of Jesus in American homes, churches, and workplaces" in the World War II era (117–118).

> During the 1990s [art historian David] Morgan solicited opinions from a variety of Americans on Sallman's *Head of Christ*. One woman told him that the picture was "an exact likeness of our Lord Jesus Christ." Another reported, "When I look at it in prayer, and when I am the most in need, I see not only a painted portrait, but the face of the real, the living Christ" [118].

Another admirer wrote

> There is something about Warner Sallman's pictures that makes me feel ... that this artist had felt Christ's presence when he made the images ... and you can feel Christ's presence ... conveyed ... to you through his images. From the image of the head of Christ I see righteousness, strength, power, reverence, respect, fairness, faithfulness, love, compassion [Correspondence file, Sallman Archives, Anderson University].

The Sallman portrait represents perhaps the most significant mid-twentieth-century example of the kind of rescripting in which we are interested. By this point in their history, American Christians expressed a willingness to acknowledge the possibility of "truth" within texts of popular culture or popular religion created outside of any religious institution. The implication of the letters to Barton and the opinions on Sallman is that for at least some readers and viewers these texts were more "real" than the Bible. It is this association and acceptance of truth and reality with the texts of popular culture that leads to paperback novels that become the "Bible" of certain theological movements. It is also the reason why the film of *The Last Temptation of Christ* or the heavy metal album *The Number of the Beast* have been protested so seriously by American religious organizations.

Theology on the Sports Page

Many of these same issues were debated in the New York sports pages and sports talk radio after an April 22, 2001, *The New York Times Magazine* article about some New York Knicks players. In a short paragraph near the end of the article the author describes attending Bible studies two players, Charlie Ward and Alan Houston, who made comments about Jews. According to Ward, Jews were "stubborn," and had "blood on their hands" for "persecuting Jesus." Houston quoted Matthew 26 from his Palm Pilot Bible: "Then they spit in Jesus' face and hit him with their fists," and Ward then commented that Christians were persecuted "every day" by Jews; there have been "books written about this," he said (Konigsberg). The players' comments were condemned by the New York tabloids, talk radio, and the Anti-Defamation League. Ward issued a statement saying that he had not meant to offend anyone but that if "people want to be offended by what happened biblically, that's on them" (Broussard). The Anti-Defamation League's statement read: "We were shocked to read the comments of New York Knicks' players Charlie Ward and Allen Houston blaming the death of Jesus on Jews and accusing Jews of persecuting Christians. We had thought these destructive historical myths … were a thing of the past…. It is clear that Mr. Ward just doesn't get it" (Broussard).

The New York sports media reacted in various ways. On the popular sports talk show "Mike and the Mad Dog," Mike Francesa and Chris Russo asked, "What's the big deal? Why should anyone care what two basketball players think about anything outside of basketball?" Sportswriter Ira Berkow commented by writing, "Ward said: … 'They had blood on their hands.' Houston spoke of Jews who had 'spit in Jesus' face and hit him with their fists,'" seemingly unaware that these are the words from the Gospel of Matthew and not Houston and Ward, wrote, "Those are words without charity" (Berkow). Editorials in the New York tabloids, like the conservative *New York Post*, while acknowledging that there was no doubt a lot of "'right-on' surfacing in support of Wards remarks," also condemned the statements as "foolish" and "ignorant" (April 25, 2001). The situation quickly blew over. Ultimately, Ward issued an apology of sorts, and agreed to open "a dialogue" by scheduling meetings with a rabbi. National Basketball Association Commissioner David Stern, calling the statements "uninformed and ill-founded," but made the decision not to "enhance [Ward's] sense of martyrdom by penalizing him" (Berkow), and the story faded from the sports pages.[4]

Although the press differed in assessing the significance of the players' statements, the most common adjective describing them was "ignorant." But, of what exactly were Ward and Houston "ignorant"? They were likely just repeating what they had heard in churches and read in the Bible and in Christian books. What sports writers seemed not to understand, or at least did not mention, was that the players' statements were not a fanatical interpretation of a single biblical passage taken out of context, but were a literal reading of the New Testament as accepted by many Christians. As Ward said in his apology, the Bible *was* the context. Although it was uncontroversial for the press to call Ward ignorant or foolish, the New York tabloids would never intentionally be caught making a statement that the New Testament is factually *wrong*; nor, would the ADL say that the Gospels create intentionally "destructive historical myth"—a statement that would directly go against much Christian doctrine and the majority of Americans' beliefs?

While they differ in detail and tone, all four Gospels are very clear in attributing blame on the Jews for the persecution and killing of Christ. Historians point out that the Pilate that appears in the Gospels seems to have little to do with the historical Pilate. Except in the Gospels, where each book gives an increasingly positive account of Pilate (and an increasingly negative view of the Jews), history portrays him as a brutal and cruel governor, responsible for hundreds or thousands of crucifixions. The theories of motivations for the various biblical accounts are well known today and emphasize the political reasons early Christians had for not alienating the Romans, the intentional production of a religious propaganda to create difference between the new "way" and the old, the need to appeal to non–Jews in the construction of what appeared to be a new religion, and the overall improbability of events occurring as described.

Although much of this scholarship is widely accepted today, it is far from a settled matter and even in academic circles debate still rages among theologians and biblical scholars over some of these very issues. And while the media and Anti-Defamation League seemed to expect sophisticated historical scholarship to inform professional athletes, they also seemed unaware of a counter trend in the late twentieth century that has questioned these conclusions. For example, as historian Josef Blinzler says, to reconstruct the trial of Jesus from the gospel narratives one *must* conclude that "the main responsibility rests on the Jewish side" (qtd. in Pagels xxii). The quotes from Matthew cited by Houston, where Christ is abused and spat upon by a Jewish priest, and the comment by Pilate that "his blood be on us and on our children," are the very passages where scholar John Dominic Crossan objects to Raymond Brown's classic study, *The Death of the Messiah*, for not questioning the biblical version enough. On a respected academic level, then, these two scholars are engaging in much the same debate as the one in the New York sports pages.

The larger implications of this controversy can be seen by first acknowledging how widespread such views as Ward's are, and then by showing the complexities and contradictions in the media's criticism of them. The media, often by relying on a type of biblical absolute morality, point to Ward's ignorance without addressing the larger problems involved in the situation. By going deeper, we see not only a strong anti–Semitic Christian presence, but also contradictory standards that simultaneously reflect conservative ethics, liberal theology, and what Herbert Schnedau calls the "biblical urge to criticize its own ground." We can also see here a characteristically American conflict between a support of freedom of religion, separation of church and state, an assumption of a direct connection between religion, the Bible and ethics, and an idealistic belief in a democratic pluralism. By re-reading the players' comments and the statements by the press in this context, we can see the deeper relevance of this situation to the complex relationship of American popular culture to sacred texts (both biblical and constitutional), ethics, and "truth." To read and interpret the Bible as Ward and Houston did has been the norm in America throughout most of the last 200 years. So what has now changed? Do we just know better? Why, in a culture that encourages individual interpretation, should Ward's reading be regarded as ignorant? What does it mean that certain, seemingly logical, readings are no longer tolerated by many?

Christianity is ostensibly a religion of the "Book," but only when we start to look to popular religion is it obvious how important *reading* and theories of reading are. Nathan Hatch stresses, "historians have often overlooked the flood of print produced by persons depicted as stalwarts of enthusiasm and anti-intellectualism" (11). There are "books written about this," Ward said to support his position on the Jewish persecution of Christians, and his vague attempt to cite written evidence is characteristically part of the American ideology, and its emphasis on the scriptural authority of many different texts. American popular religion finds its voice not in reading the Bible, but in a flood of tracts and paperbacks.

Ward and the sports media make similar errors by failing to distinguish the Christ of faith from the Christ of history, a distinction that is impossible within fundamentalist belief. The term "fundamentalism," first used by twentieth century American Protestants, although it suggests a return to "fundamentals," and therefore an earlier, more "pure" ideology, must be seen, as scholars from Karen Armstrong to Jacques Derrida[5] have said, as a modern or even postmodern movement, which, while it may seem primitive, is in many ways a very recent ideology, trying to apply the scientific ideals of rationality and truth to texts written in a culture that thought differently about those concepts. If fundamentalist American Christianity has a theory of reading, it is that there should be no "interpretation," and that the meaning is exactly what is *there*. Polls confirm that most Americans feel this way and this ideal can also be seen in contemporary secular culture outside of religion. Many critics, for example, have pointed to the literal and biblical way in which we interpret our law and our constitution.[6] The phrase "unconstitutional" holds a power of absolute authority on the level of sin, even though it is easy to show how both are concepts in total flux depending on when and where and to and by whom it is being applied.

Ultimately, what is being debated, developed, and presented here—beyond the ethical, political, and religious issues—are theories of reading and interpretation. To use questions borrowed from literary theory: does the authority of a text reside in the text itself, in the reader, in an interpretive community, in the historical culture, or in the dominant institution? Ward's reading, which would not have raised an eyebrow throughout most of Christian history, is controversial because of conflicts between interpretive communities and because of historical forces. But what do people read when they read the Bible? As we have seen, secular and popular forces have clearly determined what a biblical passage should mean, even if it is in direct conflict with a majority of American Bible readers. For most readers, reading is based around a search for a single meaning and an absolute truth. Yet, as we have stressed throughout this chapter, reading is a complicated and plural process that, especially within the ideology of American popular religion, points to the wandering complexity of the postmodern text as well as a single literal meaning. The media commentary around the controversies surrounding Charlie Ward's comments, Mel Gibson's *Passion*, Dan Brown's *The Da Vinci Code*, and the Branch Davidians in Waco are constantly and unintentionally asserting the existence and impossibilities of truth claims.

Interpreting the Popular

The permission to read or interpret the Bible and the reliance on popular texts to develop one's belief system outside of traditional institutions form the rock of American Christianity, one that Ward and Houston were standing on when they quoted Matthew and the other books in their worship session free of the influence of more "learned" interpretation. As Hatch says, American religion challenged the public to "think, to interpret Scripture, and to organize the church for themselves" (5), but the popular reaction to Ward's comments, or to David Koresh's Branch Davidians, shows that certain ways of reading are going to be judged wrong without an explanation as to how one should read. Expecting everyday readers of the Bible to understand the sophisticated and seemingly (to some) blasphemous arguments of historical and textual criticism, cuts across much of what is supposedly "American."

On the other hand, to allow comments such as Ward and Houston made encourages a prejudice that also feels like it is against what are supposedly American ideals and moral progress. Out of our beloved ideal of democracy come the horns of this dilemma. In some ways American mainstream culture seems to be saying, "the Bible is the base on which ethics and morality is built, except when it says something unethical or immoral."

The relative nature of ethical positions is worth noting; tolerance for other religious views is not part of any orthodox religious tradition. Religious tolerance once was considered heresy, or worse, apostasy, for which one might be subject to the rack or stoning death, is now culturally accepted as the most ethical position. However, not all religious views are equally tolerated. Perennial arguments for the benefit of prayer in school assume non-heterodox environment in which all children would be praying within the same tradition. In Georgia, a recent controversy erupted over the use of yoga and mindfulness exercises: parents at a Cobb County elementary were angry about the school's use of yoga and mindfulness practices to calm students because "they believe it endorses a non–Christian belief system" (French). This is a moment where tolerance for the religious views of others runs into deep mistrust of the Other. The parents were most disturbed over students coloring mandalas and greeting each other by saying "Namaste" which they saw as religious practices intended, in their view, to proselytize students into Hinduism.

In the reader comments section of the story in the *Atlanta Journal-Constitution,* many readers took the view that New York sports journalists did; they remarked on the "ignorance" and "idiocy" of the anti-yoga dissenters: "As long as we have this kind of intervention in our public schools we will always have an ignorant and uninformed citizenry! Yoga has as much to do with religion as gymnastics." Although intended to support the school's use of yoga, these supposedly tolerant views show an equally misinformed understanding of religious practices. Actually, yoga is not entirely divorced from its religious Hindu roots despite American commercialization and secularization of it. This reaction assumes as much moral absolutism as those it opposes. The idea is that tolerance is good and therefore has always been a part of traditional religious orthodoxy. There is just as much ignorance in disregarding the religious background of yogic practice as there is in saying that it will "lead to devil worship."

Some of these same issues were again played out in the media less than a year after the Ward/Houston controversy when the National Archives released sections of Richard Nixon's tape-recorded White House conversations that revealed an exchange with Billy Graham in which Graham admitted that although because of his support of Israel, Jews "swarm around me and are friendly with me…. They don't know how I really feel about what they're doing to this country." Graham went on to state that if Nixon were to be reelected "we might be able to do something" about the "stranglehold" Jews exercise over the media. Although Nixon's Chief of Staff, H. R. Haldeman, had reportedly previously written of Graham and Nixon discussing "Satanic" Jews (Greenberg), the media expressed surprise at Graham's comments. The Anti-Defamation League called Graham's statements "chilling and frightening" and their statement said that it was "shameful that one of America's most respected religious leaders and a spiritual advisor to Presidents believed and espoused age-old classical anti–Semitic canards" (ADL press release 3/1/2002).

Our aim in raising these issues is not to support or to condemn Ward, Graham, the Pope, or the media; rather we want to make a much larger point that the culture out of which they speak is more contradictory than many recognize. The problems of reconciling fundamentalism, literalism, pentecostalism, and existentialism are not atavistic links with a superstitious past, but are new and growing parts of contemporary culture, religious and secular, and a true understanding of them is necessary to understand the dialectical relationship America and Americans have to religion and morality and that popular culture has to the beliefs and practices of popular religion.

When Mel Gibson was arrested in the summer of 2006 and insulted the Jewish officer who arrested him before accusing the "fucking Jews" of causing "all the wars in the world," it was more than the meltdown of a troubled movie star, more than the revealing of his suspected anti–Semitism; it becomes, within American popular culture and religion, an actual theological event. Though many will question, as in the case of Charlie Ward, the importance of what a celebrity thinks of the role of Jews in the cosmic future of the world, what happens is that the arrest and following tirade become part of the text, part of the story, part of the apocrypha. If *The Passion of the Christ*, like *The Da Vinci Code*, is a modern-day apocryphal Gospel, and if the film determines how people think of the death of Jesus, then, for the current generation, at least, the story of Gibson's arrest will alter how they perceive and process the film; it will change their relationship to Christianity because it, like every text of popular culture, engages in the process of rescripting, revising and recreating the sacred out of which most determine meaning in their lives.

Conclusion

In September of 2015 Pope Francis visited New York City. He spoke at Madison Square Garden, the United Nations, and the 9/11 Memorial, he rode in a motorcade through Central Park, he led prayers at St. Patrick's Cathedral, and he led a mass at Madison Square Garden. He spoke in Spanish and English, he was on the front of every New York City Paper, television stations—

local and national—covered his every move, mass transit systems changed their schedule, and wherever he went he was surrounded by adoring crowds of people taking pictures of him on their phones. Filmed, photographed, tweeted, Facebooked, and Instagrammed, it was one of the biggest spectacles of celebrity culture in the history of the country.

At the same time, just feet away from the Pope's procession down Fifth Avenue, was an interactive exhibit on *Saturday Night Live*, mounted to celebrate the 40th anniversary of the show. The exhibit was designed and curated to chronicle the show's history, featuring memorabilia includes props and showpieces from the show, while at the same time taking visitors through its notoriously hectic weekly schedule. In the final climactic room of the exhibit—a replication of the actual control room—was a single display case (which the security guard was specifically calling attention too). In the case was perhaps the most famous object in the history of *Saturday Night Live*— the photograph of Pope John Paul II that singer Sinead O'Connor tore up on the air in 1992. The photograph had been carefully put back together and was placed by itself with a placard describing the event and titled: "Sinead O'Connor, Musical Performance, October 3, 1992."

What is most revealing about this juxtaposition of the Pope and the *Saturday Night Live* exhibit is that it perfectly dramatized the contradictory and complex roles that celebrity and popular culture are playing in the American Religious experience. On the one hand, we have the Pope, essentially a medieval institution, but one that is being celebrated with the most postmodern technology and as a media celebrity on the scale of and through the same channels as Kim Kardashian or Beyoncé. On the other hand, an act that was at the time almost universally condemned[7] as a disrespectful act, even by the show that presented itself as being subversive, is represented with an object displayed as a type of religious relic. Has the museumification and restoration of the torn photographed domesticated O'Connor's act? Does the restored Pope John Paul II in a display case now occupy the same position of respect that a living Pope Francis does? Or does American popular culture now allow all these multiplicities to exist unproblematically and uncontroversially at once—a Catholic relic, a blasphemous act, and a celebrity pope— on the same high profile block of New York City.

What these incidents ask us to question is the way people read and internalize important religious narratives and the way they supply, often unconsciously, religious context to popular culture. If we believe polls, most Americans must believe that Christ's birth, life, and death are the most important events in the history of the world. Yet, as has been demonstrated, it is not the Bible that provides the texts that are most influential, but instead paperback and digital guides to Christian belief, novelists like Bruce Barton and Dan Brown, painters like Warner Sallman, filmmakers like Mel Gibson, singers like Beyoncé, and television shows from *The Walking Dead* to *Game of Thrones* to *South Park*. While the theological or historical debates are important and still continue to be fought, the role of the popular is often downplayed, although it may be even more important. Once again, deep theological tensions, and issues of canonicity, scriptural authority, and belief and unbelief are worked out, not in our churches and seminaries, not in our university classrooms, but in our popular culture.

CHAPTER 2

"Jesus Is Standing at Home Plate"
Baseball and American Christianity

I don't know if there's a record-keeper up there or not. But even if there weren't, I think we'd have to play the game as though there were."—Robert Coover, *The Universal Baseball Association, Inc.*

Reading Religion and Baseball as Culture

The topic of baseball and religion is an often romanticized one. In the opening scene of the film *Bull Durham*, Annie Savoy speaks of her faith in baseball: "I believe in the church of baseball…. I've tried 'em all, I really have, and the only church that truly feeds the soul, day in, day out, is the church of baseball." In W. P. Kinsella's novel *Shoeless Joe*, he writes "a ballpark at night is more like a church than a church." While no doubt baseball fans often truly feel this kind of reverence, our aim in this chapter is to go behind this iconic image, to treat baseball as a text, not as a ritual or as a pastime, and to try to use the game as a window into the history of our national religious psyche.

What we are interested in exploring is the way that America's different and unique religious epistemology manifests itself in the game of baseball. To try to look at one's own culture entails finding fresh ways to see what is most familiar, and, as Jacques Barzun famously advised, "Whoever wants to know the heart and mind of America had better learn baseball." Furthermore, to understand America's subconscious, we need to understand that while situated within the Judeo-Christian tradition, our popular religions and our religious imaginations are and have always been different. American Religion, as religious historian R. Laurence Moore says, is a "curious and somewhat unique national passion … quite like baseball" (3).

36

By looking for religious echoes in the game of baseball, we are seeking different ways of understanding our cultural heritage. We will not be discussing baseball *as* a religion. This has been done in various ways, seriously and otherwise, before. We have just cited examples of baseball as religion in literature and film, and there are numerous scholarly approaches to the idea of sport as religion or as religious ritual: the idea goes back as far as ancient Greece or the Mayan ballgame. But there is more to be learned by looking at sport *and* religion. As Moore suggests in *Selling God,* "the history of religion in the United States has suffered from being placed in a category separate from the general issues of understanding culture" (8) and part of our intention in this chapter and in this book is to put it back.

If the study of religion, then, is necessarily a study of culture, and if we look at popular culture for what it reveals *about* a culture—essentially for why it is popular—then for the same reasons, we need to examine popular or lived religion. Popular religion, as we defined it in first chapter, means not the stated theologies and creeds of institutionalized churches, but a religion that is communicated primarily in ways outside of these traditions. More than theological discussion between professional clergy or theologians, popular religion is what people use to make sense of their lives. And popular religious thinking finds its way into the subconscious of the populace, emerging, often in disguise, in our popular culture: our songs, our television shows, and our sporting events.

From a historical perspective, shifts in American religious thinking are directly related to baseball in that the breaking from Puritanism in the 1800s allowed adults to play games. By 1888, Protestant minister Washington Gladden could say that he no longer believed that salvation "involved the sacrifice of baseball" (qtd. in Moore 153). But to look at the relationship from a more anthropological perspective, we can paraphrase Clifford Geertz in saying that baseball is an American way of reading American experience, a story we tell ourselves about ourselves (448). In his *Interpretation of Cultures,* Geertz characterizes sacred symbols as "function[ing] to synthesize a people's ethos ... the picture they have of the way things in sheer actuality are, their most comprehensive ideas of order" (90). This American idea of order is both determined by and inclusive of its religious epistemology. Ultimately, baseball exemplifies anthropologist Claude Levi-Strauss's notion of the functioning of myth as "not how men think in myths, but how myths operate in men's minds without their being aware of it" (312). If we accept that baseball operates as a Straussian myth, while serving the kind of ordering function described by Geertz, then baseball and popular American religion are always present in any artifact generated by the culture, even when the culture itself is unaware of this function.

Church and Game: 1800–1900

Calvinism and Puritanism are often cited as being the heart of the American religious consciousness, but it is the nineteenth century's radical refashioning of the Christian experience that spawned the unique forms of religion that are still prominent today. If, as many recent historians and religious scholars have stated,[1] American religion really begins in the second half of the nineteenth century, then its development almost parallels baseball. American Christianity and baseball developed together, inheriting certain values from Europe, but also self-consciously carving themselves into American institutions. What does each say about the culture from which it springs? If we see them as arising and developing in tandem, does looking at them together give us any insight into their cultural relevance, and can doing so tell us anything about their future?

From their beginnings, American Christianity and baseball have gestured back toward some imaginary golden age when things were good and pure. American Christianity looks to an original primitive church of the early Christians, untarnished by 2000 years of history. Baseball fans tend to insist upon an earlier, untouched, more honest version of the game to which we need to return. As early as 1867, *The Ball Players' Chronicle* complained that baseball "seems to be no longer participated in for the mere pleasure of the thing" (qtd. in Goldstein 67). The most respected baseball stars, ones we feel know and love the game (Cal Ripkin, Derek Jeter), are affectionately called "throwbacks"; our favorite parks (Fenway Park in Boston) are considered "old-fashioned." From a cultural studies perspective, the need for a rural idyllic past, and the controversy over the game's origin,[2] are not as important as realizing that we have a need for such myths and such controversies. The "good old days" feeling that is in both baseball and American religion refers not to a former time, but to an essential part of the thing itself.

Americans in the first half of the nineteenth century, perhaps invigorated by their victory in the Revolutionary War, began creating a new type of faith and religious experience. Although rooted in European Christianity, it rapidly developed its own personality. For Harold Bloom, "what makes the American Religion so American is that the Christianizing of the American people, in the generation after the Revolution, persuasively redefined what Christianizing meant" (28–29). Americans were infused with a spirit of individualism, a sense of rebellion against authority, and the faith and arrogance to create something new.

The American ideal of democracy, according to some scholars, was the defining force in nineteenth-century religion. No longer was God brought to the congregation by an anointed and educated clergy, but both congregation and clergy looked to the common person to find God. True virtue was associated with "ordinary people," and an individual's spiritual convictions were not subject to clerical re-interpretation. As early as 1839, America's camp meetings were referred to as "festivals of democracy" (Hatch 58). Not only could anyone define salvation on their own terms, but anyone could become a religious leader. Despite complaints by traditionalists of "illiterate ministers," multiple new religious movements led by lay persons gained momentum throughout the century. Baseball, arising in the same period, shares many of the same features. The concept of a batting order is profoundly democratic; no matter how good a hitter you are, you have to wait your turn. Michael Jordan or Lebron James pretty much always get the last shot; but in baseball the last out may come down to little-known Bobby Thomson, with Willie Mays waiting helplessly on deck. In the most documented at bat in all of baseball lore, Bobby Thomson, of course, then went up to hit a game winning home run, the most famous moment in baseball history and an event we will return to later in the chapter.

Keeping pace with apocalyptic predictions and camp meetings, nineteenth-century baseball had the "snap, go, fling of the American atmosphere," as Walt Whitman said, and an early description of a team's roster is a Whitmanesque celebration of democratic ideals: "the pitcher was a former stonemason; the catcher, a postal employee; the infielders worked as compositor, machinist, shipping clerk, and compositor. Among the outfielders, two were without previous job experience and the other worked as a compositor. The team substitute worked as a glass blower" (Folsom 35). Far from its English roots, and early fraternal organizations, baseball may have "begun as a gentlemen's game, but its demands proved to be democratic, the game insisted on conditioning and skill, not on social breeding" (Folsom 35).

Early baseball is related to the free spirited, democratic, and somewhat coarse religion of the time, but one of its parents, cricket, like the roots of American Christianity, is a more reserved and refined European practice. British-born journalist Henry Chadwick, an early baseball supporter and player, represents this American "conversion" from cricket to baseball. A former cricket player, he found baseball's pace more representative of the American psyche: "Americans do not care to dawdle over a sleep-inspiring game all through the heat of a June or July day. What they do, they want to do in a hurry. In baseball, all is lightning; every action is swift as a seabird's flight" (qtd. in Ward 8). Like the upstart indigenous religious sects, baseball consciously set itself apart from any European or Old World pedigree.

Another advantage baseball had over cricket was its portability. Baseball fields, unlike the carefully prepared grounds of cricket, could be set up anywhere: a backyard, an empty lot, even a Civil War battleground. Whitman, a baseball fan and prophet of American religion, comments on the effortless transformation of wildness to ball field and, at the same time, pays homage to his beloved democracy (no one piece of land is better or worse than another):

> I remember—it is quite vivid—a spot off on Long Island, somewhere in the neighborhood of our old home—rough, uncultivated, uncared for—choked with underbrush—forbidding: people coming would avoid it—it was that kind of place: put to no practical uses untouched.... I left the neighborhood—was away for years: wandering, seeing living: went back again: the whole face of it was changed: now a baseball ground, a park ... it had required but little work to effect the transformation—simply clearing away the brush: now it is a perfect spot of its kind—a resort [qtd. in Folsom 52].

The baseball field was to the cricket field as the camp meeting was to the traditional church. Like the baseball field, the camp meeting was a portable sacred space, not a temple in Jerusalem or a building in London, but Moses and the people in the wilderness.

Like the American churches and clergy, early baseball moved further away from its Old World roots by becoming more working class. The Atlantics, Brooklyn's dominant team in the 1860s, was one of the first organized teams to be predominantly working class. As in the churches, this resulted in battles of class and in disparaging remarks about the unwashed or uneducated. Respectable Methodists in Philadelphia split from lay-led congregations, "the wealthy and respectable minority against the poor majority," according to a minister (Taves 95). The Prince of Wales commented that American baseball "offended" the English "love of fair play" (Ward 29), and in the churches this more confrontational style also offended visiting English Bishops and more traditional clergy in American churches. For example, in the 1820s Bishop Daniel Payne stepped in to stop a "singing and clapping ring" taking place after his sermon. His congregation refused to stop: "sinners won't get converted unless there is a ring," he was told (Taves 102). The official English Methodist response to the American camp meetings was this: "it is our judgment that even supposing such meeting to be allowable in America, they are highly improper in England, and likely to be productive of considerable mischief; and we disclaim all connection with them" (Hatch 50).

Like the American congregations who created their own forms of worship reluctantly allowed by church leaders, baseball players bucked against genteel traditions of fair play to develop a game more suited to their taste. Faster pitches, curve balls, bunting, and stealing were all initially regarded as legal but morally dubious. Along with other traditionalists, Whitman was suspect of these changes, and questioned the ethics of new pitching techniques: "in baseball is it the rule that the fellow who pitches the ball aims to pitch it in such a way the batter cannot hit it? gives it a twist—what not—so it slides off, or won't be struck fairly?" (qtd. in Folsom 47). Yet, the new, more aggressive methods won out in the end.

If baseball needed to separate itself from cricket, and the class, authority, and intellectualism it represented, then it also consciously separated itself from "rounders" and other "childish" games of the time. Baseball was going to be serious business, not descended from children's play. The concern for early baseball supporters like Henry Chadwick was that baseball, "this manly pastime," be separated from such "primitive and simple" games (Goldstein 44). From the beginning, not only players but the baseball crowds were part of this "manly" and rough style. Early baseball star and entrepreneur Albert Spalding even said that the fan's harassment of umpires was part of a democratic right to protest tyranny. However, like the "Shouting Methodists," the enthusiasm of baseball fans was initially regarded with a somewhat condescending air, especially by outsiders. George Bernard Shaw wrote:

> What is both surprising and delightful is that the spectators are allowed, and even expected, to join in the vocal part of the game. There is no reason why the field should not try to put the batsman off his stroke at the critical moment by neatly timed disparagements of his wife's fidelity and his mother's respectability [Ward 79].

Both churches and ball clubs dealt with the question of whether to try to curb participants' excitement. "What ... can any club do?" a baseball executive complained,

> Can we restrain a burst of applause or indignation emanating from an assemblage of more than 15,000 excited spectators...? He who has witnessed the natural excitement which is ever the attendant of a vast miscellaneous assemblage knows full well that it is an utter impossibility to prevent the crowd from expressing their sentiments in a manner and as audibly as they please [Goldstein 32–33].

In nineteenth-century churches, as well, the enthusiasm that was originally regarded as vulgar became an essential part of the ritual. And as Moore points out, Christian enthusiasm was not that different from theatrical or sporting events: "Whenever people rush down aisles, fling themselves in the straw, and cry for salvation with mighty sighs and groans, other people become spectators" (15). These characteristics of both baseball and the American religion are what enabled them to become part of America and not just European imports.

America's Games: Heroes, Theologies, Statistics and Pastorals

As American baseball and religion entered the twentieth century they were wildly successful, both in America and abroad. Figures from Babe Ruth to Billy Sunday became enthusiastic if somewhat uncouth ambassadors, and writers from Grantland Rice to William James proclaimed the uniqueness and Americanness of their respective subjects. To continue to trace shifts in the development, perception and participation of both in the twentieth century is beyond the scope of this chapter, but we can go deeper into an analysis of some areas.

Baseball, as has often been noted, is open to many mythical or religious analogies. The trip around the bases—a hero venturing forth from home to encounter and overcome dangers to victoriously return home again—embodies what literary and biblical critic Northrop Frye calls a "U-shaped pattern" which he sees as containing the entire Bible. A pattern "in which man … loses the tree and the water of life at the beginning of Genesis and gets them back at the end of Revelation" (169). The hero can only be saved by returning from his Exodus or to his Garden of Eden. More than just the archetype of a religious quest, baseball presents a quintessential American hero on an American quest. In Robert Coover's postmodern novel, *The Universal Baseball Association, Inc.*, his protagonist remarks on this aspect of the sport:

> Motion. The American scene. The rovin' gambler. Cowpoke and trainman. A travelin' man always longs for home, cause a travelin' man is always alone … like a base runner on the paths, alone in a hostile cosmos, the stars out there in their places, and him trying to dominate the world…. Probably suffered a sense of confinement there in the batter's box, felt the need to strike forth on a meaningful quest of some kind [141].

The American Christian, as well, is only truly religious when she is alone with Christ, her personal relation with Christ is primary. As Stephen Prothero observes, "while evangelical hymns largely ignore the church, the sacraments and the trinity, they are obsessed with Jesus" (24). For Stephen Marini, "if modern evangelical hymns can be reduced to a single term, it would be nearness to Christ rather than the otherness of the sacred" (qtd. in Prothero 77). Yet despite the "friend we have in Jesus," the American hero is always a loner, a mysterious Shane rolling into town to deal with things alone.

This claustrophobic American hero, striking forth on a solitary, self-assigned mission, from John Wayne to Batman, also represents the American search for salvation. American religion, in some form or another, whether apocalyptic, Calvinist, Universalist, or Adventist, has been obsessively concerned with the specifics of salvation—how, who, when, how many—a salvation that is entirely personal. American salvation, as Bloom points out, is a "one-on-one act of confrontation," that cannot come through the community or the congregation (32). Baseball reflects these modes of thought. Like the heroic confrontation, like the American Christian, baseball creates a constant one-on-one tension. The pitcher may have his team behind him, the hitter has a bench rooting for him, but all fades away into batter against pitcher, pitcher against batter. A contest that is no less than life or death.

Death, as Bloom and others say, is the father of all religion, and the fear of death is particularly part of American religion and culture. In baseball, the fear of death is unconsciously buried in the language and machinations of the game. In his journey around the bases, a runner must avoid being put out, or worse yet, being part of a "twin-killing." One way of avoiding this deadly fate is being put out of danger by a teammate's "sacrifice." While other sporting events, like the Spanish bullfight and the Balinese cock fight, have been interpreted as being about sex and death, baseball is more about personal salvation and personal reflection, not about the reality or beauty of death, but about the ultimate defeat of it. Baseball's often mentioned unique time structure is actually an opportunity to cheat death. As Deanne Westbrook says, the progress of the game is measured by deed, not by a clock, and it is potentially infinite (100). If a team can just keep a rally alive the game is conceivably endless, and, in fact, each inning and each at bat is theoretically eternal.

A characteristic paradox or tension in American religion is its pull towards a simplification or domestication of complex thought, and an opposing creative movement towards new religions at the same time. We can see the first half of this paradox in the characteristic American anti-intellectualism and in the craving for a simple old-fashioned space. The association of this nostalgia with baseball is demonstrated in commercials for "Good Old Time Country Lemonade" that use "Take Me Out to the Ball Game" as background music. On the other hand, one thing American religion did was to open up the possibility of new religions, new prophets, and new Gods. This desire for both tradition and innovation is the same contradictory thinking that makes "same original formula" and "new and improved" two classically effective American marketing campaigns.

One way in which American Christianity domesticates its European models is to consciously make its theology less ambiguous. European and Eastern Christianity, for example, have grappled with and developed complex explanations and images of the trinitarian character of the divine. The unfathomable and irresolvable nature of the concept is often cited as part of its mystery and ultimate truth. American Christianity, on the other hand, has developed as one of its characteristics either a non-emphasis on the trinity or a denial of the concept all together (Conkin 316–318). Rather than construct difficult questions, American Christianity often tries to offer basic answers to simplified problems. "Stop suffering," the sign in front of a Brooklyn church reads, "Today at 10 a.m., 4 p.m., and 7 p.m." Necklaces and billboards across the United States in the 1990s read, "WWJD" (What Would Jesus Do?), as the answer to life's dilemmas. Bumper stickers and T-shirts say simply, "Know God. Know Peace," a phrase that would make little sense to Thomas Aquinas or Søren Kierkegaard for whom Christianity was a lifelong struggle and cause of anxiety.

To extend our analogy, we can say that from the outset baseball has been a game of clearly drawn lines: safe or out, fair or foul, strike or ball. Like American religion, it attempts to suggest simplicity and a democratic availability. Thomas Boswell speaks for American Christianity as well as baseball when he says, "instead of celebrating mysteries, baseball rejoices in the absence of mysteries and trusts that, if we watch what is laid before our eyes … we will cultivate the gift of seeing things as they really are" (qtd. in Ward 193). The idea that it is possible to see things as "they really are" is central to American Christianity, most clearly in the claim to "read" the Bible and not "interpret" it. We can also see a parallel to the relationship between the mysterious Christ of Europe, who Augustine saw as "an enigma and as through a glass," and the American Christ who "walks and talks with you" and is a "friend." For influential nineteenth century theologian Horace Bushnell, "we want no theological definitions of God's perfection; but we want a friend whom we can feel as a man" (qtd. in Prothero 63). The American Jesus is indeed more like a teammate, "not a first century Jew, but a nineteenth or twentieth century American, whose principal difference is that he already has risen from the dead" (Bloom 65). American saw themselves as the New Jerusalem and their battles as those of the original Christians. They used events from the Hebrew Bible to help them understand their situation: the camp meetings were Moses in the wilderness, and confronting the American Indian was Daniel in the Lion's den.

Baseball, as a sport of the book, does the same thing. The past is always part of the present; an event is made more meaningful by its relationship to a glorious, more perfect past. When Andruw Jones, a centerfielder for the Atlanta Braves, raced back to catch a line drive directly over his head, the radio announcer called the play, "back, back, back, Jones has a chance. Oh! Willie Mays!" This seeming non-sequitur is clear to any serious baseball fan, who knows, with just the mention of the name Willie Mays that Jones made the catch, and that, like Mays, in a play that happened in the 1950s, Jones caught the ball over his shoulder running with his back to home plate. Baseball, like religion, has sacred "texts" from the past that continue to shape current perceptions.

American Christians, although they might not be able to cite the verse, know that "Jesus loves me," because the "Bible tells me so," and American Christianity, although not a learned intellectual tradition, has often accepted the "book" at a level unique to Western culture. Unlike the European, Jewish, or Islamic emphasis on commentary, exegesis, and interpretation, a characteristic American take on the Bible is that it alone offers all that is needed. Fundamentalism has been valued over interpretation, and American fundamentalist Christians claim not only that the Bible cannot be wrong, but that to *interpret* it is to warp the meaning. The standard American Bible has always been published without any commentary. While not trying to draw too close a parallel here, baseball has come to accept its book and its numbers as a form of absolute Truth. And while new statistical analysis and reinterpretations of baseball history may flourish among baseball scholars, the general public changes slowly. Like new complex theological arguments, modifications of the game's lore tend to remain in the hands of the professional. Two examples of this are the refusal to let go of baseball's myth of a rural origin, and the slow acceptance of new baseball statistics or "sabermetrics" (taken from the acronym for the Society for American Baseball Research). A "runs created per 27 outs" statistic may define a hitter's value more than a batting average, but it won't get you recognized as a "batting champion" in the *Sporting News*.

Baseball's "book" is best represented in its obsession with recording every play. As is often pointed out, how many other sports can re-create a whole game by looking at a sheet of paper afterwards. From its origins, baseball kept close records of its numbers. Henry Chadwick was one of the first to get newspapers to publish baseball statistics, and he commented on their worth:

> many a dashing general has "all the gilt taken off the gingerbread," by these matter-of-fact figures, and we are frequently surprised to find the modest but efficient worker, who has played earnestly but steadily through the season, apparently unnoticed, has come in, at the close of the race, the real victor [Ward 8].

In other words, statistics are meant to show who earned what, who worked the hardest, and who deserved the glory, which perhaps explains why the reaction to the use of steroids and other performance enhancing drugs has been so much stronger in baseball than in other American team sports.

Baseball's numbers reveal its own mythology and belief system. "Numbers don't lie," we often hear, but of course they can and do. What is easy to forget is that the numbers we choose to record are by no means the obvious ones or the most important. By looking more questioningly at our everyday baseball box score, we can examine what a psychoanalyst would call the structural unconsciousness of its language. For one thing, baseball statistics reinforce and reveal aspects of the game we have been discussing, such as the focus on the individual confrontation between pitcher and hitter. Early baseball box scores did not record pitching statistics, only hitting and fielding. But as the game matured, the pitching numbers became important and fielding statistics (except for errors) faded away. A pitcher's wins and strikeouts and a batter's average and home runs became significant measures of their personal battle. In another example, the game's obsession with recording "errors" and "earned runs" reflects a culture obsessed with one's own individual responsibility for his or her salvation. There is always a winner and a loser; there is always fault to be found. As Roger Angell points out, the game provides a perfect, finished balance. Each hitter's credit represents a pitcher's debit, and vice versa (12).

On the other hand, a player's "on-base percentage" does not include reaching base on a fielder's error. While the statistic is intended to represent a player's ability to get on base, if he reaches on an error, he does not receive credit. Like Christian salvation, reaching base must be personally earned. Yet paradoxically, an unintentional feeble six-foot roller down the third base line can count as much as a 350-foot line drive single off the wall. Again, like American salvation, while it must be earned, the process is unimportant: one's status changes, salvation happens instantly and only the end result is important. Product is always emphasized over process. It is interesting to imagine what baseball statistics we would keep with a different religious orientation. Had America remained determinedly Calvinist, for example, or if baseball had evolved (which it probably could not have) in a Buddhist country.[3]

Baseball's language also reveals its unconscious epistemology or, in the words of the poet Wallace Stevens, "what we said of it became a part of what it is." As the language of baseball has developed, it has also increasingly emphasized the personal confrontation of the pitcher/hitter. Bradd Shore discusses the difference between "playing" and "being." One "plays" first base, but cannot "play" hitter, pitcher, or catcher. Frank Thomas cannot play batter, although he "plays first base." You have to "be" the batter (125–126). A player is identified in the wider world, of course, by the position he "plays," but in the game the ontological condition of being is reserved for moments of vulnerability. To some extent to be at-bat is to be imperiled; the fielders occupy determined positions which they defend by their "play." But, the base runner, the batter, the pitcher and the catcher are involved in battle. For the batter and base runner it is a battle for survival. One may be "safe" at first, but it is only the initiation of a series of transactions that allow the danger of death at every turn. The status, however, changes instantly, a player can become what he does, and, in baseball, confrontation and salvation are personal.

The ultimate salvation in baseball is to score, to reach home. Bart Giamatti—former major league baseball commissioner and Yale English professor—addresses the familiar topic of "home," by asking "why is it not called fourth base?" As he points out, "home" is an English word that does not translate into other languages, and it creates a sense of not only returning to a promised place, but also of a sense of flux. Home, as he says, "is a concept and not a place…. Home is where one first learned to be separate and it remains in the mind as the place where reunion, if it were to occur, would happen" (100). Metaphors of home still dominate romanticized descriptions of baseball and of what it should represent to our society.

Much has been written about the shapes of baseball, but, as usual, these writings are contradictory. Westbrook sees in the field a "gigantic transformation of the mandala, one of the oldest and most ubiquitous metaphors for both cosmos and self, outer and inner space" (112). Shore notes that "baseball is the only American sport that does not use a symmetrical field, defined by sides and ends. The baseball park defines a tension between an ever narrowing inner point, called home, and an ever widening outer field" (125). Yet for Giamatti, "baseball believes in ordering its energies, its contents, around threes and fours. It believes that symmetry surrounds meaning, but even more, forces meaning. Symmetry, a version of equality, forces and sharpens competition. Symmetrical demands in a symmetrical setting encourage both passion and precision" (90). The idea that baseball's meaning is due both to its asymmetrical and its symmetrical organization is American contradiction at its best, and is further revealing of the cultural connections between baseball and religion.

The shape of the field does offer a sense of the infinite; the foul lines extend outwards forever. In former rules, a ball that curved foul after it cleared the fence was a foul ball, so that theoretically a ball remained in play to infinity. In discussions of shapes and fields, baseball has been identified as having two centers. Depending on how you are reading, the center of the field is either the pitcher's mound or home plate. But linguistically the center of the field is home plate. A pitcher walks *out* to the mound but runs *in* to cover home plate on a wild pitch. The broadcaster describes a runner stealing second base as "there he goes," but stealing home is always "here he comes."

For a Buddhist, there is no center; for St. Augustine, the trinity forms a complex divinity that is not locatable; but for an American Christian, there is no doubt about the center. As professional baseball player turned superstar preacher Billy Sunday put it, "All other religions are built around principles, but the Christian religion is built around a person, Jesus Christ" (793). The traditional television view and the location of the press box further enforce baseball's sense of a center from which all emanates. The game is perceived and written about from this angle. Michael Scot, a minor league radio announcer, notes that if the game were called from center field, home run calls would sound more like orgasms. Instead of the traditional "going, going, going. Gone," we would hear, "coming, coming, coming. Here! Yes!"

A center always implies origin, and as we have seen both baseball and American Christianity insist upon the idea of a rural and unspoiled Edenic origin. This is not, of course, unique to America. Unspoiled pastoral green meadows have been a part of the human imagination since Virgil's *Eclogues,* and Eden goes back to … well, Eden. But baseball has one of the strongest modern-day associations with the pastoral. "The green geometry of the baseball field [is] more than simply a metaphor for the American experience and character…. [It] is closer to an embodiment of American life" (Giamatti 48). For Giamatti, we should never underestimate the "power of an enclosed green space" on the American religious imagination (42). While other sports perhaps share this aesthetic, the pastoral is always tied up in beginnings, origins, and the myth of the garden, and baseball with its mythical rural beginnings and its long history offers that. Giamatti writes that the "enclosed green field of the mind" can offer solace to those who feel the "need to think something lasts forever" (8, 13). Yet how much of this is truly baseball, and how much is the imagination of a baseball loving Renaissance scholar? David McGimpsey is probably right when he says, "baseball fans generally watch games not to commune with the fields of green in a quasi-religious way, but to see their team win" (3). And in the same vein, people go to church not to grapple with theological questions but to improve their chances for salvation or to talk to friends. American Christianity is not St. Augustine. Baseball is not Virgil.

The point here is not whether you associate baseball with the pastoral or not, but that culturally and historically we have needed and used that association. In his classic study of the American Pastoral, Leo Marx identifies two types: the first is popular and sentimental (Whitman's baseball of parks and picnics), and the second imaginative and complex (5). It is the second, of course, that is more interesting, and that we can see in American Christianity and in baseball. Marx develops the idea of the pastoral in nineteenth century America as something that rises out of the image of our country as the site of a new beginning (similar to how we have discussed religion and baseball). He demonstrates how the imaginative pastoral is never just peaceful, but must contain a "counterforce" in order to capture our imagination (25). His central metaphor for this counterforce, and indeed for the contradictory American epistemology in general, is *The Machine in the Garden*. He points to examples of nineteenth century American pastoral from Nathaniel Hawthorne to Thomas Cole, who introduce trains into peaceful scenes of nature. (The baseball metaphor for this could be its violently active infield surrounded by great expanses of primarily empty grass; just imagine the view from the top of the upper deck.) Baseball and America's need to maintain a sense of rural old-fashioned origins, at the same time that they are aggressively refashioning and denying origins, is an example of the pastoral garden planted with the seeds of its own destruction. And yet these are the very seeds that allow for continued growth and interest.

The Messiah Is On Deck

This characteristic blend of nostalgia, religion, and baseball was captured in a hit 1952 gospel song, "The Ball Game," by an otherwise little known gospel singer and songwriter Sister Wynona Carr, that compares spiritual life to a baseball game. The song, which opens with "life is a ballgame," sets up a series of comparisons between playing baseball and living a good Christian life. At the end, the song's chorus repeats, Jesus will be standing at home plate waiting to welcome you as you finish your journey. Set in a simple old-fashioned gospel style, the song consciously suggests a folksy and moral American past to which both baseball and religion nostalgically desire to return. Everyone can play the song assures us, which asserts our cherished democracy, an important concept in the formation of both American Christianity and baseball, although the word "can" suggests that some may not be included. In later verses of the song, first base is "temptation" and second base is "sin." The metaphor of the perilous trip around the bases, as we have seen, is a familiar one used to refer to everything from sacred pilgrimage to mortal life to sexual conquest.

The song also draws our attention to some contradictions in the culture and practice of the sport and the religion and, by metaphorical extension, to the culture at large: both worship and baseball are communal rituals, but are also intensely individualistic; both are democratic events that glorify cheating or have practiced exclusion based on race or gender; and, even in their formative years, both were almost instantly infused with the sense of an "old-fashioned" morality. Baseball continues to embody these contradictions. While life is a game, one must play fair, the song says. Yet hidden ball tricks, knockdown pitches, and spitballs have become a romanticized part of the game—even of its glorious golden age—"In the old days we wudda put him on his ass." No other sport has so developed and encouraged the anti-authority mentality that stretches from "Casey at the Bat" to fiery argumentative managers from Earl Weaver to Bobby Cox.

Finally, the song portrays Christ as waiting at home plate; in other words, a supportive teammate who will greet you as you score a run, give you a high five and pat you on the butt. This image accurately depicts the American Christ, who is not a mysterious part of the trinity, but a tangible and human acquaintance. "We may converse with Him as one man converses with another" (587), Joseph Smith—the creator of arguably the most American-based theology ever practiced—preached. Hymns and tracts consistently refer to him as our "friend." If Christ greets you at the home plate, he must be playing the role of the on-deck hitter, on your side from the start, cheering you out of the box, around the bases, and, if needed, he will ultimately be given a chance to hit and to bring you home himself.

The base runner, the song says, must avoid pitfalls and danger as he works his way home. As the only member of his team in fair territory, the base runner, always surrounded by the enemy, is a metaphorical symbol of the American Christian in a perpetual battle against the forces of evil. As early American preacher Jonathan Edwards warned, "one that stands or walks in slippery Places is always exposed to fall" (347). Each American's spiritual trip around the bases is also made alone; however much teammates and fans can cheer one on, whatever base coaches tell the base runner, the decisions are ultimately his. This experience is characteristic of American Christianity.

Religious leaders in the early nineteenth century did not look to sages, history, or books for answers, but "espoused convictions that were essentially individualistic" (Hatch 6). This attitude is shown in the 1820s by a woman named Lucy Smith, who wrote, "There was not then upon earth the religion which I sought. I therefore determined to examine my bible and ... to endeavor to obtain from God that which man could neither give nor take away" (qtd. in Hatch 43). The creative approach to interpretation and salvation was even more evident in her son, Joseph, who, as the founder of Mormonism, created a whole new sacred text in which he wrote of Christ's visit to what is today the Americas. If Christ *were* to visit America, what better position for him then as some sort of permanent on-deck hitter, greeting each base runner as he crossed the plate, and threatening to come to bat himself?

Becoming Virtual

What now? Where does any of this lead, and does it tell us anything about the future of baseball, religion, or culture? If we were to somehow transport a game from 1900 to the present time, put everyone in modern day uniforms, and put it in Yankee Stadium, your average fan would probably not notice a difference. By the same token, if a local Methodist minister preached a sermon first delivered in 1900, using current language patterns and events, his congregation would hardly sit up. Does this mean nothing has changed?

In this final section we want to use baseball and some of the connections we have made, to open up some larger questions about American popular religion. Because American baseball and religion come out of a dichotomous white/black, fair/foul, safe/out, and heaven/hell paradigm, they find themselves in tension with what is arguable an increasingly relativistic and postmodern world that is questioning our knowledge of such concepts as binary truths. From scientists like Albert Einstein to postmodern philosophers like Jacques Derrida, reality has become more dependent upon individual perception—on one's experience rather than on an objective "out there." The study of religion increasingly focuses on what people do rather than what they believe. While religion and baseball can appear to be in opposition to these epistemological and experiential shifts, they have also, unavoidably, become part of it.

Experience has always been a definitive concept in American religion. The unique American God is experiential, and is known to exist because he can be felt. If we are looking at baseball and culture—baseball and religion—we need to look most closely not at the objects themselves, but at how they are perceived and experienced. Although both baseball and American

Christianity are often regarded as troubled institutions, over 70 percent of Americans still identify themselves Christian, and more people than ever before are watching and going to baseball games. What is their experience?

The experience of a twenty first century baseball fan is one of a multi-layered reality. Baseball, and sports viewing in general, has become more complex, a network of connections, one leading to another with no logical flow. The game as a self-contained unit is no longer the typical experience. With radio, television, smart phones, and the internet one can follow a whole season without seeing a game in its entirety. A typical fan can sit and, using a remote control, flip back and forth between up to ten or more games on cable television. If fans miss a big play they rewind the DVR or watch it later on their ESPN app, or on the MLB cable station. Through a computer or satellite radio fans can listen to almost any professional game in the country, major or minor league, or they can go to a web site to check on the progress of their fantasy or rotisserie team (updated in real time), a roster they have picked but based on the performance of real life players.[4] The concepts of "team" and "game" have become different. If a televised game is boring, viewers cut to another one. With rare exceptions, major league teams almost completely change their players within two years. The team is an empty symbol, a simulacrum; like many contemporary religious symbols, like information on the internet, it stands for something that exists in a materially inconsistent: a sign with an unstable signified.

The possibilities that the internet has offered to baseball are a model for new ways of thinking about religion as well. It is already a cliché of this new century to define modes of thought by talking about the internet, but, as theologian Graham Ward points out, the internet is the "ultimate postmodern experience ... the ultimate in the secularization of the divine ... a God who sees and knows all things, existing in pure activity and realized presence, in perpetuity" (xv–xvi). A religious thinking that has also become postmodern encourages the blurring of virtual and real. Religion in cyberspace is represented by hypertext Bibles and the *Idiot's Guide to Religion On-Line,* but it is also more complex than that. In a culture that has been open to new gods and new sacred scriptures, this new way of viewing the world goes straight to the core of American spirituality. American popular culture has developed into a post–Christian one where the multitudes of American Gods have begun to blur and erase each other. Contemporary baseball has not moved away from its connections with American religion, but has continued to develop along with it. Does baseball produce fans or do fans produce baseball? And if the experience of God or of baseball is now one of blurred edges, no beginnings or endings, and no definitions, how do we proceed?

Two American novels often identified as "postmodern" offer some insight into these changing perceptions. In Robert Coover's novel, *The*

Universal Baseball Association, Inc., J. Henry Waugh, Prop., the protagonist creates a whole fictional world of baseball and life with dice and charts in his small apartment. The players in his league are rookies then veterans; they marry, retire, become managers, and they die. Henry lives a "real" life of loneliness and drinking, but his only pleasure is in the manipulation of his baseball league. At the end of the novel, Henry himself seems to disappear, but the players continue on, unaware of the death of their creator. Coover's book is an expression of our attempts to understand our own history, our alienation, and our questions as to origins and reality. The book creates a postmodern world where the boundaries between virtual and real, fact and fiction, and history and narrative are blurred or dissolved. The ending of the novel presents us with a society unaware that its creator no longer exists, and with no answer as to what they are doing there. It asks us, through the language of baseball, the existential questions of our time: Is there a God? Did we create him? Are we crazy? Is he?

Don DeLillo's expansive novel *Underworld* is a demonstration of how America's obsessions with baseball and religion now exist in an ambiguous world of past and future and of truth and fiction. The novel uses Bobby Thomson's famous 1951 home run as a transcendent event around which DeLillo builds his web of the next 50 years of American history. In the novel, the actual baseball that Thomson hit acts as a sacred relic, as the idea of it connects characters across the country and across generations; the ball is found, lost, sought after, desired, and worshiped. We are never really sure if it is the authentic ball itself that characters claim to possess and as Todd McGowan says, although the ball is *the* object, "no one seems to have it. Even the person who actually has the ball is unable to posses it because its value lies in its absence" (125–126). In the same way, Jesus is still, as Sister Wynona Carr's song suggested, the on-deck hitter, but "on-deck" in the sense of an anticipated messiah, only present through absence. A messiah by definition can never arrive, just as an on-deck hitter never comes to the plate. And in our imagination, present and absent, secular and divine, baseball and religion will continue to represent, change with, and determine our popular culture.

CHAPTER 3

Consuming Faith
Porn, Advertising and Religion

The whole system becomes weightless, it is no longer anything but a gigantic simulacrum ... an uninterrupted circuit without reference.
—Jean Baudrillard

Representation is reality.—Catherine MacKinnon

Calvin Klein has always been a thought-provoking brand. Their advertising has always been progressive. Brooke Shields was a child when she was quoted as saying "nothing comes between me and my Calvins." Was that child porn? In my opinion, it wasn't then, and it isn't now.
—Craig Lawrence, President of One.1K

Prologue

While the desire for God in American popular religion includes a desire for containment of an increasingly chaotic social system, the ever expanding, ever insistent, ever voracious culture of consumerism subtends a system that is equivalent to a national, and increasingly global, dogma that surpasses all others in its zeal, creating in its adherents an overwhelming desire to acquire and consume goods and services. Without this overriding desire, Western culture would crumple. The desire-creating systems clash in particularly interesting ways in the commercialization of Christmas, whose religious message is subsumed by and devolves into orgiastic consumption, which has come to be assumed by every sector of the economy, dubbed "the war against Christmas" by Christian groups and Fox News.[1]

In direct contrast to the explicit message of humility and proscriptions against vanity of the major religions of Western culture, as constituents of a culture of consumerism we are regularly bombarded with the message that it is of vital importance that we acquire material wealth, and, more importantly, that we use that wealth to buy more and more products, which in turn will become symbols of our wealth. Advertising instills a desire in its viewers/readers through an elaborate system of metaphor in which the desire for the product ultimately becomes conflated with other human desires. The desire for wealth, power, companionship, social status, romance and God's love are all used to sell the consumer goods and services. But, the most commonly used human desire by far is the desire for sex; and yet, sexual desire itself discomfits most American religious groups.

For many religious groups, there is no metaphor or allegory in the biblical text. Increasingly, however, while many maintain this scriptural truth, the focus of American Christianity is not so much on the book but on the personality of its founder. As we have said before, America has become a "Jesus-centered" country, rather than focusing on scriptural, creedal or doctrinal principles. The commonplace for most fundamentalist and evangelical Christians in the United States has been for a personal relationship with Jesus, a relationship that emphasizes the person of Jesus rather than his divinity or position relative to the other persons of the trinity, as we will discuss in our chapter on the God of film. The desire for the divine is fulfilled through a literal interpretation of Jesus as the incarnate word of God. The carnal embodiment of Jesus gives fulfillment to those who seek an unmediated relationship with divine. This chapter will analyze the intersection of consumerism, advertising, pornography, and popular religion. Developing themes of allegory, desire, faith, and the real, as they are negotiated and recreated at this intersection, reveals a uniquely American national religion full of characteristic contradictions.

Advertising Desire

The model sits recumbent inside a shopping cart in a mall parking lot. Her legs straddle the outside rails of the cart, a mischievous smile plays on her face. She shares the cart with several bowling balls, one of which lies between her legs. The image seems to elicit two simultaneous responses; she is both consumer and consumed. In another pose she sits in a semi-darkened theater, between her spread legs an impossibly large tub of popcorn; the colors are vibrant primaries; red predominates. She is young, dangerously young. There are other poses, all of which seem to signify without words her availability as commodity.

In one she is sitting cross-legged in a round beanbag chair. In another she pushes back her long hair from her face while looking unfocusedly away from the camera. Another pose shows her leaning against a very colorful wall looking down toward the viewer, her hand poised at her jeans' waistband. In yet another pose, she slouches back in a nondescript booth of a nondescript diner and overdramatically applies lipstick with her mouth opened wide. Her face in each of these shots is heavily made up, with distinctive and gaudy blue eyeliner and shadow and bright red lipstick. The combination of bright, primary colors, soft pastels, unsubtle makeup, and playful poses serve to give the model an even more youthful appearance than she already possesses. In none of these poses are the jeans she is wearing very clearly depicted. Indeed if there is any subtlety in these ads at all, it is in the non-description and non-particularity of the clothes they advertise. The only text accompanying these images is "GUESS JEANS" written in a bright red, Roman, capitals on a white background.

This ad campaign, which appeared on New York City subways in 1999, was an early example of the now common campaigns that occupy all the available ad space of a subway car, so that no other advertising images are visible. In their ubiquity, they reveal a certain kind of power, a condition that can be seen as a microcosm of the marketplace at large. The flood of advertising images dominates our senses, with the exception that rather than the cacophony of ads we usually associate with chaotic cityscapes like Time Square or Shinjuku, Tokyo, these present a unified field of images all pointing to the same product. Other than this monopolist power, the ads themselves were not that unusual or even remarkable. They employed a fairly common structure in advertising, one easily recognized by most members of the culture. The use of a young attractive woman in suggestive poses is meant first to attract attention, and create an association between sexual desire and acquisitive desire. On some level too, there is the idea of transgression. The shots of this young woman are meant to cross some line of modesty or, more precisely, appear so to have done.

At the time, what most drew our attention to this particular ad were stickers pasted to some of the posters which read, "Boycott Guess Jeans. This is child pornography," and signed Men Against Violence Against Women (MAVAW). What interests us now has to do with some definitional issues. First, how was MAVAW defining child, pornography, and violence? And, what makes it possible for them to read these ads as pornographic, violent, or abusive to children and/or women? And more broadly, what is it in our cultural epistemology that makes this kind of advertising simultaneously so offensive and effective? Since this ad first appeared, the advertising universe has shifted sharply toward online advertising. This change has made the role of viewer participation even more a central part of advertising campaigns and has shifted participatory action central to the experience and strategies of both creating and perceiving advertising.

With the revolution in mobile devices and social media, most of the money and attention in advertising is moving toward the digital. According to media assessment company Strategy Analytics,

in an overall pot that it estimates at nearly $187 billion, digital will account for just under 30% of that—28%, or $52.8 billion, to be exact, putting it nearly $30 billion behind TV ad spending. However, growing at a rate of 13% this year, and up 2.5% on 2014's share, digital remains the fastest—growing of any category [Tech Crunch].

In 1999, the digital portion of that pot was non-existent; now it "is expected to overtake TV advertising in size by 2019, with the former reaching $83.9 billion on the back of a 2014–2019 compound annual growth rate (CAGR) of 11.15%" (marketingcharts.com). Interestingly, market forecasters predict that public transit advertising—as part of what the industry calls Out-of-home or OOH advertising—"has the strongest prognosis of the traditional media types" (marketingcharts.com).

Subway and bus ads often deploy shock value to grab attention, and are open to commentary from the riding public, often in the form of graffiti or other visual content. This direct interaction between the public and the ads makes them a fertile site to probe the relationship of advertising and offensiveness. In spring of 2014, a New York plastic surgery practice began advertising breast augmentation surgery at a flat rate, using the image of a noticeably augmented pair of breasts in a tight, but revealing top, with a label that read "made in New York." As with the old Guess Jeans ad, these ads attracted a number of comments on their offensive nature. Some comments are written directly on the posters, others are attached in various forms: including a handwritten "poem" crudely stuck on with masking tape:

Women are deeply beautiful.
This idiotic ad is a farce and cannot encompass the humanity you hold.
Human beings are deeply beautiful.
Fuck advertising, and have a lovely day in this gentle,
brutal, love-filled and sorrowful world [Reddit].

Others use pre-printed stickers that pronounce the ads "oppressive to women," as well as other stickers, which feature a 1971 picture of Gloria Steinem and Dorothy Pitman Hughes with the caption: "this insults women and pisses us off." It seems most of the conversation generated by the ads was about getting them taken down. Even New York Governor Andrew Cuomo's office attempted to remove the ads from the subways, sending a letter asking the MTA to reconsider its standards. The doctors' group second attempt, in spring of 2015, was a much subdued variation on the theme; a young model is shown from about the waist up; it is clear that she is nude, but rather than showing her breasts there is a caption which reads: "DREAM BIG." "Dream" appears just to the left of her body and "big" occupies the space where her chest would be. This ad did not provoke as much commentary, and is described by one marketing observer as "elegant."

The ad seemed a recalibration to tone down the shock value of the first ads; but in summer 2015, they were back on the "offensive," treating NYC subway riders to a series of ads featuring "average looking" women holding up fruit to their chests. In one version the model holds tangerines in one pose, and looks sad; but, in the other pose she holds a pair of grapefruits, and looks happy—without captions. While this ad is not really salacious in the way ads that are often called pornographic might be, it certainly presses more muscularly on the theme of body shaming women into "fixing" themselves. These ads also garnered a number of comments with stickers that mostly called it oppressive to women.

A strong argument can be made that plastic surgery characterized as necessary for women to reach some hetero-normative ideal of beauty is oppressive to women. But, there are two issues with attacking the ads in this manner: the first is a purely commercial one. Doctors Plastic Surgery (the imaginative name of the physicians' group behind the ads) is not particularly interested in oppressing, insulting, or pissing off women as much as they are in offering them a service, which some women do seek. Yelp reviews for the office are actually quite positive, and most of the women gush about the service including one who says, "I must admit I was very skeptical at first because I saw their ad on a NYC subway. I called anyway and as soon as I walked in I was immediately comfortable." This customer's response may reveal something of how these kinds of ads work. The ad did not initially appeal to her; she suggests that she called the office despite rather than because of the ads. But obviously she would not have called if she hadn't seen the ad. So while even she might have considered the ad offensive, she was still willing to give them her business. Here, we are not arguing that the ads are not sexist—they certainly are—but they are so within an established complex matrix of cultural constructs. One of the issues with hegemony is that many strands and strata of culture, which tangle together to comprise it, make it difficult even to assess exactly how its force is exerted on the whole social system. The point is that if everyone in the culture reads the ads only through this lens and reacted univocally, the ads would never work, and neither would every other ad that uses this strategy to sell product.

The other issue is conceptual and has to do with reading through representation to what is signified; that women are made to feel like they need these services is a function of the objective position in which the culture places them. In other words, the ads by themselves cannot really be read as oppressive; instead their oppressive nature only functions in concert with the cultural constructions of gender, which while changing is still primary established along patriarchal lines. It is only through understanding the context of a culture that is always already oppressive to women, that we can read a symptom of the social condition of women through what is offered purely as commercial enticement.

As with Guess, the doctors are using shock value to attract attention to their product. While both Guess and the surgeons must walk a thin line between shock and offense because ultimately they are commercial enterprises that stand to lose their viewers' custom by going over that line. In a free-market economy this is supposed to be the check on corporate violation of community standards. Advertisers, the theory goes, can regulate themselves because they would be loath to transgress community standards to the point of losing business. But that presumes a homogenous community whose standards function across the market. Advertisers like Guess, Calvin Klein and others have discovered that they can offend a plurality of the population while still engaging and appealing to much smaller but quite profitable segments of the population.

Calvin Klein has been a pioneer in this kind of advertising, and continues to find ways to shock the public. In 2016, he once again made news and raised public outrage with an ad campaign that included a picture of model Klara Kristin shot up her dress, with the words "I flash in my Calvins." The shot mimics a form of pornography referred to as "upskirt," which is described by the National Center on Sexual Exploitation, who consequently started a petition to make Calvin Klein suspend the campaign, as "a growing trend of sexual harassment where pictures are taken up a woman's skirt without her knowledge, or without her consent" (Feldman). The statement from the Center goes on to express concern for how this ad might influence the culture:

By normalizing and glamorizing this sexual harassment, Calvin Klein is sending a message that the experiences of real-life victims don't matter, and that it is okay for men to treat the woman standing next to them on the metro as available pornography whenever they so choose.

Oddly, this kind of negative reaction to ads like these does not serve to stop them, but rather can only help Klein. What Calvin Klein discovered many years ago after charges of child pornography for his ads was that negative publicity was good for business. When asked by the *Huffington Post* "if she thought Calvin Klein would ever stop putting out these types of ads," Jean Kilbourne, senior scholar at the Wellesley Centers for Women and creator of the film series *Killing Us Softly: Advertising's Image of Women*, was adamant in her response. "No, never," she said. "Why should he? He's making a fortune, getting a huge amount of attention."

While Klein tries to scandalize the public as a marketing strategy, more traditional advertisers tend to protect their brands from negative publicity, which would, as we said, normally act as a check on advertising excesses. But groups who only wish to make a political point have no such concerns or check on transgressive expression. A 2010 ad campaign sponsored by a group calling itself American Freedom Defensive Initiative (better known as the SOIA, or Stop Islamization of America), a group that the Southern Poverty Law Center considers a hate group, placed Islamophobic ads on New York and Boston transit, including one that read: "In any war between a civilized man and the savage support the civilized man. Support Israel. Defeat Jihad." As with the other transgressive ads, commentary on these, on subways and buses, has been extensive many are almost completely covered with the overlays that say things like: "Stop Hate," or "RACIST." Because these ads represent an attack on a foreign demographic, analyzing them can help us to talk through some of the assumption made in the ads aimed at women.

The Guess Jeans and breast augmentation ads, like other cultural texts, call for interpretation; they require a series of internal and external cues that will allow most members of the culture to recognize, yet look past, the available sexual tension and focus instead on the product; whereas pornography, by its very nature, requires the focus to remain on sexual arousal. If the ads remained purely pornographic, Guess would not sell very many jeans and not many women would be buying implants from Doctors Plastic Surgery. To interpret these ads as pornographic or oppressive is to misread the presented analogy as strictly sexual or misogynist and to misunderstand the intention of both pornography and advertising.

This misreading interprets literally what is offered allegorically, an attempt to circumvent, or render unambiguous, that which is always accepted as complex and unavoidable in the culture, the relationship between commercial and sexual desire. One is absolutely essential; the other must be controlled. Because sexual desire and the desire for God's love are incompatible, this misreading sets up a contradiction between American consumerism and its religious mores. But, the AFDI ads do not participate in the same meaning-making system; they do not offer an analogy of a political position, which the reader must decipher and render in a different mode or register. Instead, the ads are bluntly racist; the example we cite proposes that Israelis are "civilized" and the Palestinians are "savages." The AFDI does not need to protect its brand from boycott, or be concerned that they may offend subway riders; *this* is their brand, and their intent is specifically to offend a large portion of the population to which they are "advertising." To rise to this level of offense, the doctors would have to say something like: "Flat-chested and worthless? Just $3900 can make you a valuable woman with a big rack?" and Guess: "don't be a frump; buy our clothes and look like a hot underage call girl." The ads may metaphorically imply this, which makes them sexist, but they can't come right out and say so literally. There is no subtlety or contextualization necessary to read through the AFDI ads because they focus on an outsider group. Because they involve political speech, they are protected by the first amendment. Unlike the surgeon's ad, the MTA did try to remove them and ultimately, the MTA voted to ban political ads altogether and the federal judge upheld the general ban.

We might think of advertising as working by exposing the general population to a representation of a product that might attract some of the public to it; in the meantime not offending the broader population with that representation. But, in this case the goals seem to be the contrary; AFDI seems to actively want to offend most of the public in order to get its political position "out there" and to present that political opinion in the most belligerent form so as to generate the most attention.

Desire for the Actual

We can see here three main themes involving consumerism, advertising and popular religion. First, consumers are able to read through the suggestively "pornographic," or offensive, in advertising and establish a desire for a product because they have been trained through the construction of an elaborate allegorical system that requires a deep understanding of its hidden messages. Advertisers might use sexually alluring material as a stand-in for acquisitive desire and their audience understands and does the interpretive work to get there as a consequence of their social and cultural development. In the breast augmentation ads, for instance, the doctors do not have to create the idea that larger breasts are better than smaller ones; if this were not already an accepted ideal in the culture, the ads would not succeed in either creating a desire for their product or offending anyone.

While advertising uses allegorical distance, the opposite is true of the unquestionably pornographic. "Hardcore" pornography is always purely mimetic. The whole point of the pornographic image is to be, well, graphic; there should be a one-to-one relationship between that which is desired and that which is perceived. Paradoxically, this one-to-one structure comes closest to the literalist scriptural doctrine of most American fundamentalist Christians, who see scripture as not only inviolable, but also representative of a *literal* truth, and who stress the importance of a personal relationship with their God that is not mediated by institutions, images, or even the biblical text. Opponents and viewers of pornography are likewise encouraged to interpret the text for themselves at the same time they see the texts as actual or "real."

Second, the prevalence of consumerist faith overrides all other concerns for community and moral standards, including concerns about defining, mitigating, or legislating the obscene, profane, or pornographic. Since much

American Christianity has developed a close relationship with the ideas of patriotism and capitalism, this sets up contradicting and competing paradigms.[2] Because of consumerism's overwhelming impetus toward "capitalizing" human desire, efforts to curb, delimit, or otherwise regulate the presumed pornographic in advertising will ultimately fail.

Third, the overarching construct, underpinnings and economic well-being of an advanced capitalist society depend upon a system of universal belief or faith in consumerism; the nature of capitalism requires and breeds a culture of acquisitiveness that verges on, perhaps even overshadows, religious fervor. Indeed many of the strategies employed in the selling of products to the public by advertisers are in direct opposition to most American religious attitudes. This conflict would seem to set up a critical contradiction that would negate one of these institutions, but they instead are inextricably linked. This link can be seen in the way American capitalism and religion relate to and employ desire. Desire for a product is not entirely unlike desire for God's love, or for a set of guiding principles which will allow us to live better lives. Whether God is seen as literal, metaphorical, or impossible, the god-idea always indicates and generates desire. Whether through the image or the idea, absence or presence—desire always indicates a lack of some sort. Desire desires desire. Religious revivals always take place in the shadow of crisis where there is a perceived lack of spiritual coherence and a desire to return to an Edenic past of purity and innocence.

God exists, as some theologians have said, primarily or even exclusively in our desire for him.[3] Pornography and advertising can also produce this construction of meaning through desire. Since American texts of popular culture and popular religion have rescripted how we read and think about the sacred, and if our concept of God is at least partially a desire for God, then both advertising and pornography have also rescripted desire in a process that is partly theological, a process that cultural critic Mark C. Taylor calls "adverteasing":

> What makes adverteasing so seductive is the repeated promise yet inevitable denial of fulfillment. Signs evoke real satisfaction only to "reveal" another sign that defers gratification. If the sign is always a sign of a sign and never the real thing, there is no end to the excessive quest for satisfaction. Desire is sacrificed on an altar that figures crucifixion but not resurrection [*Nots* 207].

The "literal" nature of scripture as read through fundamentalism accords well with the representational "real" of pornography. Rather than the literal truth or an essential verisimilitude, advertising functions strictly in the allegorical mode. While the central dominating dictum for advertising in this culture is that "sex sells," there is an inherent contradiction; while most people believe this truism, they do not believe it applies to them. It seems that sex does sell, but only to other people. Even those who feel that there is too much sex in the media incongruently agree with this premise. That is, although they themselves see this use of sexual imagery as offensive, they agree that it has certain allure to others.

There seems to be a critical disconnect between the methods employed by advertisers and the fundamental mores of the society to which they advertise. There is a boundary—this is generally accepted—beyond which advertising which attempts to titillate becomes pornographic, but the boundary itself is not in fact agreed upon. The difficulty in distinguishing between the pornographic and the non-pornographic can best be overcome by reconsidering these categories in light of their respective rhetorical strategies. The pornographic uses mimetic verisimilitude in creating sexual desire in its viewers; the desire in this case remains always sexual, always literal, and creates a simple relationship that necessitates no intermediary step. Seen in this context, pornography, marketing, and religion are not in conflict, but instead work together in a process of defining and framing the borders of acceptable behavior and morality.

It is not a coincidence that America's three major obsessions are sex, money, and religion. Guess, Victoria's Secret and other advertising is successful not despite religious disapproval, but because of it. We could think about pornography and fundamentalism as synesthetic practices. Like the fundamentalist Christian who wishes to establish an unmediated relationship with the person of Jesus through a written or visual text, the viewer of pornography wishes to experience visually what is usually a tactile occurrence. By contrast, questionably sexualized advertising is always necessarily an allegory or extended metaphor for sexual activity, in which there is a displacement of sexual desire for consumptive desire, and is therefore always non-pornographic. The images of advertising partake in the paradoxical conjoining of the belief in a literal text and the open interpretation that make up American Christianity's paradoxical relationship to the Bible. To read the allegory of advertising as pornographic is therefore to read it as a literalist or fundamentalist Christian.

God and Desire

The interaction between religious faith and the marketplace often results in paradoxical situations, yet there is a reciprocal relationship between the two. The marketplace informs the ways in which religious faith is shaped, disseminated and understood, just as faith *in* the marketplace is determined and understood in the same terms as religious faith. While the two systems would seem to be at odds they actually function together in many ways. As in the *South Park* episode featured in our introduction, the economy itself becomes a sacred entity which must be appeased, one in which we must have faith, and which has great power over us and yet exists only because of our faith that it does exist.

On the one hand, the culture of consumerism readily yields to the pornographic gaze and its power to seduce buyers. On the other hand, the Judeo-Christian tradition negates and attempts to stem sexual desire and redirect it toward a human desire for God. American consumer culture and popular religion coexist in a perpetual tension in which each attempts to keep the other in check. As R. Laurence Moore shows in *Selling God*, this relationship is at times problematic and at others symbiotic. Religion often makes use of marketing techniques developed in consumerist culture, while consumerist culture uses religion as a backdrop against which to set its cultural productions. For marketers, religion comes to define a boundary against which a transgressive impulse seeks to push.

Beginning early in the nineteenth century, American religious leaders became aware that they would need to compete in the marketplace of ideas in order to draw new converts to the fold and attempt both to control and attract the "coarser" elements of social freedom. As popular religious movements began to borrow from new rougher trends of popular culture, as we noted in the previous chapter, the more established churches denounced what they felt were dangerous precedents. Early on, congregational Protestant ministers railed against the "hucksterism" of revival shows and camp meetings of the "Second Great Awakening," as well as the sensationalism of the popular press and the sheer commercialism of the young republic.

If our definition of popular religion as "the religion that surrounds us in our everyday lives" and "the ways that ordinary people use religion to make sense and give meaning to their lives," then the question becomes: how did it get to be that way? How do these religious practices come to surround us? Religion and American Christianity, in particular, have had to compete in the marketplace of ideas with other ways of making sense of the world. Partly because faith in the American economic system has become indivisible from both its form of government and its predominating religious practices, what has developed is a religious free-market, in which "consumers" of religion have choices of a variety of religious practices. Many Christians today, do most of their scriptural reading online where the sacred text, thus, must necessarily be read from a locus shared with the profane consumerism of advertising including some that would be considered "porn" if we apply MAVW's definition. This is even further complicated when we think about the fact that most people now get their pornography, advertising, television, music, newspapers, and scripture through the same digital devices.

One consequence of this free-market has been a splintering of Christian denominations. "Mainline" denominational churches have been losing parishioners for years, while smaller, often more fundamentalist churches, have been growing. In the meantime, the 2014 Pew Research Center Religious Landscape Study showed a sharp rise in the number of Americans who identify themselves "religiously unaffiliated," also known as "nones" (as in, none of the above) from their previous study. For religious studies professor Matthew Hedstrom "Spirituality is what consumer capitalism does to religion." In his words,

> The millennial approach to spirituality seems to be about choosing and consuming different "religious products"—meditation, or prayer, or yoga, or a belief in heaven—rather than belonging to an organized congregation. I believe this decline in religious affiliation is directly related to the influence of consumer capitalism.

Religious "nones"—a shorthand we use to refer to people who self-identify as atheists or agnostics, as well as those who say their religion is "nothing in particular"—now make up roughly 23 percent of the U.S. adult population. This is a stark increase from 2007, the last time a similar Pew Research study was conducted, when 16 percent of Americans were "nones." During this same time period, Christians have fallen from 78 percent to 71 percent (Pew Research Center). This period has also seen the rise of social media to dominance among media outlets. The challenge to save souls (or, maintain followers) has become even more mercenary since the publication of our first edition.

In-Corporate Church

What makes the United States different from theocracy is that conservative religion has had to compete in the marketplace of ideas almost since the inception of the republic. The outcome of this situation is the inherent commercialization of religion. Religion competes not just against other philosophical positions, but also against its own image as commercialized.

From the tent revivals during the Second Great Awakening in the nineteenth century to stadiums and megachurches packed full or parishioners, Promise Keepers, "hipster" Christians, and Billy Graham's last great crusade at Flushing Meadows at the beginning of the twenty-first, American religion has attempted to broaden its appeal through modes that are often indistinguishable from crude commercialism. According to Moore, in the early days of the republic:

> Americans remained a religious people because religious leaders, and sometimes their opponents, found ways to make religion competitive with other cultural products. Although nineteenth-century Protestant ministers and many entrepreneurs of commercial culture on occasion furiously attacked each other, they had to learn to work the same audiences using a market model that compelled them to adopt techniques of persuasion rather than coercion [38].

On occasion, the churches themselves have been in conflict over the manner in which the "good news" was being spread. "Some [Protestant leaders] warned about the dangers of commercialization and suggested that the only obligation of religious leaders toward the reading public was to ensure that those people who wanted devotional material got the real thing" (Moore 34). Ultimately, the system of religious commercialism becomes tied in with the consumer culture and what develops is a vortex of influence where each affects the other in foundational ways. For example, as Moore notes, "the work of the American Bible and Tract societies as it influenced commercial culture laid the groundwork for mass communications and for mass movements generally" (76). Commercial culture within the American capitalist system develops side-by-side with religion and with advertising's manipulation of various human desires. As advertising develops, it becomes more and more dependent on the use of women's sexuality to manipulate these desires.

Market forces, however, have also always led to uneasy compromises between religious leaders and the ever-evolving marketplace. From the early days of radio broadcasting, the "good news" has been fraught with the dangers of being tainted by the more unseemly and grosser elements of commercialism. Televangelism, which remains with us today, is one of the ways in which popular religion has been broadcast to the nation. This approach can be seen variously as either an efficient and effective way of evangelizing or an opportunistic pyramid scam that allows some to take advantage of the vulnerable and gullible and get very rich. One of the most popular forms of broadcast ministries is the "prosperity gospel," which offers the message that God wants us to have money and luxury items as signs of our spiritual wealth. Washington Post columnist Cathleen Falsani writes that this idea, "an insipid heresy whose popularity among American Christians has boomed in recent years, teaches that God blesses those God favors most with material wealth" ("Prosperity Gospel"). Proponents of this theological position include Lakewood Megachurch leader Joel Osteen, and the appropriately named Creflo Dollar, who in 2015 asked for and got $65M to buy a luxury Gulfstream G650 jet to "safely and swiftly share the Good News of the Gospel worldwide" and "because it is the best, and it is a reflection of the level of excellence at which this organization chooses to operate." Prosperity theology often functions according to a "seeding" principle; the idea is that if you give Dollar money for his plane, God will reward you with your own financial recompense. The paradox that a Christian church would espouse a theology of material wealth is obvious, but it also resembles some of the dissonance between faith in free market capitalism as juxtaposed to Christian doctrine on the value of material wealth. Also significant to our point here is that awareness and condemnation of some of these practices reached a broader audience through popular culture, when, in 2015, John Oliver dedicated a sequence of episodes of *Last Week Tonight* to this ethically dubious practice.

The absolute faith in capitalism and the free market supported by most Americans is interrelated to the religious impulse to control and contain social morality. In this relationship, however, faith in the free enterprise system is always anterior to any religious impulse. Religious leaders again and again raise the danger of privileging the economic over the spiritual. In the post–World War II period, a number of Protestant writers struggled to establish a priority of place for a Protestant identity in the American marketplace. Protestant writer Paul Hutchinson's *The New Leviathan* of 1946 shows the uneasy relationship between religion and the marketplace, "disturbed by the idolatry of free-enterprise economics. [Hutchinson] quoted his friend Halford E. Luccock's satirical dictum: 'thou shalt not upset the applecart'" (Marty 141– 142). Luccock and Hutchinson very well understood the position of religious doctrine in its relationship with the marketplace. It is a relationship that highlights a number of contradictions of American culture and religion and also draws our attention to larger questions of representation, reality, presence, and desire. These are questions about who determines the value of speech: what is profane and what is sacred, what is real and what is merely representation?

In the twenty first century, this relationship remains no less complex or uneasy, and, in fact, conflation of the real and the virtual in the worlds of gaming, marketing, and advertising, has further complicated this association. In order to reach more people, established denominational churches have had to market themselves in non-traditional ways. Once marginal sects have come to be mostly accepted within mainstream American religious landscape largely through marketing campaigns; Mormons, Seventh-Day Adventists, Jehovah's Witnesses, and Scientologists have all moved beyond cult status to occupy a more mainstream position. In many cases, they accomplished this shift in public opinion through advertising campaigns that present their denominations as normative and American and yet, as offering something fresh and new at the same time. The LDS Church has used TV and internet advertising to "normalize" Mormon belief through the "I am a Mormon" campaign; and the Church of Scientology has run ads in the past four Super Bowls, asking viewers to ask a "question that lies at the intersection of technology and spirituality: Who am I?" (2016 Super Bowl advertisement).

Scientology presents a particularly interesting example. The history of Scientology as the creation of sci-fi writer and all-round eccentric L. Ron Hubbard is of recent date, even younger than the Mormons who date back to the nineteenth century. Hubbard initially created Dianetics as a mental health therapy, but turned into a church for convenience. Like the Jehovah's Witnesses, Scientology used a direct marketing method: sending droves of followers into the streets to get passersby to take a copy of *Dianetics* or take their free "personality test." While the organization has been considered a religious organization (and tax exempt) since 1993 and before that from 1957 to 1967, it was not originally designed as a religion. Hubbard is famously known to have said "You don't get rich writing science fiction. If you want to get rich, you start a religion," or some variation of that statement as early as the 1940s.

The Church that he founded, however, is one often noted as operating much more like a corporate entity rather than clerical one. And yet, despite its aggressive litigiousness, infiltration of the IRS, and apparent mercenary goals, the organization has been able to use advertising to reshape and project its self-image to the world. Through marketing, these churches have been able to "normalize" the practices of their faiths, which have become a part of the everyday religion that surrounds us: a part of the way in which American experience spirituality. These would be extreme cases of religious groups using the tools of the marketplace to either establish or further their "brand," but even more established denominations have used similar tactics, and, in fact, it is now common to see churches such as the Times Square Church advertise on the New York City Subways. From tent revivals to internet click-bait, American religious movements have always participated in the same sandlot as other commodities, often employing advertising techniques that other Christians have found questionable or even crass.

Mad Real

Because the appeal to desire is so effective in these techniques, the pornographic gaze again frames these issues in several important ways. While other representations are more easily distinguished from the real, depictions of sexual activity require a more complex assessment. Part of the question has to do with the conflation in the free market between human desire (of various kinds) and their commodification. Paradoxically, these questions of desire, representation, reality, and commodification can be addressed just as easily in a discussion of American religion and specifically the evangelical movement; in the interplay between market forces and religious zeal, expressions of desire and meaning often take on arrangements similar to sexualized desire.

The desire for a relationship with a clearly identified God whose meaning can only be confirmed through some form of real presence within a personal relationship is analogous to the need for presence that arises out of the consumptive desire created in advertising copy, a desire that can only be fulfilled through actual consumption of product or the redemptive power of a personalized deity. The whole idea of the real gets complicated by the creative force engaged in the very act of desiring; however, by definition, the pornographic does not yield desire, but satiety.

It would be difficult to talk about the this aspect of advertising and ignore the television show *Mad Men*, which chronicles the loosening of social mores in modern advertising through the cultural revolution of the late 1960s, as well as depicting the complex correlation between desire and consumption, and to some extent the emptiness of that consumption. In the show, Don Draper represents a new creative voice in the advertising world and also perhaps one of its most prescient and sophisticated philosophers. In analyzing the connection between desire and consumption, Don says, "Advertising is based on one thing, happiness. And you know what happiness is? The smell of a new car. It's freedom from fear. It's a billboard on the side of the road that screams reassurance that whatever you are doing is okay. You are okay" ("Smoke Gets in Your Eyes" 1.1). At a deeper lever the show deals with existential dangers of creating and perpetuating a culture fixated on desire for desire's sake. Early on in the show Don defends his profession against an obvious critic of consumerism:

> Roy: You hucksters in your tower created the religion of mass consumption.
> Don: People want to be told what to do so badly that they'll listen to anyone.
> Roy: When you say "people," I have a feeling you're talking about thou.
> Don: And I have a feeling that you spent more time on your hair this morning [points to Midge] than she did ["Babylon" 1.6].

Roy refers to the notion of consumption as a religion, implying that there is deceptiveness in both religion and the cult of consumerism. He sees what Don does as lying to the public and more significantly creating a system that enslaves people in a vicious cycle of work for superfluous goods. In equating consumerism with religion, Roy suggests that advertising serves as a kind of gospel. Don's retort suggests that people are so gullible that any religion will do, while pointing out that Roy himself is one of those people. Don's argument is something like: if it wasn't us (advertising), then someone else would be telling people what to do. Cinematographically, the show functions like a time a machine; not only portraying a historical period, but also allowing the audience to experience it "first hand." The highly stylized depiction of the times suggests an impressionistic interpretation of the aesthetic of the period, rather than faithful realistic rendering. There is verisimilitude, but its focus is almost exclusively focused on a striking graphic rather than the mundane details. It is a kind of *mise en abyme*, where it self-referentially represents the period in the style of the period.

It is not, in fact, that, but a rescription created from memory and nostalgia. Some have pointed out a number of historical inaccuracies in the show, which is interesting in a show that in some facets seems so careful to capture the exact look and feel of the period. Most of the "errors" have to do with anachronism, which may indicate that the show is more concerned with highlighting broader themes of the period than in rendering a perfectly accurate historical record of events. But the complaints about these "errors" also reveal how seriously viewers are taking the show as historical representation, and how much they are interacting with the show rather than passively watching it, as they would have in the era that the show depicts. The objectives of the show are more than just to present a historical view of the period; in some sense, it creates its own reality. As the editors of *Mad Men, Mad World: Sex, Politics, Style, and the 1960s* suggest, citing a *New York Times* story about the show,

> "The Korean War created Don Draper," the newspaper of record wrote, as though asserting a biographical fact. *Mad Men*, the *Times* seemed to say, was creating a window on the nation's past through which viewers might experience America's history in narrative form. Don Draper was not fiction but biography; *Mad Men* was not television but a repository of the past [Goodlad, et al. 1].

Here reality and fiction come together in a simulacrum which creates its own evidence for itself; there is no doubt that for some viewers (especially younger ones, but some older ones too) what they know of the 1960s and advertising will be shaped by this show. The show further influenced and confused "reality" in inspiring several *Mad Men* style clothing lines and in the seemingly ubiquitous presence of Jon Hamm's voice used in actual advertising for companies like Mercedes-Benz and American Airlines. The show's observations about the ways in which goods are marketed to the culture are made even more relevant to our argument by these dialogues with notions of "the real" and the ways in which the show flirts with becoming "real."

When Peggy says to Don that sex sells, he responds sternly, "You are the product. You feeling something. That's what sells. Not them. Not sex. They can't do what we do, and they hate us for it" ("For Those Who Think Young" 2.1). Here, Don refers to people like Roy and is trying to emphasize the artistic nature of his job. He both humanizes and distances the viewer; people are products to be sold, but they can only be sold by personally touching their emotions. Don is so good at selling an idea through emotional appeal that one never knows if he is actually emotionally involved or just selling us. We are therefore left wavering in some middle space between understanding the universal "truth" his words seem to convey and knowing that he is just feeding us a line meant to elicit an emotional response much as he does with his clients.

The uncertainty about the emotional investment of its main character gives the show a cynical perspective. As Don tells Peggy when she is depressed about a break up, "What you call 'love' was invented by guys like me. To sell

Nylons" ("Smoke Gets in Your Eyes" 1.1). And, if there is a quote from the show that most encapsulates the culture of consumerism, it would be from Peggy: "Those people—in Manhattan—they are better than us. Because they want things they haven't seen" ("Indian Summer" 1.11).

Despite achieving great wealth and fame, Don is never happy. Like many protagonists of "auteur television," he is driven by invisible, impossible, and unexpressed desire. Sometimes that is depicted in the show by his ravenous alcoholic, materialistic, and sexual appetites; and, paradoxically, other times it is expressed by his attempt to preserve a kind of patriarchal order in his household. And finally, sometimes it is his running away from the very things that appear to be his most valued assets. He seems to seek something more substantial, something we could call spiritual fulfillment, or some moral stability in an otherwise amoral existence. Don does whatever he wants, whenever he wants, and, yet that is somehow still too restrictive for him. In a state of constant existential angst, he goes through women, cigarettes and scotches like it's a personal calling, but none of it seems to serve.

The show ultimately presents a view that everything—including ideas—is fungible, but some things are unobtainable or even inexpressible. It also reveals that in the modern world everything must be advertised. Religion must occupy a place in the marketplace roughly comparable to that of Guess or other advertisers. The matrix of sexual, acquisitive and spiritual desires requires that we yearn for what we don't have; we may desire a deity, but can't have him as a real presence. The divine becomes an absent/presence of which the "literal word" is its closest representation on earth; it's like those people who are "better than us because they want things they haven't seen."

Strange Bedfellows

Reading like a fundamentalist is reading like a literalist, though the divine cannot be divined, and, reading advertising as pornography is like reading it scripturally. The desire elicited by sexualized images is construed as literal sex, which is in this case a present/absence. Spiritual advertising thus functions along the same axis as sexualized advertising, though from a contrary direction.

When groups like Men Against Violence Against Women (not a Christian organization) label certain advertising campaigns as pornographic, they seem to make a feminist move against the commodification of women, which it sees as damaging. However, labeling this kind of advertising pornographic does not elucidate the kinds of dangers they see it posing. Critics of the system that allows the use of sexually suggestive images in the service of consumerism apply the term pornography to these images in the hope of discrediting them and thereby stem a chaotic morality, either from a feminist point of view: because they promote a misogynist patriarchal system that is oppressive to women, or, from religious conservative view, which sees unsanctioned sexual activity as sin against God, but would wish to uphold the patriarchal system and women's assigned gender roles within it.

This maneuver, however, establishes a false dichotomy and elasticity for the term pornographic which renders it less than useful. The discomfort with this kind of advertising lies in its commercialization of sexual desire. As we have been arguing, advertising which commodifies and fetishizes sexual desire in the interest of consumerism, always creates complex relationships of signs whereby one sign stands in for another until sexual desire is transformed into the acquisitive desire, which is widely sanctioned within the culture. For religious conservatives, the position of women as subservient to men is symbolic of a proper family relationship. For them, the problem with these kinds of ads lies not with its use of women or its potential harm to them as individuated persons in society, but rather with the incitement to lust they might ultimately create and the breach to the family unit it may thus rouse.

What both these sets of critics are concerned with is not the pornographic nature of advertising but the appeal that is made to sexual desire. Like fundamentalist Christians' approach to the biblical text, these critics rely exclusively on the literal level of interpretation, and they read as mimetic what is meant to be metonymic. In other words, they fail to see past the sexual allure to the consumptive and ultimately capitalist desire. For some feminists, the approach embodies the patriarchal power relationship whereby women are objectified and oppressed. Yet, while "real" pornography may be placed alongside images that sexually objectify women in advertising as a part of the patriarchal hierarchy that places women in a subservient position, it must logically be distinguished from this objectification. For religious conservatives the practice of using sexual desire to sell products represents a moral concern. Since sexual desire, except as constrained by very specific rules, is seen as sinful, the appeal to this desire is equally, if not more, so.

While some groups have asserted the destructive power of this type of advertising, most of the energy exerted against sexualized images has been directed at "real" pornography because an attack on advertising's use of sexual imagery is in conflict with what we would call the major tenet of capitalism, "the freedom of acquisition." Recently, Utah Governor Gary Herbert has signed a resolution, passed by the state legislature, declaring pornography a "public health crisis. The resolution came about as the result of lobbying by group known as Fight the New Drug, who engaged in a billboard ad campaign claiming pornography as a danger to public health. "The legislation and FTND's philosophy are based on the premise that pornography is addictive"

(*Huffington Post*). The *Huffington Post's* Jesse Jackman suggests that the premise is supported by poor scholarship and "pseudoscientific studies." It is worth noting that the resolution while supported widely in the state, will not really have much of an effect in controlling pornography. In some sense, it seems to be a definitional exercise.

Cultural moralists rarely can attack salacious advertising as ardently as actual pornography because advertisers must by definition be allowed to appeal to consumers in whatever way possible to get them to buy their products, and consumers, on their part, must be allowed to make their own decisions about acquiring the goods that appeal to them. This is a structure influenced by Protestant ideas of personal freedom, choice and responsibility. Faith in this system of a free market protects commercial speech against the claim that it serves solely pornographic role. The system relies on the unwritten rule that advertisers dare not transgress the moral values of the community, lest the community react by withdrawing its patronage. However, while advertising serves a primarily commercial interest in its intent, in its execution it exerts a socializing force. As fully socialized individuals in the culture, we all become subjects of the cult of consumerism (even if unwittingly or indirectly); the media, including advertising, play a major part in our system of socialization. Advertisers, thus, have a great deal of power in drawing the boundaries between socially acceptable and morally suspect. By pushing against the boundaries of community values, these advertisers redraw those boundaries. The process of becoming a gendered, fully socialized citizen and consumer of the culture requires a level of media savvy which begins early in our development. Gender markers for females and males are scrupulously instituted from the first days of life. While the role of the mass media is implicit in this socialization, it is so only because it is a part of the culture; however, every aspect of the culture—family, school, government, church— is engaged in this process.

It is within this total cultural process that children ultimately become fully mature functional adults, or not. However, the process must begin before children, particularly girls, can be considered apt sexual partners. Since the culture views women's sexuality as inherently tied to male dominance, where women perform submissive gender roles, the sexualization of girls must by definition be conjoined with the social position they are expected to fulfill in adult life. Girls are trained by the society in all its permutations (including the media) to fulfill these roles, including being sexualized objects of a male gaze rather than independent sexual beings. This process is particularly evident in the uncompromising re-inscription of traditional gender roles and resistance of equal rights for women within the religious Right. For example, the organization Silver Ring Thing, supported by a federal grant in the 1990s, and True Love Waits, both market the idea of celibacy to young women.

These organizations, described as a "product or 'brand' that is especially packaged and marketed for adolescent consumers" (Moslener 198), established their brand through rallies, white ribbons, billboard ads, T-shirts, bumper stickers, rings, and even tattoos. Another more ritualized example would be "purity balls," which are formal dance events attended by fathers and daughters where daughters make a virginity pledge to remain sexually abstinent until marriage, symbolically offering to remain by their fathers' side until then.

In the economy of sexual development and negotiation, girls become potential objects of male desire because they will ultimately take up this role in adult life. Female "beauty" is seen as the epitome of feminine objectives. Young girls are taught to be beautiful submissive receptors to an eventual masculine advance, while boys are trained to be aggressive unfeeling conquerors of female desire. Girls and women often vie in beauty contests for the glory of being crowned as the most desirable by men. Thus, these contests become a site where society's expectations of women and girls can be most closely interrogated. What is most evident in these contests is the relative commercial value of female beauty in contradistinction to any or all other attributes a woman may possess. This feature is most harmful when the contests feature young girls who learn through these competitions that their whole self-worth is tied into how physically desirable they can be in the eyes of the (usually male) judges. This arrangement is repeated in every corner of the culture.

While many laws have been enacted since the 1990s for the protection of children from pornography, Americans continue to support multi-billion-dollar,[4] multi-media activities that may actually promote the seduction of children and the incitement of pedophiles, as girls parade in age-inappropriate attire and poses that suggests their sexual availability. Recent estimates suggest that some 250,000 girls participate in these pageants annually. Some critics of the pageants suggest that they are tantamount to child abuse.

> Parents—the very people who should be the most outraged by the sexual exploitation of youngsters—have been the principal supporters of hundreds of media-hyped children's "beauty pageants." These pageants commercially flaunt kids' bodies, often converting preteen and preschool girls into sex puppets adorned with lipstick, mascara, false eyelashes, bleached hair, high heels, and satin-and-rhinestone gowns and professionally coached in showgirl postures and movements [Davidson 62].

The 1996 death of JonBenet Ramsey[5] heightened interest in and concern over these pageants, where female children participate in a process of objectification and promotion of an aesthetic that reinforces cultural ideals of feminine beauty and desirability. According to cultural critic Camille Paglia, "These pageants mark a deep sexual disturbance in the society, a cannibalizing of youth by these vampiric adults" (*NYT* 61). While the wholesomeness of these contests is continually reaffirmed by the parents of the participants, these children are as sexualized as any image in advertising. The clear message is that there is a normative idea of female beauty and that this is the ultimate goal for all women. If we are going to call the breast augmentation ads oppressive, these kinds of rituals are where young women may develop the body dysmorphia that makes them susceptible to these ads.

It is remarkable and perhaps inevitable that both these pageants and purity balls take place in some of the most religiously conservative communities in the country, where one might expect resistance from conservative Christians. The religious Right, it seems, objects to sexualization, but agrees with the objectification of girls and women, which is a major precept of patriarchal capitalist culture. Because it subverts the system by allowing the exploration of unsanctioned sexual activity, the regulation of pornography seems necessary to conservative Christians. Social conservatives paternalistically seek to protect women and girls from sexuality here, only because it falls out of the conventionally acceptable mode of objectification. However, they never question the social structure of gender roles or the position of women vis-à-vis male aggression or sexual objectification. For many conservative Christians the question is one of control and containment. They look to regulate the cultural production so that their own view of morality, including a particular sexual objectification of women and girls, is reinforced.

While many Christians as well as some feminists agree in using legislation to curb the distribution of pornography and what they consider pornographic images, they would, however, disagree on the issue of these pageants. The most strident and consistent objections to the pornographic come from two separate camps and are based on entirely different grounds. On one side, are the evangelical Christians, but on the other are radical feminists, like Andrea Dworkin and Catherine MacKinnon, who oppose the representation of women in pornography as damaging to women in general and those represented in particular. Evangelicals see these images as damaging to the family structure and ultimately to the established society, and would move to eradicate, while Dworkin, MacKinnon and others have insisted that any penetrative heterosexual intercourse is inherently damaging to women and organized around a violent power relationship in which women always play the role of victims.

Into the 1990s these two groups—of conservative Christians and radical feminists—engaged in a battle that came to be known as the "sex wars" against civil libertarians and other radical feminists (known as pro-sex feminists). In his book *Mediated Sex*, Brian McNair clearly summarizes the Dworkin/MacKinnon position:

> The objectification and fetishization of women present in much pornography is a reflection of male dominance, endorsing and reinforcing it. Its explicitness (however, we may

define that term) and its intention to arouse are not neutral characteristics of the text but demonstrations of male power. The images, and their arousals, are produced by and through the physical abuse and exploitation of the women whose bodies they depict. The arousals of pornography, by dehumanizing and objectifying women, induce misogyny, with all this implies for male behavior (in the sexual and other spheres) [48].

There is no question that this may be a serious objection to the effects of pornography. However, there is some question as to whether these are in fact the effects of pornography. Regardless, the fault lies not with pornography, but with society itself; representations of women in advertising, television shows, movies, literature, etc., necessarily convey the very same kinds of objectification. MacKinnon and Dworkin read pornography as creating these circumstances and not as representing them or participating in them. If the "arousals" of the pornographic involve "demonstrations of male power" in which women are objectified, it is because this condition is embodied in the culture. If women were considered the absolute equals of men, sexual desire would not be tainted by this power struggle (though it may very well have different power relations associated with it). Advertising and popular religion also are as much responsible for this condition and much more interested in maintaining the position of women relative to the patriarchal structure.

MacKinnon and Dworkin insist, "pornography is ... the subordination of women" (MacKinnon 290). Pornography does not represent the subordination of women; it does not cause it; *it is* that subordination. "Pornography is a form of forced sex" (290), MacKinnon writes, "representation is reality" (291). They see the representation of women in pornography as reifying the power structure. They define pornography as "material that explicitly represents or describes degrading or abusive sexual behavior so as to endorse and/or recommend the behavior as described" (quoted in McNair 132). Paradoxically, this definition both over-confines and over-generalizes the term. On the one hand, MacKinnon and Dworkin require a proselytizing role for pornography, "endorsing or recommending" the abusive behavior. On the other, the slipperiness of the term "describe" as used in the definition allows Dworkin and MacKinnon's work itself to be considered pornography by their own definition.

When MacKinnon says that pornography is not a representation, but is, in fact, the thing itself, she is restating a view embraced by fundamentalist Christians that what a text represents can *become* real. In the same way that Sallman's *Head of Christ* or Barton's *The Man Nobody Knows* appear to viewers and readers as the "real" Christ, the woman's experience in pornography is reality itself—"representation is reality." This notion participates in a blurring of the line between the "real" and the signified, an idea that expands meaning in both directions. On the one hand, what is seen on the screen has a kind of "real presence," as if it were happening in the room; but, it is simultaneously the thing it represents and a symbol for a much broader understanding of the circumstances of women in the culture. What pornography depicts as sexual activity is, in fact, that activity, its representation, and the actual oppression of women. Reading it this way ignores the fictive context of pornography, while also raising its connotative power.

Girls Gone Wild

Pornography exists and is effective in its intent of arousal because it explicitly represents desires that are always implicitly present out in the culture. Advertising works with the same implicit desires (for sex, money, God), but maintains their implicitness in representing them to us. In the American context, the impulse toward these implicit desires is always conflicted by alternating impulses. Religion to some extent operates upon the same system of desire, but also seeks to control or mitigate transgressive human urges while filling some of the space with desire toward the godly. When viewed broadly, U.S. history can be seen as cycles of chaotic freedom alternating with periods of severe restriction and attempts at containment. The connective tissue of these periods is the open marketplace and religious engagement.

While the "sex wars" relate principally to the distribution of softcore and hardcore pornography, the use of images of women and girls in advertising was largely ignored by both the MacKinnon/Dworkin camp and their religious counterparts. Some "pro-sex" feminists have argued that the real damage done to women and girls is not through pornography, but in the mainstream media. Furthermore, feminist critic Lisa Duggan argues that pornography's existence serves some social functions, which in fact might benefit women. "By challenging Judeo-Christian ideals of what sex is for and how it should be organized (i.e. exclusively within marriage and monogamy), pornography subverts the very patriarchy which so disadvantages women" (in McNair 78). Pornography, these feminists argue, can be liberating to women because it can allow them to rescue their own sexuality from the patriarchy and give back the power that is routinely taken away in mainstream media. The pervasive use of women as commodified sexual objects in advertising is readily available to the society at large and much more stringently reinscribes patriarchal notions of sexuality than pornography. The position of women in American society certainly does not derive exclusively from representations in pornographic material. Since advertising is a much more "legitimate," much more public medium, and more central to socialization than pornography, its influence on society at large and the condition of women specifically is significantly greater.

While advertising is adept at exploiting allegorized sexual desire it has created over the past hundred or so years, it also capitalizes on the concern over how much "sex" is too much. Advertisers make use of the controversy over ads that probe the limits of this allegorical scheme. Concern about child pornography in advertising may have begun with Calvin Klein ads featuring a very young Brooke Shields in her Calvin Klein Jeans, and continued with Kate Moss. In 1993, Calvin Klein bus ads featuring a very young Kate Moss, dressed only in Calvin Klein underwear, inspired a great debate about the propriety of using models that appear to be underage in ads of this kind. Ultimately, the ads were pulled amidst allegations and protests that they were representative of "child pornography." Moss was not in fact underage at the time of the ads, but her body type (slim hips, undeveloped breasts and "waiflike" thinness) made her appear even younger than her actual age of nineteen.

Themes of a sexualized child present in the Klein/Moss ads are explored by John Leo in a *U.S. News and World Report* article:

> Here and there, her photos flirt with themes of masturbation (fingering her breasts under her bra), bestiality (posing nude with a large dog), incest (under a towel, apparently nude, being hugged by her brother) and violence (bare-breasted, with blackened or bruised eyes, holding her hand over her mouth and looking upset) [27].

In each of these cases, the themes require some allegorical interpretation in order to be read as sexual or violent. One has to read what is absent through what is present in order to arrive at a definition of the ads as child-pornography: why is posing with a dog necessarily bestiality? How do we know through visual representation that it is her brother she poses "apparently nude" with, and how does posing imply incest? The subjective nature of these assumptions can be easily discerned in the language used to describe the ads as pornographic:

> In her ads, Moss often *looks like* a vulnerable and compliant child, stripped for sexual use. "The message of these pictures is that she is very young and very available," says Linnea Smith, a North Carolina psychiatrist and anti-porn crusader. Other commentators have noted the theme of Moss as a slightly soiled and exploitable street urchin. Harper's Bazaar says she *looks "like* a kid from a latter-day Fagin's gang." The naked child, staring vacantly and helplessly at the camera, is a staple of child pornography. One of Moss's photos shows her cringing nude in the corner of a huge sofa, with legs locked and arms pressed to her breasts, *as if* bracing for an impending sexual assault [Leo 27, emphasis added].

These descriptions, brimming with merely suggestive, subjective and figurative language, such as "as if," and "looks like," reveal some of the problems of interpretation. None of the poses or situations described can be literally read as either pornographic or involving a child. And yet, these commentators can read through implied symbolism to the absent presence of sexual desire. The commentators here are not privy to some ultra-critical eye, which allows them to read through the meanings of the ads, but rather are individuals socialized to do precisely what the ads require them to do, though perhaps a bit too well.

The ads sparked a debate that opens up two lines of questioning. If a major part of "society" deemed these ads as "child pornography" (which appears to be the case), why was Klein not prosecuted according to the law? And if a significant portion of the culture saw the ads as offensive, pornographic or obscene, why did Klein's sales increase? Klein's technique is effective because it pits a number of market forces against each other at several levels of the culture. On one side, are those who are offended by the advertising, this includes a large percentage of conservative religious groups. Once they react to the ads in the ways Klein anticipates, the advertising becomes a news story and as a news story it draws attention from civil libertarians who read the issue as involving censorship and first amendment rights. The controversial nature of these political disputes attracts the attention of Klein's young consumers who may or may not have been attracted to the fashion, but are attracted to the transgressive nature of the advertising. Once the controversy reaches a peak, Klein pulls the ads and makes a contrite apology. This assures that more liberal critics see the transgression as an honest mistake and forgive him.

Although Klein was forced to pull the ads by consumer groups, and apologize for them, and while a judicial investigation was launched into the nature of the ads, he never faced criminal charges. What, then, is the difference between these ads and "real" child pornography (i.e. the kind that is criminally punishable by law)? And what definition of pornography is being used to determine that these ads are or are not indeed pornographic?

Let us propose, for a moment, a different set of circumstances that might even further problematize the definition. If Klein had used a model who was sixteen but, rather than Moss's prepubescent body, revealed fully-formed breasts and hips—if she appeared to be older, rather than younger—would the ads have attracted the same amount of controversy? Would her appearance have had an effect on the cultural definition of "child" or "pornography?" By legal definition, a sixteen-year-old is legally and, in most cases, culturally a "child." But in this case, the portrayal is not of a child but of an adult; so that, although she legally and even culturally may be a child, the model comes to represent a simulacrum of an adult. For all intents and purposes, the child in this case becomes the signifier of a mature woman and thus would elicit no significant response in terms of the sexualized nature of the ads. What is represented becomes real; like MacKinnon's definition of pornography and fundamentalist Christian readings of the Bible, what is presented to us is what is there, appearance is everything.

We should note that it is the representation of the child in an "adult situation" that so mobilized the protesters of Klein's ads, so that a representation of an adult in the same situation would not elicit the same response. Advertising in all media makes use of scantily dressed mature women in more provocative poses than those used by Klein. Yet, these are rarely called into question as pornographic. We can safely assume that the cause of the problem in the Moss case was not the nudity, whether assumed to be pornographic or not, nor the actual age of the model, but rather Moss's particularly childlike appearance, in other words, representation. In this case it seems there is some leakage or slippage between the terms "pornography" and "child." There is something in the definition of the term "child" that seems to have an effect on whether or not the ad can be considered pornographic by the public. If the "child," posed in a particular way, appears to be a child, the ad may be considered pornographic, but if the ad features an older looking child or an actual adult, the definition of pornographic seems to disintegrate. That is, material that in no way would be considered pornographic when featuring apparent adults becomes pornographic when the participants are, or rather can be identified as, children.

At about the same time as the Klein/Moss ads appeared, an "adult actress" using the name Traci Lords was discovered to have been only fifteen years old when she began making pornographic films. When this fact was discovered, she had already made over 80 films and was one of the most popular performers in the industry. This discovery leads us to two separate and rather intriguing discussions. Does authorial intention affect a change in definition for child-pornography? And what agency, if any, does the "child" in such a case actually have?

No one who saw the movies before the discovery was made could have imagined that Lords was underage. Given her appearance, one would have assumed that she was a young but mature woman. So we have here something like the hypothetical case we alluded to above. The representation in these movies was not of an immature girl, but of a fully developed woman. Lords comes to mimetically signify a fully sexualized adult female; as such, she is symbolically tied to "normal" adult sexual desire. Once her real age was discovered, however, her image becomes tainted with pedophilic lust, and the symbolic arrangement, by which she represented an adult, is broken. In fact, one of the outcomes of this revelation was that to certain men her videos became even more desired, now as pseudo-legal child pornography. For these men, the real becomes the unseen present. Lords's films become more sexually desirable although nothing within them has changed and what has changed is absent from the films.

What is important in both of these cases—the model in advertising and Traci Lords in film—is the ambiguous and contradictory nature of the response. In the case of advertising it is the *apparent* age of the model that becomes *real*— as signifier the 19-year-old becomes underage. On the other hand, in the case of Traci Lords, the opposite seems to be true. When her actual age becomes known her films are legally defined as child pornography, despite her appearance. They become illegal to sell, increase in value, and even apparently increase their power to elicit sexual arousal. What is significant here is that in both cases there are contradictory forces at work within the creation of meaning and the representation of the real. Like the stylized depiction of the 1960s in *Mad Men*, or faith in the deity of the economy in *South Park*, the real becomes contingent on how we understand it. Representation becomes reality, and reality becomes representation depending on our view of them.

To conclude, let us return to the Guess ads. As would be expected in a predominantly Christian, capitalist society, the modes of interpretation are determined through the interaction of these very strong forces. The reaction to the pornographic depends upon the pre-established Christian context against which it defines itself. Any reading of artifacts from this culture must necessarily incorporate the reaction to America's Christian context. Pornography defines itself against this backdrop. What is sinful or transgressive is *so* because of its relation to a Christian ethic. When pitted against the consumerist drive and its creation in the culture, however, this ethic cannot stand.

The contradictory responses to these portrayals of women in many ways mirror the American public's relationship to religion and the Bible. In each case we have the assumption of a literal truth—a dissolution between the borders of representation and reality—while, at the same time a freedom exists to choose not only one's response or interpretation to a text, but to actually create an alternate reality that replaces or changes that text. Like the relationship between popular culture and popular religion, what appears to be contradictory is often just as easily seen as symbiotic and creative. This paradoxical sense of reading an image is perhaps most dramatically indicated in religious popular culture by the numerous instances where Christ has been seen embedded in the images of billboards, an event that simultaneously contains elements of religion, advertising, and desire. We see what we want to see, what we need to see, in images designed to inflame our desires. This circularity whereby the real and the virtual become indistinguishable, where God and desire become signs for each other, is always at work in the American marketplace, American popular religion, on our smart phones, and in the American imagination.

CHAPTER 4

Absolute Contradictions
Perceptions of the Spiritual
and the Religious in Popular Music

*If religion functions both to explain the world—providing models for how
we live, tenets of faith and empowerment, and comfort for when they
don't work—and to offer a sense of contact with something greater than
oneself, then heavy metal surely qualifies as a religious phenomenon.*
—Robert Walser in *Running with the Devil*

*It's like here comes the Catholic Church saying "Sex goes here and
spirituality goes there," … but I say, No they go together.*
—Madonna (from *Truth or Dare*)

Absolutely Abstract

In this chapter we will look at works from several genres of popular
music that have directly interacted with ideas of popular religion. Using
Madonna's song and music video "Like a Prayer," John Coltrane's jazz suite
A Love Supreme, and British heavy metal band Iron Maiden's *The Number of
the Beast* to set up our frames of analysis, we will then look at two songs and
music videos from the twenty-first century: Matisyahu's 2005 "King Without
a Crown" and Kanye West's 2004 recording, videos, and live performances
of "Jesus Walks." Although the possible example are almost endless, we are
choosing a divisive popular music video, an iconic jazz album, a controversial
heavy metal album, and two powerful but complicated representations of
religion in reggae and hip hop in order to demonstrate similarities across
genres as well as to point to a few genre-specific characteristics that are significant in their negotiation of religious meanings through radically different
forms of popular music. In each case, we see ways in which music can employ

and play with traditional religious symbols and signs, using them as bearers of meaning and subverting or distorting their cultural associations at the same time. Through their critique and re-imagining of institutional and popular religion, we find not only both a rejection and an acceptance of religious practice and experience, but also forms of rescription—ways in which thinking through music influences how we see religion and its texts and practices. Finally, although it may not be the primary "meaning," each text and its surrounding discourse also reveals a negative or indirect path to an understanding of the sacred—a recognition of the desire for religious or spiritual experience, but also a marker of the absence of God or a divine presence. By musically and socially enacting the impossibility of assigning essence or meaning and in the process questioning their own autonomous existence and communicative intelligibility, these pieces of popular music participate in the contemporary re-imagining of religion and the doubt that accompanies contemporary faith.

The central topic in this chapter stems from our larger interest in the intersections of popular culture and popular religion, which focuses on the action of texts in their creation, perception, and effect. What does it mean to say that a piece of music is spiritual or religious? Or to say that music is immoral, blasphemous, or satanic? Where does the source of the spirituality lie? Is it determined by the music or the lyrics? Is it in the effect on the listener, the intent of the composer or performer, or is it something inherent in the music itself? Works of a "spiritual" nature have become more fashionable within popular music and popular culture, and religion has become a more common academic topic, yet not enough attention has been directed to *why* we perceive a popular works as spiritual or religious. In trying to answer these questions, it is important to conceive of works of popular music as complex historically and culturally situated texts, whose "meaning" lies in verbal, sonic, and visual codes as well as in the web of surrounding discourse. So although our choice of musical works may seem somewhat arbitrary, what we are especially interested in—and this is a much larger issue—is how contemporary cultures have constructed objects or experiences as spiritual or religious.

The issue of whether an album or a piece of music is an object or an experience is also connected to the irresolvable ontological contradictions that form the core of our argument. The tension between the two ideas of music—as object or experience, as solid or as ineffable—is ultimately a theological question, made even more complicated by digital technology that has made music streaming the dominant form of distribution. The desire for a god-presence leads to the idea of music as an object, but it is also as a subjective experience through which popular music demonstrates its role in religious ideology. We will concentrate mostly on the reception of the texts, primarily in the United States, and on the texts surrounding the work and the music itself, which is part of our point—that meaning is created outside of the traditional art frame that still dominates much writing about music. Religion or spirituality is never *in* a text; whether it is the Bible or a rock song; meaning of any kind is culturally created and contextual, so a work of spiritual or religious art is always a cultural process in process, its multiple meanings intertwined in the complex theological and epistemological contradictions of the culture.

* * *

Perhaps more than any other art form, music inspires an insistence of presence, while its abstract nature guarantees an open meaning, and thus, in its undecidability music approaches the contradictory nature of divinity that we have been locating in the texts of popular culture. Victorian author Walter Pater famously claimed that all art aspires towards the condition of music; many religious thinkers have also used music's abstract nature as an ideal model for comparisons to the indescribable character of religious experiences. Yet music's often textless text creates possibilities for subversion as well as creation as it indicates an ultimate contradiction of absence and presence. Music can inspire or accompany worship; it can replace traditional religious experiences; it can challenge or protest religious roles; it can complicate and problematize the relationship to the divine and can itself become a sacred text. Because the popular normally exists within a clear linguistic frame, the meaning of which music itself cannot escape, popular music participates in the discourse and practice of popular religion in ways that both reaffirm and deny its spiritual qualities.

Popular music, according to most definitions, begins in the late years of the nineteenth century with the rise of minstrel shows, ragtime, jazz, and the sale of recorded cylinders and sheet music. With roots in Negro spirituals and blues, almost all popular music can be shown to have some connection to religious traditions, but an antagonistic and dialectical relationship between popular music and popular and institutionalized religion existed almost from the outset, as cultural and religious conservatives associated popular music with prostitution, crime, simple mindedness, "primitive" urges, racial inferiority, and a general immorality. Although jazz is now used as a symbol of sophistication, is taught at Juilliard, and occupies its own branch of Lincoln Center, for much of its history it has been perceived as an outsider, and as a rebellious and dangerous music played by black people and drug addicts. A 1921 article in *The Ladies' Home Journal* by Anne Faulkner entitled "Does Jazz Put the Sin in Syncopation?" warned parents of the evil properties of the popular new jazz music. Faulkner found evidence for the "evil influence" of jazz in "immoral conditions" among young people, in the "demoralizing effect" on workers who had "indulged" in jazz music, and in the negative effects upon the human brain "demonstrated by many scientists"

(32–34). As dated as her language may seem today, her sentiments echo more recent denunciations of popular music, often also couched in the language of morality, pseudoscience, and religion. As we shall see with Iron Maiden and Madonna, the act of calling something evil or blasphemous is an act that emerges from within religion and is related to the text's role as a religious work or experience. Although at points in its history it has been the most popular music in the world, heavy metal music has always defined itself by its outsider status. More than any major genre, metal has been associated with religious condemnation and is regarded as "satanic," a characterization that many metal bands have encouraged through their lyrics and their consciously self-fashioned images. Madonna's song and video, which depicts her kissing a black Jesus or saint figure and dancing in front of burning crosses, was controversial from the outset, especially inciting protests by religious organizations.[1] More recently the shift in blame has moved more to video game and online material, but it is still common to hear commentators, like Bill O'Reilly blaming, for example, rap music for the explosive violence in Ferguson, Missouri.[2]

On the other hand, from "shout-outs" to God in hip hop and the use of traditional Santería and voodoo drumming in Latin dance music, to "praise" rock and Christian metal, to claims of spiritual ecstasy in electronica, the relationship between popular music and popular religious practices has never been more evident. In many ways the cooperative relationship between popular culture and popular religion is most obviously seen in the power of popular music to influence worship practices, create alternative spiritualities, and inspire religious sentiments. Popular songs routinely incorporate the music styles, language, and visual images of the church into music, videos, and performances. There are almost no popular religious practices that don't incorporate some forms of music making or listening, usually (as opposed to much institutionalized religion) influenced by popular styles. The fastest growing branches of American Christianity—storefront Pentecostalism and mega church evangelism—make use of the musical styles of popular music and the visual style of music videos. Accompanying the increase of these popularized forms of worship, in recent years the presence of religion in popular music has increased visibly, and the separation between religious and musical practices has, as in other popular genres, often blurred.

Human interactions with music parallel religious practices in that they negotiate the private and public. Recent technology has shifted the tensions between the public and the private even to the extent of forcing us to redefine what we mean by these terms. So while, on the one hand, the majority of music listening is now extremely private—experienced through headphones and curated through online platforms—on the other hand, fans can communicate and share music and musical experiences across the globe regardless of age and location. Furthermore, a growing music festival culture and large-scale electronic music events encourage massive groups experiences, often compared by listeners and critics to religious camp meetings.

Despite (or because of) the trend toward more overt references to religion within popular music, and the historical link between popular music and worship, there has recently been an expressed need for more scholarly work in this area. Michael Gilmour emphasized this point in his 2005 book, *Call Me the Seeker: Listening to Religion in Popular Music*, claiming that "there does not appear to be as much scholarly energy devoted to the links between religion and popular music compared to, say, television and movies" (vii). Gilmour organizes this collection of essays around three standard categories: the religious sources behind popular music, the religious themes in popular music, and religion and the audience of popular music. As we discussed in the preface, categories like these establish artificial boundaries between culture and religion, and conceal ways in which popular culture and religion re-create, re-write, and re-contextualize each other. While Gilmour's organization is still useful, we would suggest that the relationship of religion and popular culture is so conjoined as to make any such categories limiting. To see how popular music really interacts with popular religion it is necessary to move beyond this type of typology.

For example, in his introduction, Gilmour argues that popular music draws from and interprets themes of major religions, and that they are important to study because "insight and profundity can be found not only in the traditional canon, religious or otherwise, but also in unexpected places" (viii). Gilmour's statement that "profundity" can also be found in "unexpected places" such as popular music seems to summarize his conclusion, but, for us, this assertion is an accepted starting point. What he ultimately points to in *some* popular music, we assume in all popular culture. As opposed to identifying places where popular music draws from and interprets a canonical text therefore occasionally providing the "insight" of a sacred word, from our point of view popular music cannot help but draw from and interpret religious themes—one of our assertions in this book is that, in its very nature, popular culture necessarily draws from popular religious discourse, and therefore *must* be part of popular religion itself. Furthermore, we would not make the claim that popular texts can *also* be profound, because we do not privilege the power of insight or profundity in traditional sacred texts. As we show throughout the book, popular culture not only interprets or imitates the nature of sacred texts; products of popular culture actually take on the role of sacred texts and sacred experiences in and of themselves. By looking to find religion *in* popular music, Gilmour and others assume a certain stability to the meaning of "religion" and then look for remnants of it *within* popular music. For example, in *Pop Cult: Religion and Popular Music*, Rupert Till insists on a strict separation of the sacred and the profane and defines "religion" according to such large institutional concepts as the Reformation, the Enlightenment, Augustinian philosophy and Neo-Platonism against which the profane activities of popular music can be oppositionally compared. We would question the assumed boundaries here and rather than assume something called "religion" can be "inside" a text of popular music, we would look and listen to the role that each can and must play in defining and creating the other. Popular religion has been at least partially created through interaction with music, and we can just as easily look for music "in" religion—neither one has an autonomous or privileged status outside of the other.

Hip hop music, with its shout-outs to God, its obvious debt to Pentecostal preaching styles, and protests against it by conservative religious organizations, is at the center of many recent discussions of this issue. The book *Noise and Spirit: The Religious and Spiritual Sensibilities of Rap Music* by Anthony Pinn poses as its guiding question, "Is there anything of religious significance in rap music?" (xx). From our viewpoint this question is not applicable and our response is "How could there not be?" While these books make important interventions into the field, like many works addressing popular culture and religion, they seem to be limiting their questions by a too traditional and non-questioning definition of religion. To claim that a song or musical piece can be "religious" also implies that it could be religiously insignificant. But to insist on that separation is to again create artificial boundaries between two interlaced areas, and to insist that we can somehow stand outside of religion and popular culture, viewing accurately where one begins and the other ends.

What Gilmour and Pinn's readings of popular music share is an awareness of the role of popular music in the expression of recognizable religious tropes as communicated through either song lyrics or the images of a music video. They use different methodologies, but both focus on how music uses traditional religious language, themes, or images in ways that promote either a traditional religious understanding or an anti-religious one. However, it is just as important to look at how this field of popular culture plays a role in understanding religion outside of proclaiming itself as sympathetic or antagonistic to accepted belief systems. Instead of citing references to God (or Satan), images of crosses, or the trance-inducing properties of electronica, we should look for deeper connections that reveal themselves in less direct ways.

Music is almost unique among popular art forms in the emphasis fans place on the actual perceptual experience; while most of the critics and thinkers we have cited so far point to the importance of the text of music and its relationship to religion, fans more often than not point to the religious-like experience of listening. Additionally, while critics and scholars find faith or blasphemy in lyrics and narrative, fans find it in the experience of music itself, often without referring to the lyrics at all.

In ways more varied than many of the other popular forms discussed in this book, the experience of listening to music has been more commonly discussed in religious or spiritual terms. Recently, some critics have joined fans in locating the spiritual within the listening experience. Gordon Lynch, for example, points to how popular music audiences use their experience to construct alternate spiritual identities or systems of meaning. His focus is on the claims by club goers that he associates with forms of spirituality. In another work that uses concert-goers as subjects, *Traces of the Spirit: The Religious Dimensions of Popular Music*, Robin Sylvan studies the spiritual reactions of the audiences of rock, heavy metal, electronica, and hip hop. He interprets these reactions as a form of religion, descriptions that many of his subjects did not identify as religious. In doing so he extends the definition of what "religion" means. The need to define "religion" in new ways is, in this case, a direct result of ways that music can reshape a religious experience. In turn, then, these texts of music become sacred or sacrilegious because of interplay between the religion and the popular culture.

What still needs to be asked is why these music experiences need to be redefined as a form of the religious or the sacred. What is it about music that produces the desire to describe it in these terms? Is it music's perceived abstract nature that encourages listeners to turn to the lexicon of religion to describe their experiences? Is this related to the common practice of incorporating religion in music's lyrics? If lyrics can be perceived as dangerously subversive or blasphemous, is it then possible for music to be blasphemous through its aural qualities alone? Ultimately, the age-old question behind these questions is how music communicates religious ideas.

The abstract relationship between music and an idea is difficult to define, variously debated, and questioned throughout Western history. It is useful to explore some of the historical roots of these interrogations especially in terms of the concept of "absolute music," an eighteenth and nineteenth century movement in which music "as music" was perceived as more pure and more spiritual without attaching any "extra-musical" content. To absolutists the "meaning" of music lies exclusively in the musical process alone; the "language" of music can refer only to itself, not to anything outside of music. Until then the prevailing idea of music—going back to Plato— was that it needed *logos*: language as an expression of human reason. Either music had to contain words or it needed to be supplied with a program or a story.

Around 1800, a whole new way of thinking about music developed.

According to advocates of "absolute" music, words were "outside" of music, and purely instrumental music was no longer considered "beneath" language, but above it and, in fact, contained the essence of a truly spiritual musical experience. Absolutists insisted that this "wordless" music would be "elevated" above speech. Gradually the idea of absolute music became the aesthetic paradigm of nineteenth century musical culture. While generally considered in the context of instrumental classical music, the idea that music is more pure and absolute when considered outside of "extra-musical" texts is still a dominant way of thinking, especially outside of academic music scholarship. Performers and listeners commonly insist on the importance of focusing on the "music alone" as a transformative force. This "pure" music, then, is justified on the grounds that it is a *more* religious experience *because* it is not connected to a text; it is more immediate and more authentic. American religious ideology tends to seek the authentic in the popular and to favor the experiential over the doctrinal.

This process of authorizing or authenticating the sacred out of the popular and, in fact, making new texts even more sacred than the original is the basis of American popular religion. The questions at the center of the relationship of popular music and popular religion revert back to issues discussed in the debate over absolute music. Ultimately, they ask what kind of music leads one to the divine or the transcendent experience, an interrogation that leads to the ontological questions of defining just what it is one is aiming towards. Is the proper target of devotion the traditional Judeo-Christian personal figure that could be addressed or is it a more abstract "Absolute" that is an experience beyond words?

This debate over whether instrumental music or the singing of lyrics is a more spiritual or religious experience is one useful model to discuss modern popular music and religion, but this traditional debate has been given a characteristically American and postmodern twist. To understand the complex relationship, we must go beyond religious lyrics or anecdotal accounts of transcendence. Like other forms of American popular culture, music involves the space between the shifting creative process and the desire for absolute stability that characterizes American religion: a tension between creative and absolute presence, an employment and subversion of accepted religion and the creation of new religious experiences. We can also find this tension expressed in the different experiences of live music versus music on an LP or a CD versus music accessed from a digital "cloud." The popular music examined in this chapter demonstrates this tension by showing the desire to imbue music with divine (or satanic) essence, to locate the true meaning within the creator and the object, and yet each text also is revealed to exist only in a contradictory web of associations, discourse, and experience.

Twentieth Century Models: Sounding the Sacred in Pop, Jazz and Metal

Madonna's "Like a Prayer," John Coltrane's *A Love Supreme* and Iron Maiden's *The Number of the Beast* achieve their religious or sacrilegious status through a complex web of associations that reflects deep paradoxical theological themes imbedded in our culture. The perception of spirituality or of religiosity that surrounds these texts seems to find its ground and language in the verbal and visual texts that are part of the packaging of the music: Madonna's video images, Coltrane's liner note prayer, Iron Maiden's song titles and album covers. Conversely, the language of fans and critics attempts to move away from the surrounding texts and tries to attribute an unquestioned spiritual content to the music alone, making a conscious and determined break from the surrounding verbal texts. These cases are more interesting because they come from genres that have been—at various times—commonly perceived as threats to traditional and conservative ways of life often associated with institutionalized and popular religion, and, in the case of Madonna and Iron Maiden, they have prompted intense protests from American religious organizations. Our discussion of Madonna's song and video and the discourse that it generated will primarily serve to introduce the concepts, issues, and arguments that we will then use to examine other genres and pieces of popular music.

The structural and contradictory aspects of American religion on which we have been focusing are essential in understanding the relationship between popular music to religion; to reiterate our central thesis: American religious ideology comes from a powerful literal belief in the Bible and therefore a related belief in the essential power contained in a text, a belief which is largely separate from institutionalized religion. This concept of literalism is contrasted with an equally strong belief in the individual rights to religious interpretation. This simultaneous literal belief in the word and power to reinterpret the word allows for the creation of new religions, new sacred texts, and the encouragement of radical interpretations of religion, and of what is religious. This contradictory belief system is central to the American evaluation of popular texts. If the U.S. Constitution, for example, can come to be treated as a sacred text, then it is presumable that a piece of popular music can be perceived as containing the very presence of either a sacred element or a satanic one. Americans approach texts of popular music with this same fascinating, creative, and contradictory epistemology. The openness to confer sacred status on new texts and yet a persistent literalness to what they perceive as essentially religious and even "biblical" results in complex creations of and reactions to texts that take part in a theological dialectic of tradition versus rebellion, chaos versus order, and absolute presence versus the uncertainty of absence.

Throughout American history, music has been at the center of religion and culture and naturally plays a complex and important role in defining and reflecting how we practice and understand each. "Like a Prayer," *A Love Supreme* and *The Number of the Beast*, and their reception in the United States, play into this cultural vortex. They borrow or incorporate religious and biblical language and images at the same time that they participate in testing limits of perception, question the concepts of freedom and stability, and pose the paradox of the essential and created religious meaning of signs.

An American Madonna

More than thirty years after she debuted, Madonna continues to be major player in the popular music scene. In the 1990s she was a favorite topic for popular music scholars, cultural critics, and religious fundamentalists, each of whom had their own take on her role in American society. And, although her aggressive and open sexuality, and provocative stage shows and music videos have drawn the condemnation of religious and cultural conservatives who claimed her image and music taught a girl to behave like a "porn queen in heat" (qtd. in McClary 1), she also has been given credit for opening up new ways to experience and express sexuality, feminism, spirituality and even religion.[3]

Madonna's "Like a Prayer," a song from the album of the same title, was released in 1989 and as a music video shortly thereafter. The video, one of the most recognized of the twentieth century and voted the *Most Groundbreaking Music Video of All Time* for the twenty-fifth anniversary of MTV, has probably still attracted more contradictory critical and popular attention than any other music video. It was immediately protested by Christian organizations who saw it as blasphemous, crassly commercial, or even as endorsing cross burning, but it was also praised for its honest depictions of discrimination, rape, and faith. The song itself features a minor key introspective melody and a contrasting up-beat funky dance section that is catchy but unremarkable: a good Madonna song on a best-selling album at the peak of her popularity. It was the video, however, directed by Mary Lambert, that immediately generated controversy and debate, and, perhaps surprisingly at the time, intense scholarly discussion. The basic plot of the video shows Madonna as a young woman who witnesses a black man being arrested for coming to the aid of a white woman who had been assaulted and stabbed by a white man. Madonna's character in the video, after going to pray in a small countryside church, then decides to testify in favor of the black man. This fairly simple plot, however, is woven into a complex montage of images which include Madonna kissing what appears to be a black saint (St. Martin de Porres[4]) or, as it is more often read, a black Christ, and dancing provocatively in front of burning crosses.

This video received a lot of attention within the media—both positive and negative—and perhaps more than any other music video inspired scholarly analysis of its religious meanings. Leading cultural studies theorists as well as well-known musicologists (Susan McClary) and philosophers (Mark C. Taylor) used the video to explore new ways of addressing this issue. The video, as religious studies scholar Mark Hulsether writes, points to the "need for greater attention to religious dimensions of other popular music"; he sees the video as "among the more powerful statements of some major themes of liberation theologies." Hulsether points to its "focus on combating sexual violence, its call for solidarity against racism, and its heavy emphasis on the gospel choir" (84–85). Most important for our purposes is how the video for "Like a Prayer" became a central text that attracted critical attention from different perspectives on the subject of popular music and religion. Although the lyrics of the song point most obviously to Madonna's familiar theme of conflating sex and religion, the video presents a more plural and complicated message that cuts back and forth between what seems to be a dream and reality. For Carla Freccero "the puns, reversals, and circularities of this video, in combination with the lyrics, are dizzying" (175), and the video offers many possibilities for alternate readings. The video opens with a striking short montage that shows Madonna (wearing a cross), accompanied by distorted guitars and sirens, running through a vaguely surreal landscape, past a burning fire; we see a jail door slam, a burning cross, a white man attacks a white woman, a small old-fashioned wooden church, and the arrest of a black man. The rest of the video then presents a somewhat more linear plot, but within a layered plural narrative and a complex symbolic, visual, and musical structure. The video is full of ambiguous religious images: Madonna seeming to give herself stigmata, ecstatically prostrating herself (or masturbating) on an altar, kissing the black "Christ's" feet and then lips, and dancing in front of burning crosses.

The video is structured through a series of binary oppositions: the inside of a church and the outside world of fire and violence, black and white, the Catholicism of saints and stigmata and the black Protestantism of a gospel choir; sex and religion; reality and fantasy; the pipe organ and electric guitars, and, as Susan McClary points out, the musical struggle between the theme of "mystical timelessness" in D minor and "exuberant physical celebration" in F major. McClary's close reading of the musical language points out how the religious tensions expressed through the music rely on the use of semiotic codes: the sound of an organ for oppressive institutional religion, the feel of gospel music for religious ecstasy. For McClary, musically and thematically, the song and video succeed in joining together these perceived opposites: "No longer self and Other, they become two flickering moments in a flexible identity that embraces them both" (15), or as Mark Taylor suggests, "the distance separating the purity of the angel from the impurity of the whore is less than it initially appears, the two might even be one" (*Nots* 194). Ultimately, this song is about "multiple rather than unitary identities" (McClary 15). But multiple identities are always problematic within a monotheistic culture, where the idea of a stable unified self is indissolubly linked to the idea of one unchanging God, and the irreducible paradoxes presented in the song and video discomfort traditionalists, while simultaneously suggesting spiritual possibilities for its fans.

Taylor, writing from the point of view of a philosopher and a radical theologian, sees the video in a more subversive and abstract manner. Through Taylor's reading, Madonna's video suggests the transgressive and non-institutional religion that lies outside of any dogma. Madonna's Christ, as Taylor points out, gives in to sexual temptation, but "this is his glory, not his sin" and "the Kingdom is not elsewhere, it is *present*" (203). For him, when the black Christ leaves the church it is because Madonna has been "able to lure Christ from the pedestal that holds him captive." In other words, Madonna—in a classic move of American popular religion—tries to "release Christ from bondage to the Church" (*Nots* 200), expressing a distrust of creeds, theology, and institutions. The striking image of Madonna dancing in front of the burning crosses is not a moment of blasphemy, but a celebration of transcendence through sexuality, through dance, through dream, and through music. The video, then, suggests a symbiotic view of sex and religion, sacredness and profanity, but also a view of religion without a resurrected Christ, a church without God, as well as God and Christ without a church. What the video and the various interpretations of it offer is a play of presence and absence, emblematic of the contradictory play in American religion and the perception of popular music, that lays the groundwork for our investigation of other forms of popular music.

John Coltrane's A Love Supreme

As it becomes more common in the twenty first century for young people to characterize their identities and religious practices as "spiritual but not religious," it is important to look back at how the phrase "spiritual" became an identifiable part of the experience of a popular text. Although jazz is now debatably considered a genre of "popular music," we can use an iconic piece of jazz from the 1960's to demonstrate some of the complicated and contradictory ways in which religion and spirituality were first included in discussion of recorded music and popular music culture. John Coltrane's *A Love Supreme* was released in 1965 and instantly became an extremely popular album for what was essentially an avant-garde jazz suite. From the outset, musicians and listeners discussed this work in religious or spiritual terms. Coltrane's wife, Alice, in an often-quoted statement describes his appearance after finishing the first sketch of the piece as like "Moses coming down from the mountain" (qtd. in Kahn xv). Alice Coltrane's comments hint at the cult that was built up around John Coltrane after his death—he was commonly referred to as a saint or a prophet, and it was pointed out that he shared initials with another religious "JC." But despite the almost universal acceptance of the work as a "spiritual masterpiece," its reception opens up revealing questions about how the concept of "spiritual" gets woven into popular texts, and in the process develops a new meaning.

Coltrane's *Love Supreme* has been called "one of the best-known examples of jazz's religious sensibilities" (Pinn 11–12). But what does it mean to point to *jazz's* religious sensibility? Regardless of the fact that a genre of music (and a vaguely defined one at that) cannot in itself really *have* a religious sensibility, Pinn's evidence for his statement focuses on events and texts outside of the sonic experience of music. He specifically cites Coltrane's written notes about his album, his self-described "conversion" experience, and the formation of the Church of Saint John Coltrane, African Orthodox Church. While each of these "texts" is a fascinating juxtaposition of culture and religion, they hardly make a case for the music itself having a religious sensibility. Again, where do we locate this message of spirituality? Words? Music? Artist? From its mythical genesis to its influential popularity as an album to its iconic status in jazz history, *A Love Supreme* enacts the very ontological and theological questions at the intersections of religion and music.

The album is a thirty-three-minute, four-part suite, broken up into four tracks or movements: Acknowledgment, Resolution, Pursuance and Psalm. The album was both revolutionary and characteristic for its time. Like several of the leading jazz musicians of the '60s, Coltrane was breaking with the complicated fast moving chord and harmony changes of '50s bebop music. Instead, *A Love Supreme*, like the music on Miles Davis' *Kind of Blue* (on which Coltrane played) allowed long stretched out improvisations over unchanging harmony, which gave the soloist greater freedom to experiment (In some ways echoing the "spiritual" experience of a live Grateful Dead or Phish concert.) *A Love Supreme* was also an example of the large-scale jazz suites that were important in the '60s, works which were often identified with larger cultural issues, such as civil rights, poverty, or war.

Scott Saul says of *A Love Supreme* that it confirmed "jazz had gone from being seen as the 'devil's music' … to a resonant expression of spiritual uplift"

(254) and this language and sentiment is found throughout popular jazz writing. Ashley Kahn's book on the making of *A Love Supreme* repeatedly describes the suite in religious terms. For Kahn, *A Love Supreme* "transcend[ed] his category and time" (xv), its "message has remained constant" (xvi), and was "created as a gift to the Divine." The album, according to Kahn, has an "undeniable spirituality" (xx) and is "what a speech on the Washington Mall was to Martin Luther King, what a mountaintop sermon was to Jesus Christ" (xix). Kahn admits "many who came into direct contact with Coltrane rely on the language of religion to express their feelings for the man and the album" (xix). Kahn makes each of these assertions with certainty, as if they were essentially unproblematic. But what does it mean for something to have an "undeniable spirituality"? To say that a piece of instrumental music has a "message" at all, much less that it has remained "constant," is to instantly impose an outside perspective and frame upon an abstract text.

On the liner notes to the album Coltrane offers a note addressed, "Dear Listener," that begins, "all praise be to God whom all praise is due." The note explains that he had recently experienced a "spiritual awakening," at which time he asked to "be given the means and privilege to make others happy through music." Then he explains that although he had previously "entered into a phase which was contradictory to the pledge and away from the esteemed path" he has now "been duly re-informed of His omnipotence, and of our need for, and dependence on Him." The letter ends by proclaiming "His way is in love, through which we all are, it is truly—a love supreme—." He also included a full poem, "A Love Supreme," a free-form poem of thanksgiving that circles around the word God and repeats phrases like "God is," and "thank you God." The poem consistently refers to God or the divine as "it" ("It is merciful"), similar to Christian mystics for whom to even name God was a reductive act. Coltrane does not go this far, alternating between "God" and "it," but this odd disconnection between a divine force and its name could be read as discomfort with both language and music's ability to signify. The question, can music point to God or only to an "it," reflects the arguments over absolute music and also reveals a discomfort about the necessary relationship between language and the divine.

Commentary on the poem included with the album reveals the inherent contradictions. Kahn is clear that for him the spirituality of the poem exists in the person of John Coltrane, although he will claim just the opposite when discussing the music:

> Had Coltrane been clearer in his liner notes, the poem's subtle structural role would undoubtedly have been more widely understood and appreciated. As it turned out, this aspect of the composition became part of the album's mystique; a secret to be discovered and shared by a few [123].

By identifying the poem's role as a "secret," Kahn is clear about pointing to a specific artistic and spiritual role that the poem contains that could have been revealed by its creator, the prophet, John Coltrane. The poem, like purely instrumental music, is perceived as containing a message or a secret because of its abstract nature. The poem is read by Kahn as a guide to the music, and as a carrier of a secret that cannot be uncovered. What is revealed is the desire for absolute presence; what is demonstrated is the impossibility of this presence.

It is important to have a sense of the musical elements of the suite, as listeners, musicologists, and musicians have pointed to specific aspects of the music as evidence of its spiritual or religious essence. After the opening of the suite, a brief cadenza by Coltrane, the piece begins with the famous F-Ab-F-Bb four-note theme in the bass. There is nothing unique about the pattern itself—it is essentially a blues lick—but because of the way it is used on the track it becomes significant to our discussion. The extended solo by Coltrane that follows is based almost exclusively on these four notes; his style features a flurry of fast notes, diminished scales and chords as well as his famous tenor saxophone "screams." The four-note theme returns at the end of Coltrane's solo as he transposes it into multiple keys before the theme is chanted: "A Love Supreme, A Love Supreme." The association and repetition between this four-note theme and the chanted title suggest an attempt to textualize the music; to make the music speak in non-abstract language, almost an incarnation of the music. The two middle movements are more traditional, if equally inspired, post and late bebop jazz and the final Psalm is a long hymn-like tenor saxophone solo that more or less corresponds to the wording of the devotional poem Coltrane included in the liner notes, each syllable of the poem being rhythmically imitated on the saxophone.

While the whole piece is generated out of the opening four notes, the wild explosions of improvisation set up a dialectical, even adversarial, relationship between control and stability and exploration and freedom. This relationship can be expressed in theological terms: while the corresponding chant (on the same four notes) supplies the four note foundation with a literal religious interpretation, the free and challenging improvisations explore another recognized aspect of spirituality. Many musicians and scholars, especially in the field of jazz, point out that the "rejection of received harmonic and tonal practices was often made in the name not only of ideological freedom but also, precisely, of spiritual fulfillment" (Radano 108). This idea of spiritual fulfillment is directly opposed to the traditional use of "harmony" as a metaphor that links tonal music and spiritual balance. Instead, avant-garde styles, which are often accused of resisting accepting views of religion, are seen as a path to spirituality. These almost opposing descriptions of divine or spiritual experience depict how musical expressions of religious sentiment are viewed through an always already perceived frame within which music belongs.

Because of musicians' and listeners' desire for a pure musical experience that is analogous to a religious one (and vice versa), they often resist perceptions that all experiences are culturally constructed; the always already present origin of culturally created meaning challenges their (equally constructed) ideal definition of artistic and religious experience. Paradoxically their search for authentic and pure musical transcendence forces them to frame the musical experience with non-musical knowledge and characterizations. These dilemmas are apparent in the comments of musicians who have performed later versions of Coltrane's suite. As Kahn points out, with a typical vocabulary, "anyone approaching A Love Supreme does so with an entire fellowship looking over one's shoulder" (Kahn 202). It seems that musicians not only need to justify why they feel they can or cannot play the work, they also need to locate the source of its spirituality and therefore run into the same questions that we posed at the beginning of this chapter, like where does the source of the spirituality lie and is it determined by the music or the lyrics or some other element? Saxophonist Frank Foster sees no need to perform the work and finds the source of its spirituality in Coltrane: "nobody could add anything to the music that John didn't do himself" (Kahn 202–203). Reviews of recordings and performers often accuse the performers of lacking proper respect or religious perspective in their performances. For example, while some reviews of Wynton Marsalis's big band version of the suite praise the music for how it "speaks in prayer to a higher being" (Santella), others conversely, complain that it does not "reproduce the original quartet's concentrated religious turbulence" (Litweiler). Although performances and arrangements of the piece have become more common recently, they are still often framed and marketed—as was the 2015 performance of Marsalis's big band version in New York City's White Light Festival—as Coltrane's "spiritual testament to his art and hypnotic hymn to God."

A Love Supreme, as an album, as a musical experience, as a basis for improvisation, and as a site for theological expression dramatizes a desire for God and for transcendence; within the American ideology, this need gets expressed by a need for essence and for something solid. Yet the music can actually be seen to demonstrate the opposite—the slipperiness of any claim of divinity, and the ontological impossibility of a text becoming or pointing to a God or transcendence. Any meaning of music is created by cultural context, and likewise, the idea of God is an experience—to the extent that we can understand it—created by symbolic systems; yet such systems can only demonstrate their inability to represent God. Divinity and spirituality necessarily exist, at least partially, in their failure.

Iron Maiden and British Metal in America: Satanic as Transcendent

If Madonna's "Like a Prayer" was, in some ways, the beginning of scholarly engagements with religion and popular music and Coltrane's *Love Supreme* an early example of popular music being constructed or perceived as spiritual, then metal music provides another model of important intersections of popular music and popular religion. In choosing an Iron Maiden album as a musical example, we take on an example of a musical genre often the aim of vitriolic criticism for being satanic, blasphemous, and immoral, while attracting religious-like disciples who characterize the experience of listening in transcendent and spiritual terms. Through the reaction of the American public to what they perceived as new, other, and either revolutionary or threatening, Iron Maiden, a British band, like the Beatles, offers a better look at American culture and helps emphasize the unique national tastes and attitudes. It was not until the band's *Number of the Beast* tour of America that the album was linked to ideas of the satanic by American evangelical and right wing groups, still perhaps the most enduring legacy of the album.

There is no denying the existence of a literal, intentional, antagonistic, and symbiotic connection between twentieth century heavy metal music and religion. Metal bands with names like Judas Priest, Nazareth, Possessed, Testament, and Atheist release albums with titles such as *Haunting the Chapel* and *Hell Awaits*; sing songs called "Seven Churches," "Welcome to Hell," and "At War with Satan"; and put on ritualistic performances to fanatical crowds of fans who perform defined rituals (including the famous "devil's horns" hand salute), and claim extreme out-of-body experiences which they describe in pentecostal terms. Ignored as serious topic for academic study until the '90s, metal is no longer (at least in some circles) considered a strange choice for intellectual investigation. Yet heavy metal music has only occasionally been discussed in the context of popular religion. Like many discussions of the relationship of popular music to religion, writing about metal generally slights the sonic experience of the music in order to point to select verbal passages or to compare their roles as ritual. For example, in "Metallica and the God That Failed: An Unfinished Tragedy in Three Acts," Paul Martens discusses the band's paradoxical representation of God and religion at different stages in their history, by focusing almost exclusively on lyrics, and what the band *says* about religion and God, rather than on the music as a religious experience or on how listeners construct ideas about religion using their reactions to the music. Fans, in contrast, claim religious experiences from listening to music whose lyrics they claim not to know or understand.

Neither approach captures the full impact or cultural importance of popular music which is always constructed by sound, lyrics, ritual, and spoken and written commentary.

Like *A Love Supreme*, Iron Maiden's 1982 album, *The Number of the Beast*, was both a commercial success and musically groundbreaking. *The Number of the Beast* was the number one album in the UK and subsequently became a top ten hit in many other countries, and the band became the most identifiable component of what was known as the New Wave of British Heavy Metal (NWBHM). The music featured the operatic tenor vocals of Bruce Dickinson, a new more musically tight sound of two guitars playing in precise unison as well as expanding the harmonic language, a more active and less static bass line, and sudden shifts of key, time, tempos, and dynamics not previously explored in metal. It also differed from established American metal in its more modal and less blues based sound, faster tempos, and lyrics borrowed from mystical and religious texts.

Helping to set the post-apocalyptic background for the music, the cover of the album pictures a colorful landscape dominated by two cartoonish figures: a smaller red stereotypical devil figure and a larger corpse-like monster—"Eddie," as he is known to the band's fans—who is controlling the devil marionette-like with green strings. Closer examination shows that similar green threads hang from the devil's fingers as he too controls someone or some creature down below; perhaps even another representation of Eddie. The back cover of the album (the inside jacket on the CD version) featured, along with pictures of the band, a quote from the Book of Revelation which was also intoned ominously on the album.

> Woe to you, Oh Earth and Sea, for the Devil sends the beast with wrath, because he knows the time is short.... Let him who hath understanding reckon the number of the beast for it is a human number, its number is Six hundred and sixty six [Rev. 12:12–13:18].

Other song titles also reference religious and apocalyptic themes: "Children of the Damned," and "Hallowed Be Thy Name." Although well received in England and in Europe, it was understood quite differently in America. Noticed mostly for musical innovation before, on their United States tour Iron Maiden was accused of being "satanic," and protesters staged prayer interventions and large record burnings. What is most revealing about these protesters is that they ceased burning records when they realized that they were perhaps releasing devil-fumes into the air, after which they merely smashed the albums. For these protesters, then, the actual vinyl *contained* the "real presence" of evil, an example of American religion and its tendency to both literalize and create—in this case creating a new presence of Satan which literally existed in the molecules of mass produced record albums.

On the other hand, many American metal fans identified listening to the music and going to their concerts as a religious experience that one fan described as "seeming to raise me up out of my body so that I didn't even exist anymore." Fans of the music of Iron Maiden, as Robert Walser puts it, "draw on the power of centuries worth of imaginative writing to make sense of their own social experience and to imagine other possibilities" (Walser 160). Walser, author of an acclaimed cultural studies and musicological analysis of metal music, writes that "if religion functions both to explain the world—providing models for how we live, tenets of faith and empowerment, and comfort for when they don't work—and to offer a sense of contact with something greater than oneself, then heavy metal surely qualifies as a religious phenomenon" (154). What does it mean to call metal a religious phenomenon? This aspect of metal has not been totally ignored, as one sociologist referred to Led Zeppelin as "liberation theology in vinyl" (Donna Gaines qtd. in Walser 154), and as Sylvan claims, heavy metal provides "an entire meaning system and way of looking at the world, a surrogate religiosity" (163). If whirling dervishes search for a spiritual transcendence, then so do head bangers and stage divers. The religious camp revival meetings of the nineteenth century were described and defiled much like the heavy metal concerts of today for being too loud, too sexualized, and too dirty. Deena Weinstein points out that the typical heavy metal concert "bears a striking resemblance to the celebrations, festivals, and ceremonies that characterize religions around the world" (232). Citing Durkheim, she compares the way metal and religions bring together normally isolated groups to celebrate and indeed to become conscious of themselves as a subculture. Heavy metal concerts, for her and for many fans, are experiences of ecstasy that embody a sacred experience. This clearly expressed need for the concerts to resemble religious rituals imbues the music itself with more religiously expressed significance and is conversely energized and created by the sonic experience of the music.

Iron Maiden's music on *The Number of the Beast* creates a destabilizing effect on the listener, at the same time that their skill gives a feeling of security in traversing such a perilous road. The guitar solos, in their free-soaring flights above the rhythmically strong and steady beat of the bass and drums, suggest the same dialectic of freedom versus stability that we commented on in *A Love Supreme*. Walser points to the dialectic that is "set up between the potentially oppressive power of bass, drums, and rhythm guitar, and the liberating, empowering vehicle of the guitar solo" (54). Iron Maiden's music explored the freedom further, as the drums and bass ventured away from the static, giving listeners an even more liberating experience. We can also see this same dialectic of power versus freedom enacted in the Madonna video for "Like a Prayer," where the constraints of the church are contrasted to the freedom of dancing outdoors, and where multiple identities are contrasted to unity. In each of these cases, the music experience mirrors the paradoxical ideology of an American popular religion that clings to unity (fundamental-ism) and also celebrates the freedom to explore, and create within faith.

Although heavy metal is less formally analyzed, fans of metal and Iron Maiden exhibit the same paradox of reception. Walser sees Iron Maiden as offering a religious "empowerment that is *largely musically constructed*, but which is intensified by ritualistic images that sanctify the experience" (Walser 154; emphasis added), and fans insist on the same pure, musically created experiences of transcendence. Yet this transcendence falls on both sides of the American religious experience: it can come through a stable unchanging rhythm or through a radical creativity. Transcendence can result from head banging or air guitaring; through the hypnotic, steady, pulsating beat, or through exhilarating improvisation.

As with Coltrane and Madonna, it is the extra-musical elements that provide the spiritual context for reception of the album. These elements create a condition which resembles the contradictory epistemology of belief in an inerrant sacred text while emphasizing every individual's right to interpre-tation, which we have been arguing is central to American popular religion. Heavy metal's embracing of themes and images of chaos borrow directly from the chaos monsters and language of the Bible, particularly the Book of Rev-elation. Even in attempting to create a sense of chaos and disorder, metal musicians—in a culture that is so redolent with Christian symbolism—must incorporate recognizable monsters from its sacred text in order to create symbols and images that resonate with members of Western culture. The fig-ure on the album cover is shown manipulating a devil-like caricature, and so opens up a space within the mythology. Iron Maiden enters that space and so whatever chaos it can create takes shape out of a preexistent system, which it ultimately reaffirms. Chaos, although often viewed as antagonistic to tra-ditional religious thought, is in reality a necessary balance or struggle between order and disorder, cohesion and destruction, a space and dialectic that is at the core of Western religion.

Perceptions of "Like a Prayer," *A Love Supreme*, and *The Number of the Beast* give us three contrasting twentieth century texts that set up categories of religion and popular music culture for fan and critical analysis. While each suggests different assumptions about the role of religions and have been seen as texts that contain a religious essence in and of themselves, they also tend to be described in ways that negate this. In different ways, Madonna, John Coltrane, and Iron Maiden presented challenges to preexisting structural tra-ditions and texts at the same time that they employed them, ultimately embracing the contradictions and paradoxes. They were, as a philosopher might say, part of a way of thinking of God after the death of God—a ques-tioning of the very structural elements that are seen to define them, a simul-taneous desire for and a rejection of ideas of a unified, immediate, or pure experience of transcendence or spirituality. Like Madonna's all-too-human Christ figure leaving the church to enter into a "real world" where his divinity disappears, these pieces present religious elements without religion, spirituality without God, and a near transcendent experience that yet reminds us of the impossibility of total transcendence.

Like jazz critics reading Coltrane's liner notes seeking a "secret" to reveal the "correct" interpretation, or Christian protesters identifying Satan in the fumes of burning Iron Maiden albums, the impulse to frame popular music as an autonomous unit with a single clear meaning produced by an obvious creator is the same impulse that seeks to see the Bible itself as a possessor of meaning and truth intended by its author. Yet the very process of affirming this autonomy reveals the impossibility of such self-contained essential meaning. This "essential contradiction" may, in some ways, be the aspect of these musical texts that is most closely related to spiritual or sacred tradition, and that, instead of undermining the religious, perhaps offers a sense of a transcendent experience, however subversive. This very tension can be explored and explained through theological thought that sees God as both the possessor and guarantor of all meaning *and* that which lies beyond comprehension and possibility— a God at the very limit of meaning. In other words, God, the Bible, and texts of popular music all can slip loose from their sacred moorings and resist an essentializing determinacy. And whether we pursue these texts as believers or skeptics, it is this space of undecidability we must forever navigate.

Hipsters, Hip Hop, Spirituality and the Nones

The stubborn idea that much popular music is somehow opposed to religion or religious practice has somewhat receded in first decades of the twenty first century. As mainstream churches struggle to maintain their congregations, they have more often borrowed the strategies of less traditional churches in including popular music in their services. Such movements as "hipster Christianity" have embraced craft beer and indie rock in ways indistinguishable from their non-confessional organizations. And as young people are less inclined to identify with a particular religion and yet more inclined to identify as "spiritual" or have a religious "practice," popular music often fills that space. Electronic Dance Music (EDM), noise rock, post punk, doom metal, and gospel rap all have passionate followers who insist on the spiritual or religious importance of their listening practice.

Matisyahu's "King without a Crown"

Jewish American reggae vocalist and hip hop beat boxer Matisyahu burst onto the scene with his 2005 hit "King without a Crown," an upbeat reggae tune about a desire and need for God and about waiting for the coming Messiah or Moshiach. The song, which was a top 40 hit, owed much of its popularity and fame to the buzz surrounding the striking image of a Hasidic Jew with yarmulke, full beard, and Hasidic undergarments (or *tallit katan*), beat boxing, singing, and dancing around a reggae beat. As one critic wrote, "Here was a Hasidic Jew, dressed in a black suit with a broad-brimmed black hat worn over a yarmulke, and sporting a full, untrimmed beard, who nevertheless performed toasting raps about the glories of traditional Judaism over reggae beats in a dancehall style directly from Jamaica, punctuating his performances with stage diving" (Ruhlmann).

Although fan discussions frequently centered around the difficulty of processing the religious lyrics with the music, as Matisyahu frequently pointed out, reggae, especially Bob Marley's music, is full of scriptural references, particularly from the Old Testament, and phrases of spiritual longing. From this point of view, even though many of his listeners do not see it, Matisyahu continues this practice of scriptural citation and spiritual questing around a reggae beat. The constant Old Testament references in Bob Marley's songs provided further confirmation for him—not of the divinity of *Haile Selassie* but of the God of Jacob. To listeners and viewers, however, the perceived message is complicated.

One of his most popular songs and videos, "King Without a Crown," filmed on location in New York City, captures the contradictions present in Matisyahu's performances, his fan base, and his negotiation of religion, popular culture, identify, and scripture. The opening of the song, just Matisahu's voice, is almost a type of *Nigun* (a wordless melody, common in Chasidic practice, which is intended to prove a spiritually uplifting experience rooted solely on the music and not on lyrics, a type of absolute music, if you will). The rest of the song has a fairly traditional reggae sound mixed with Matisyahu's beat boxing vocals and a rock style guitar solo. The lyrics, which are prayer-like and worshipful, are also unabashedly Jewish, using Hebrew words such *HaShem* to refer to God and *Moshiach* to mean messiah.

In the video a young man or teen age boy walks alongside a wall, head downcast and wearing a hooded sweatshirt. On the wall are various posters of Matisyahu and his band, which come to life as the young man walks by. The video negotiates two seemingly separate spaces, reflecting the two worlds of its protagonists, and the experience of living in Brooklyn neighborhoods such as Williamsburg or Borough Park where hipsters and Orthodox Jews occupy the same spaces but seem to be living in separate parallel universes. The boy in the hoodie walks the streets slowly and aimlessly, head hidden beneath his hoodie. While the verses feature shots of the young man in his urban location, during the choruses we actually enter Matisyahu's poster world, a paradoxically livelier and more fluid one than the "real" world of the streets. The video depicts a drab urban Brooklyn neighborhood in shadows and grays interrupted with occasional abstract shapes in bright colors, sometimes imitating a poster, and sometimes becoming more psychedelic (especially during the guitar solo).

The video emphasizes the importance of words throughout, both as we hear them rapped and beat boxed, and as we actually see them visually depicted in the video. A constant stream of lyric subtitles flows behind and around Matisyahu and his band; so that, as he dances and sings, he literally moves through and around the printed words of the lyrics that stream through the video; a sort of echo of Jewish mystics that encourage the experience of focusing on and engaging with the empty and white spaces around the letters of scripture.

The boy's final encounter with Matisyahu on a street corner is an ambiguous moment but significant of something being passed from an elder to a youth. In the final moment, we see the boy's picture is now on the wall behind them. The video, like the music and like Matisyahu himself, plays with blurring the lines of the "hip hop" elements of the video with Hassidic interpretations: the blending of graffiti and Jewish scripture and the echoes between the hoodies and yarmulkes that one sees in Brooklyn neighborhoods. In Matisyahu's images, music, and fan base, then, one can see a reciprocal transference of religious, cultural, and social symbols. The song not only reappropriates the Jamaican Rastafarian appropriation of ancient Jewish history, but translates it into a world where Hasidic practice and hipster spirituality exist and even began to converse.

In 2011, Matisyahu—who reportedly once had to turn down an invitation by Madonna to hang out at her Passover Seder—shocked (at least some of) his fans by shaving his beard and tweeting "No more Chassidic reggae superstar." Rabbi and blogger Eliyahu Fink called it "The Shave Heard Around the World" (qtd. in Wax). As the *Washington Post* asked just days after he shaved his beard:

> Was the Hasid in the hoodie—who is known to fuse beatboxing with Orthodox Judaism's style of songful prayer—forgoing his faith? Or was he simply dialing back his belief? Would his highly religious lyrics—like those to "One Day," which was played as background music in some television coverage of the 2010 Vancouver Olympics and asks God for a day without violence—vastly change?

More important than the answers were the larger issues of the questions. Speaking in 2012 about his Jewish practice, Matisyahu said, "I took that trip as far as I could. And then I started to find other things" (AP 7/16 2012).

In a way, Matisyahu's much debated new direction just continues the final images of "King without a Crown." The young hoodie wearing boy in the video might just as easily represent an unassimilated portion of the artist's identity. He could be Matisyahu himself before he "believed." Thus, the transformation that occurs in the song, much more in the video, and perhaps externalized in the action of shaving his head is not from a state of spiritual drift, more of personality integration. One way to read Matisyahu's "trip" might be a kind of self-rescripting. We might be tempted to see the act of shaving his head as a loss of faith. But, what if we think that the identity of the Orthodox Hassidic Jewish reggae hip hop star is only symbolic? This is a symbolic identity which could always only approximate the whole person. In other words, now that audiences recognize his Hassidic identity, he can shave his beard, and yet still be a Hassidic reggae star. Although it is much discussed by his fans, in this way, his actual religious practice may be somewhat beside the point. His music, lyrics and performance style are now essentially linked though his artistic persona to his Orthodox Hassidic identity. The song, video, and remixes of "King without a Crown" all exist both before and after Matisyahu's recent religious shifts. Like many religious experiences, the experience of listening to the song involves thinking outside of linear time. The nature and ontology of a piece of popular music allows it to exist outside of time, and while popular music is also deeply intertwined with celebrity culture, the acts of recording, sampling, downloading, listening, and remembering provide new ways to read, and news way of thinking about text and narrative.

Kanye West's "Jesus Walks"

With the bourgeoning musical genres which continue the popular discourse about and around religion, it is impossible for this chapter to provide exhaustive coverage, but it would seem especially incomplete without an example from mainstream hip hop. Far and away the most influential musical genre of the twenty first century, hip hop music, with its ostentatious jeweled crosses, its shout-outs to God on CD liner notes, its "Gospel rap," and its claims that "Jesus is my homeboy," maintains an often seemingly explicit connection to religion, although in practice a much challenged and debated one. Positioned as both self-evidently "deviant" and as connected to African American evangelical Christianity, hip hop, and the study of hip hop, is uniquely positioned to help us think through the relationship of popular culture and religion.

Studies of religion and hip hop music, like other attempts to "find" religion in popular music, often take the reductive approach of defining "religion" according to a top down model based in official beliefs and dogmas, rather than the lived practices that are constantly influenced by popular culture. Critics of hip hop are especially guilty of this as they often assume either a direct connection with or an antagonism to a monolithic "Black church." One common mistake—as we pointed out in the study of Madonna and Iron Maiden—is to find these two characterizations (deviant and "religious") in opposition. One reason the word "spiritual" has gained favour among the younger generation is that it is easier to blend with practices seen as non- or anti-religious (sex, cursing, rebellion). Like Madonna saying she wants to put sex and religion back together, Kanye West's claim in 2016 that his new album is a "gospel with a lot of cursing" is an attempt to break down these assumed borders. Understanding religion *in* hip hop, as in all popular music, involves a turning away from (although not completely losing sight of) institutional religions. If, as scholars like Russell McCutcheon and Talal Asad claim, the category of religion is created by discourse itself, than the ways in which we talk about popular music and religion makes that conversation part of our current negotiation over what religion now is.

Probably the most high profile rap song in discussions of religion is Kanye West's "Jesus Walks." In much the same way that Madonna's song and video "Like a Prayer" came to be the go-to example for undergraduate and academic studies of religion and popular culture in the late twentieth century, West's "Jesus Walks" has been in the early twenty-first. Many, often influenced by West's comments, interpret the song and videos as a daring and open expression of Christianity in a "secular" music industry. Others read it as an egocentric and performative expression of an arrogant super celebrity. Others see a subversive irony or political statement hidden in both of these readings. How literally are we supposed to take Jesus, and Devil in the song? Do Kanye fans and listeners unproblematically accept the common explanation of Kanye as a believing Christian and the lyrics as an extension of black evangelical churches? How are reactions to this song and video influenced by Kanye's later exhortations that "I am God," his album "Yeezus," or the presence of a Jesus figure on stage during his 2013 tour version of "Jesus Walks"? Like Madonna's song, the impact of the song has been expanded and complicated by the video, by the persona of the artist, and by subsequent live concert versions. If "Like a Prayer" was an expression of religion that questioned borders and categories, than "Jesus Walks" is both a more obvious expression of a form of Christianity, and a text that challenges institutional religions and the category of "religion" itself.

The song begins with an introduction of war against terrorism, racism and ourselves. As the song unfolds, it would appear that the war we're at "with ourselves" is a struggle with the sins, the lifestyles, the decisions we make that we realize are wrong. The introduction ends with a refrain that the devil is trying to break him, repeated throughout the song. Like Madonna's "Like a Prayer," the song features a traditional gospel choir, a sample taken from the gospel song "Walk with Me" mixed in with a repetitive militaristic beat.

The first verse develops the theme of fighting with ourselves, as West describes some scenes out of the lives of a few of the sinners he'll later list in the second verse. He describes the actions of thieves and drug dealers. When he gets to the chorus he gives voice to the desperation of the sinner. The release of the song was accompanied by three different videos, each offering a version of "Jesus" in the everyday world, a visual presentation much more material than spiritual. The first video featured West as a preacher with angels as his guides. The third video was a low budget, Jesus-in-the-modern-world narrative. The second and most familiar video was a flashy high budget production set in the deep south; it offers non liner images of a chain gang, girls jumping rope, a police chase through a desert landscape, and a man chopping down a tree and then making a cross, putting on his Klan robes and setting the cross on fire. Throughout the video, we see West surrounded by fire and—like all of the other people in the video—dressed in white.

The album and the song, not surprisingly, attracted critical attention from fans, critics, and scholars: "*The College Dropout* is an album of intense contradictions, a godly album awash in sin and temptation as well as an anti-academic manifesto from the whip-smart son of a college professor" (Rabin). Many conservative Christians were offended by the song, especially when seen in the context of his entire *The College Dropout* album and even more so by the article that appeared subsequently in *Rolling Stone*. As West said once in an interview with BBC Radio 1, "I just told you who I thought I was: A god. I just told you. That's who I think I am. Would it have been better if I had a song that said 'I am a nigger,' or if I had a song that said 'I am a gangster,' or if I had a song that said 'I am a pimp'?"

Kanye's informal references to Jesus fit in with the American Protestant Jesus-is-my-friend narrative. Referring to himself as "Yeezus" perhaps renders the idea of religion more palatable for his listeners, most likely millennials who at least appear to resist traditional labels and religious institutions, simply because the name is a less traditional and more modern version of "Jesus." Kanye, as a celebrity, might be seen as offering a demonstration to his listeners in the popular culture world that religion is not something to be afraid of. Religion can be quite personal, and any of us can easily become a "Yeezus." Like the Black Jesus/Saint escaping the church in Madonna's "Like a Prayer," Kanye's rhetorical move here is to push religion into the popular where it does not need to be confined within the walls of a church. In a classic hip hop move that combine braggadocio, commerce, art, and spirituality, he also makes the claim that not only is religion and Jesus part of popular culture, but that in his hands anyway, it is indeed a *marketable* part of popular culture despite resistance: "They say you can rap about anything except for Jesus."

For religious studies and hip hop scholar Monica Miller, Kanye West "gave rap music a liberation theological facelift, reminding the public of what

Jesus of Nazareth was *really* up to in the Gospels" ("God of the New Slaves" 169), or, in West's terms, Jesus was "kickin' it" with those outcasts who were "criminal and deviant." The video's blend of faith, commerce, bigotry, war, apocalyptic fire, and everyday life not only captures the cultural sense of the early twenty first century, but expresses its complicated religious sensibility as well. Kanye's Jesus—in classic America Style—walks with us, but as West reminds us, he particularly walks with the oppressed.

Kanye poses *the* two central questions within Abrahamic religions: What if God were human? Can humans become gods? These questions, found in debates over the nature of Christ in the fifth century to Mormon theology in the twentieth, are also constantly restaged in popular culture. On the other hand, in an age that claims a rise of the "spiritual but not religious" (SBNR) and "nones," especially among the younger generation, the liberation theology of Kanye West can be used to question the very definition of religious itself. Religion, as Miller writes in her book *Religion and Hip Hop*, "like gender and race, is assigned and performed for social, political, and cultural reasons" (8). West's "Jesus Walks" can perhaps seen as an example of what Miller describes as hip hop's "predilection for maintaining complexity and useful incoherence" (215). Building on this idea, we can turn Kanye's song around. His world is one in which Jesus, like the Ku Klux Klan, like gang violence, like the Kardashians, is real. But "real" can mean many things that are not traditionally religious or worshipful. If he, as he raps, needs Jesus the "way Kathie Lee needed Regis," then just how much is that, actually?

One way of understanding hip hop and sampling culture is to see it as a new way of thinking about the role of history and artistic influence. A hip hop artist, unlike a jazz musician, for example, does not merely imitate, adapt, or copy a lick from Charlie Parker, but instead can literally uses the exact recording and rework the sounds into his or her own material. Fans of the music pride themselves on their knowledge of all the historical levels represented in the sampling and the sonic landscape and will talk about the presence of 1970s B-side horn licks or 1990s Bhangra samples in a Jay Z song. The song then is not only paying homage to or "remembering" a previous musical sound, but it is literally reframing this exact sound. This flattening or conflation of history is in many ways an experience characteristic of religious experiences and scripture. A Catholic participating in the eucharistic ritual feels actually transported to the moment of the crucifixion; a reader of the *Book of Mormon* is literally reading the Book of Isaiah that has been lifted from the Hebrew Bible and placed in a new context almost unchanged in content.

In a popular music world now driven more by social media than by record sales, the type of rescripting here done by Matisyahu and Kanye West often takes place in less institutionalized spaces. While their music shares common roots in hip hop culture, their listening audiences are quite different. Yet their music and discussions of it are played out online and through various forms of new media. Even mega stars like Kanye use unorthodox strategies to market the release of a new CD.[5] These alternative venues, strategies, and distribution formats have provided popular music a different space of existing, one that can more easily exists with the less traditional forms of believe and spiritual practice that young people (particularly the "nones" and the "spiritual but not religious") claim to seek.

Contradictions of the Absolute: "What if God were one of us?"

In the days that we were finishing the second edition of this chapter, Prince died. The outpouring of articles and tributes across mediums pointed not only to the huge influence he had on the last three decades of popular music, but also to the complex and contradictory role he and his music had played in the development of the way people thought about music, music business, spirituality, sexuality, and culture. But even more than that, the initial memories, tributes, photos, and essays from fans, scholars, musicians, and writers all seemed to testify to the difference Prince had made on their lives, and were often phrased in religious terms. Peter Coviello, in a piece in the *Los Angeles Review of Books*, "Is There God After Prince" seemed to sum up these sentiments. Coviello labeled Prince "the least secular rockstar we have ever known," and wrote "Prince is hard to grieve because he is, in an only barely not literal sense, divine."

What almost none of these religious characterizations mentioned, however, was the well-known fact that Prince was a devoted member of a Jehovah's Witness Church, where he was know as Brother Nelson to church members. First a Seventh Day Adventist and then converting to a Jehovah's Witness, Prince's identified sects are two of the most indigenous strands of American Christianity and are yet sects that challenge the borders of traditional American Protestantism. As a Seventh Day Adventists, like Little Richard before him, Prince would have been surrounded by a faith that is both an American original and, as Malcolm Bull writes, "a negation of the American Dream" (*Seeking a Sanctuary* 268). As an American apocalyptic faith, inspired by the Millerite Great Disappointment of 1844, the sect can be considered almost heretical in its acceptance of extra-scriptural authority, its limitations on the power of Christ, its denial of immortal souls, and its centrality of Satan. In converting to a Jehovah's Witness, Prince moved to another apocalyptic cosmic view also heterodox in its denial of the Trinity, its fierce anti-intellectualism, and its celebration of a powerful and angry Gnostic God seeking an ultimate Armageddon victory. What does it do to think of Prince as an apocalyptical Christian that expected Christ's immanent return, and that went door to door distributed religious tracts, supported Republicans, and opposed gay marriage? To what extent Prince participated in the theology or politics of his chosen churches and to what extent he was just seeking a familiar community outside of his celebrity may never be known, but what is known is that this side of Prince adds yet another inexpressible contradiction to his persona and his music.

These contradictions point to ways in which current engagements with popular culture are part of a larger project to re-define what we think of as religion or religious. If we learn anything about religion from Prince, it is that one's religion is expressed in multiple ways beyond belief, prayer, or church membership. It is also in an ecstatic vocal scream or in the yearning or searching wail of a guitar; it is in seeming to overpower nature itself in a torrential downpour in front of millions at the Super Bowl, or to appear painfully vulnerable on stage alone with a piano.

On the day of Prince's death, English Professor Andrea Knutson wrote, "who will write and sing about desire in a way that respects women's desire and sexual being and independence? Who will do that?" Knutson, like Peter Coviello, echoes Christian theologians in the radical tradition for whom the death of their savior is not necessarily a path to resurrection, but is instead a moment that forces one to imagine an existence alone—a permanent Easter Saturday when the messiah is just dead and buried, and no stones have been rolled aside to reveal an empty tomb. In many ways Prince's "religion" and his "divinity" spring from all of these contradictions. Prince was never any one thing or one person. His whole career extended impossible questions and answers into religion: Was he saint or sinner? Holy or blasphemous? Apocalyptic Christian or sensual shaman? The answer to all of these questions is yes, all of the above.

A Prince song, like a Shakespeare sonnet, feels private and social, homo- and heterosexual, and sacred and profane. Coviello points to Prince's "hotly feminized masculinity," and his "queer blackness" before finally calling him the "sexiest fucking Emersonian in the history of the world." It is in this Emersonian embrace of contradiction and paradox where Prince's heretical yet deeply American religion is most apparent. Jon Pareles wrote in the *New York Times* obituary that Prince was a "unifier of dualities," and maybe he was, but it seems more accurate to say that he exploded them all together. Prince not only sang about and composed contradictions, he *embodied* the contradictions of celebrity, of sexuality, and of American religion and divinity that popular music continues to rescript.

* * *

Contradictions and paradoxes are at the heart of how American culture creates and enacts religion. And by contradiction, we don't mean it in the sense that "the Bible contains contradictions, therefore it is not true," but to mean that a "text contains contradictions, therefore it is an open and interpretable text." Religion is often defined as a force against chaos, a force for order, but as radical theologians throughout history have pointed out, it has also always been a force of rupture and chaos. We have pointed to the suggestion of a chaotic sacred within popular religion and the perception of popular texts. Although recent philosophy and theology have often pointed to disruptive elements inherent within Western religion, the perception of popular religions and popular texts often overlook this aspect of belief. But popular culture and popular religion also intersect in ways that are disruptive and contradictory, albeit often unrecognized by the practitioners.

These "sacred" texts, like any sacred text, cannot be said truly to contain a religious essence (as much as listeners—from head bangers to record burners—want them to) but instead they continue to define the human separation from the One. In enacting this negativity, popular music can be seen as similar to more traditional and canonical texts and experiences regarded as sacred. The Bible, as many scholars have attested, constantly resists a religious interpretation, as close reading and its multiple interpretations bear out. Although for many, prayer is when they perceive themselves as closest to God, the practice of prayer requires the *absence* of God and therefore can only take place at a distance from God.

To return to our opening question: what does it mean to say that a piece of music is spiritual or religious, or that it is immoral, blasphemous, or satanic? To ask these questions is the same as asking if the Bible is religious, or if prayer is a spiritual experience. On the one hand, the answer appears obvious, but on the other it seems clear that the Bible is religious and prayer is spiritual because one thinks it is. There is no doubt that these subjective experiences are culturally and historically constructed, but even that is a tautological explanation, and the answer is always more contradictory and subversive than it appears. Again we are left with the same questions. Where do we perceive the spirituality or religiosity to exist? And what is it about certain texts or experiences that invite these descriptions?

Moving from "Like a Prayer," *A Love Supreme*, and *The Number of the Beast* to "King Without a Crown," "Jesus Walks," and Prince outlines a type of borderland where popular culture and popular religion meet and our contention is that all popular texts exist within a space on the continuum of this meeting. It is in their contradictory perception and effect and in their complexity that they actively work to create this space. Their questioning of limit points of comprehension, their enacting of the dialectic of freedom and stability, and their dramatizing the contradictory elements of true presence are examples of how texts of popular culture reveal deeper currents of theology and religion—indeed are the texts where we do not *find* meaning but through which we create meaning for ourselves.

CHAPTER 5

The Gods of Film
Representing God and Jesus
at the Movies

The cinema has always been interested in God.—André Bazin

To analyze today's ideology, cinema is the best.—Slavoj Žižek

"The Walrus and the Carpenter" [is] an indictment of organized religion. The walrus, with his girth and his good nature ... obviously, represents Buddha, or with his tusks, the Hindu elephant god, Lord Ganesh.... Now, the carpenter, which is an obvious reference to Jesus Christ ... represents the Western religions. What do they do? ... They dupe all these oysters into following them and then proceed to shuck and devour the helpless creatures en masse ... to me it says that following these faiths based on mythological figures ensures the destruction of one's inner being.... Organized religion destroys who we are ... out of fear of some intangible parent figure who shakes a finger at us from thousands of years ago....

—The Angel Loki in *Dogma*

In the Beginning

When Moses receives the Ten Commandments in Exodus, God explains the rationale for each; for the second and third he commands:

Thou shalt not make unto thee any graven image, or any likeness of anything that is in heaven above, or that is in the earth beneath, or that is in the water under the earth. Thou shalt not bow down thyself to them, nor serve them: for I the Lord thy God am a jealous God, visiting the iniquity of the fathers upon the children unto the third and fourth generation of them that hate me [Exodus 20:4–6].

In this passage, scripture paradoxically shows both the majesty of this God and his humanity. He is a "jealous God," a most human quality; this is a God concerned with its position in a divine hierarchy. He is at once humanized and unapproachable. No longer the God of Genesis who visited Adam in the Garden, there is no room in this construct for a "personal relationship." God dictates from on high and must be feared and obeyed. Abraham's response, to obediently attempt to murder his innocent son against all possible rational or ethical reason, is exemplary of the proper human reaction to God's will. This is the God of the Hebrew Bible; vengeful, punitive, almost peevish and generally bad-tempered, a deity who is most concerned with its own glory, and most certainly not funny.

The Abrahamic tradition of unquestioned allegiance, obedience to and fear of God represents the proper response to this God, who requires it, but the Christian Bible and subsequent Christian interpretations shift some of the focus in this arrangement. The incarnation and sacrifice of Christ determines a different kind of relationship between God and humanity. Although the biblical Christ is not obviously divine, Christianity's need to establish Jesus as divine and then as part of a Holy Trinity created narrative and theological contradictions and complexities resulting in multiple heresies, sects, schisms, and complicated compromise doctrines. This difficult and complex theological construct is simplified in the American context by a focus on a "personal relationship" of humankind to the incarnate god, and by a decreased emphasis on the concept of the troublesome trinity. The personhood of the new American Jesus is simultaneously more accessible and more vulnerable than the first person of the trinity. Although popular religion often tends to simplify Jesus into a friend and companion, popular culture's conceptions of God and Jesus return to the unanswerable questions and irresolvable issues of the representation of divinity debated by early rabbis and the Christian fathers.

In American Christianity the primacy of God the father in relation to Christ the son has been reversed and most of its cultural capital invested in Christ, or more accurately in the person of Jesus (with a noticeable trend in some circles towards privileging the Holy Spirit). What ultimately develops within this structure of popular culture is a singular God rather than the complex and confusing Trinitarian theology of orthodox doctrine. Ironically, the need for a singular and stable god has resulted in multiple gods and multiple Christs. For many American Christians, it is difficult to understand that the Jewish and Islamic God is, at least textually, the same as the Christian one. This reveals not ignorance exactly, but the level of self-constructedness to which current evangelical and other popular American Christian movements are dependent. The contradictory impulses to hold the Bible as literal, singular, unerring and God-authored, while also asserting one's freedom to interpret it for oneself, preserves popular religion's ability to define itself in contrast to other faiths and not through links with them.

Jesus, as the American God, has literally become a new figure, a twentieth-century phenomenon with contemporary characteristics and issues, and with a distinctly modern multiple and fragmented personality. While this manifestation is apparent throughout popular religion and popular culture, film is perhaps the medium best suited to reflect and create these new and rescripted divine figures.

From its beginnings, film has had an active, if uneasy, relationship to religion, and many early classic films were religiously themed (*Samson and Delilah, King of Kings* and *Sign of the Cross*). Protestant resistance to graphic depictions of God as idolatrous notwithstanding, these films focused on dignified and accurate representations. More recent films, however, have been more radical in their imagining and representing religious subjects, and while this has often resulted in controversy (*The Last Temptation of Christ* for example), they also provide a lens through which we can observe another intersection of popular culture and religion. We can see and most closely interrogate the shift from a doctrinal orthodoxy based on the theology of the trinity to a popular conception which places the person and the personality of Jesus Christ as the godhead through examination and contrast of two relatively recent films, Mel Gibson's *The Passion of the Christ* (2004) and Kevin Smith's *Dogma* (1999). These films approach the representation of the divine from contradictory perspectives, while maintaining a level of cultural capital that allows them to speak to and for popular beliefs. Through very different approaches and for very different populations, these movies create for themselves and for the culture at large what French sociologist Pierre Bourdieu calls "culturally symbolic capital" which is negotiated through commercial and artistic frameworks that bound what he calls "the field of production." We will return to this idea at the end of the chapter. Even more recent films, for example Darren Aronofsky's *Noah*, continue to restage these tensions. *Noah*, in particular, shows an awareness of the old Hollywood biblical epic and the ironically postmodern, and it can be read as both experimental and traditional.

Our focus in this chapter will be to contrast these films and to show that while their contradictory representations may be at odds, the overall effect is the reflection and formation of a new understanding of the sacred. *The Passion*, for example, has been understood by many believers to have a direct connection to religious history and to actual faith; when asked about the movie, Pope John Paul II is reported to have said, "It is as it was."[1] The *National Catholic Reporter* quotes an unnamed source at the Vatican as saying that "while Gibson may be a bit idiosyncratic theologically, his heart is in the right place." The Vatican official also predicted, "There will be conversions because of this film" (Allen). The notion that the movie might serve a proselytizing role for the church by providing an accurate representation of scriptural sources for the Passion brings the idea of rescription of the sacred more into focus. Even more dramatically, because the movie is accepted in these terms and sanctioned by the Pope, it thus becomes to some extent, as we discussed in our introduction, a new sacred text with a certain level of legitimacy and authority.

The movie, as we shall see, does not necessarily reflect an accurate picture of the Gospels' version of events, just as *Noah* takes editorial license with its biblical sources. In fact, Mel Gibson has acknowledged that much of his script comes from a late-eighteenth and early nineteenth-century German nun, Anne Emmerich, whose visions were written down as *The Dolorous Passion of Our Lord Jesus Christ.* This conflation is not new; the incorporation of legends and traditions to bolster the rather thin description of the Passion in the Gospels has been practiced since the medieval passion plays, from which Gibson's film takes its form.

The insistence on a rendition faithful to the evangelists serves only to lend the work scriptural sanction, but, even following the Gospels closely, is impossible, and already presents an unsolvable textual and representational problem because their narratives are not in agreement, and any representational choice is a privileging of one text over another. For example, the scene in Gethsemane in Matthew, Mark, and Luke takes place immediately after the Last Supper, which is a Passover meal, but in John this scene occurs the night before and only includes the capture.[2] In determining which Gospel to follow, clear editorial choices must be made, and Gibson's decision is evidently to choose from various sources including all of the Gospels (primarily John), but not relying exclusively on them. This kind of co-mingling of different sources in order to create a coherent text is precisely what we have been discussing as rescription, and although it can be found throughout Christian history, takes on a new form within the participatory nature of American popular culture.

For believers, like their reception of the Warner Sallman painting *Head of Christ, The Passion* becomes a new and more "realistic" way to experience the sacrifice of Christ than just reading the Bible or going to church. Because the "real" is experienced in a more immediate way through graphic representation, the painting or the film becomes more real, more accurate. Questions of inaccuracies, which crop up immediately, are beside the point; the reception has more to do with a willingness to believe, an impulse that is, of course, always shaped and reshaped within the culture, and by the characteristically American privileging of experience over creed. Living through the film becomes a sacramental act, a more dramatic and ultimately more tangible form of communion; this is my body which you will see scourged for you, this is my blood which will be spilt for you.

Why Hast Thou Forsaken Me

Representations of God the father in contemporary films tend to be less about accuracy of scripture and/or doctrine and more about a general faith or belief. Because of this, they assume more freedom, and have the possibility of showing the humorous side of God. In *Dogma*, the main plot is set in motion when a doctrinal change made by the Catholic Church causes a series of reactions. The fallen "muse" Azrael uses the loophole created by Cardinal Glick's "Catholicism Wow" campaign to encourage renegade angels Loki and Bartleby to walk through the arch of a church in New Jersey, thereby to be absolved of their sins, to prove God wrong, and thus to end all of existence. Bethany, the "last scion" (described as "the great great great great great great great ... grandniece of Jesus Christ"), is tapped to stop the angels from entering the church. After many trials the group composed of Rufus (the black 13th apostle), the Metronon (the voice of God), Serendipity (a muse) and two prophets (Jay and Silent Bob), manage to win the day as Bethany figures out that God is trapped in the body of an old man being kept alive at a nearby hospital. The overall effect of this plot is to reveal a more human and more vulnerable God. "See, I told you she was funny," says the Metronon, as God (now played by Alanis Morisette) unprepossessingly walks around in flip-flops, does a handstand from which she crumples to ground, and pokes a woman on the nose when she asks about the meaning of life. While the God of movies like these tends to be funny, a sense of invulnerability allows for deeper theological questions than representations of the son.

In the 1940s and '50s, film representations of God depicted the God of Abraham in grand style. Movies such as *The Ten Commandments*, *The Bible* and others show this vision of God at work. They generally attempt to stay true to both the stories and spirit of the Hebrew Bible, while creating an unimpeachable God whose distance from human weakness is insurmountable. These films invest a large portion of their cultural and financial capital in "getting it right," to a certain level of biblical accuracy. The attempt is one of verisimilitude, correctness, an approach to the real. They were made to be film epics, showing the grand narrative of a Judeo-Christian past. And in popular culture, they are accorded a certain level of iconic power and symbolic cultural capital by virtue of their subject and their careful approach to it. Rather than being seen as idolatrous or controversial, these films thus accrete a level of cultural and devotional clout, but their representational choice is due in large part to the cultural attitudes and narrative system of film at that time. It would have been impossible to make a movie like the remake of *Bedazzled, Bruce Almighty, Saved,* or even *Noah* in that era. On the one hand, it would not have been part of the idiom filmmaking of the period, but on the other, the important religious tenets which would be seen as being ridiculed in the movie would have prevented such a film from being acceptable to the culture, and thus not financially viable. Culturally, the role of God in films of that time focused on his holiness.

In a sermon on the holiness of God's nature, online minister David W. Hall quotes at length from scripture to show how:

> God is intrinsically holy.... All he does is holy; he cannot act but like himself; he can no more do an unrighteous action than the sun can turn dark. God is holy primarily and transcendentally. He is the original pattern of holiness. It began with him who is the Ancient of Days. God is perfectly, unalterably, and unchangeably holy [www.apocalypse soon.org/xfile-35.html].

In more recent films, however, God's unalterable holiness has become sullied by its connection with humanity. Once it becomes connected to human nature the possibility of a perfect holiness is diminished. Only as long as God remains above, unmixed with human emotion, can it be seen as purely and perfectly holy. As God becomes more human, as Christ gains primacy, God is portrayed as weaker and more fallible. As we noted earlier, Slavoj Žižek characterizes Christianity's essence as residing in a divine and "fundamental imperfection" that is revealed through God's need for Christ. This essential imperfection manifests itself when God, through the humanness of Christ, realized his own weakness and an "impenetrability of God to Himself." It is at this moment that "God the Father Himself stumbles upon the limit of his own omnipotence" (*On Belief* 146).

God as the author of the universe, or the Bible, comes closest to the limits of his omnipotence at the moment of Christ's passion. As we saw in Chapter 1, Christ-like Tigger in Walt Disney's *Winnie the Pooh* cannot alter the end of his Book, and the absence of God is most conspicuous at this moment of crisis. God, as divine, is most palpably absent, at the very instant when he is most vulnerable in his incarnate self as the son. *Dogma* and *The Passion* recreate this moment, albeit in very different ways. The story of Noah, especially as depicted in the 2014 film, is another dramatization of God's self-doubt and weakness. American religion reenacts this gesture when it replaces God with Christ, an act that implies the inadequacy of the father to fulfill humanity's need for companionship. Film depictions of God reflect this double creation of weakness, as God tends not only to be more human than film Christs, but also in need of human assistance; God demonstrates an overall susceptibility to human weaknesses and characteristics.

God's interaction with humanity becomes more ordinary and eventually cruder in contemporary film. An extreme example is seen in *Dogma*, when, in reaction to having met and being kissed by God, in the form of Morisette, Jay confesses, "you wanna hear something sick. I got half a stalk when she kissed me.... I couldn't help it, the bitch was hot." In this version, God (the father) becomes considerably less holy, more mundane, flawed and human.

Partly, because Christ's nature is already human, it becomes much more dangerous to represent him in anything approaching this kind of vulgarity. Christ may be mocked by Roman guards or the Sanhedrin because this represents a scriptural "fact," but this physical treatment of Christ out of the biblical context is strictly off limits. Christ's divinity must be reiterated and insisted upon in contradistinction to God's humanity which never really reaches the level of doctrine or profanity.

Within American Christianity, the correlation between a divine Christ and human God presents an interesting paradox or contradiction. The majority of American Christians view Jesus as a personal savior and see themselves as involved in a personal relationship with him; their attitudes and connections to God the father is less specified. Philo/theological questions about the nature of the Holy Trinity are not regularly interrogated in the context of popular belief. The focus in the United States on Christ as Lord and Savior diminishes the role of God the father and only attributes to him an almost mythical or legendary status, which contradictorily allows for certain liberties to be taken with depictions of his character. This view allows movies to represent God as comical or to present him in situations that, from a strictly orthodox or doctrinal perspective, might be called blasphemous, but paradoxically reaffirm the presence and power of God in the culture because they never completely escape from his presence.

The God who lays waste to Sodom and Gomorrah, floods the earth, and confounds the speech of the builders of the Tower of Babel because "now nothing will be restrained from them, which they have imagined to do" (Genesis 11:6), in its human form as Christ becomes more merciful and understanding, and much more approachable. God's "only begotten son" occupies the role of bridge between humanity and the deity; humankind's familial relation to this person of the trinity becomes fraternal rather than filial, and simultaneously creates a vulnerability and close familiar bond that God could never have. And yet depictions of Jesus in film have remained, for the most part, serious and less open to more "human" variations upon his character (even *Jesus Christ Superstar*, despite the fact that it is a musical and has a definite "hippie vibe," is quite serious and conservative in its depiction of Jesus).

Jesus at the Movies

Just ten years ago, when our first edition was published, the range of physical depictions of Jesus on film was most represented by Mel Gibson's then recently released epic *Passion*. Among the lessons that Gibson taught Christian-themed filmmakers, was that movies piously focused on religious subjects had a ready mainstream audience that could pay off financially.

Paradoxically, in many ways, the greatest influence of *The Passion*'s success was to open up a space for variety in the depicting of Jesus on film. While portrayals of Jesus or New Testament themes continue to be dominated by earnestly serious, sometimes doctrinaire, representations, *Washington Post* chief film critic Ann Hornaday describes 2016 as

> a year that has encompassed the Coen brothers' extravagant parody of 1950s Hollywood Bible kitsch (and sincere portrayal of discernment) in *Hail Caesar!*, the modern-day drama *God's Not Dead*, and the period pieces *Risen* and the *Young Messiah*. When a lavish, state-of-the-art remake of *Ben-Hur* opens this summer, we will have come full circle to precisely the brand of lurid swords-and-sandals epic the Coens skewered so affectionately just six months earlier [Hornaday].

What has emerged in the years since *The Passion* is broad range of Jesus themed movies with markedly different tonal and theological qualities. Jesus may no longer be out of range of humorous interpretations, but he is both a marketable draw for audiences and remains a serious subject. The treatment of Jesus on film in the early part of the 21st century, while more open, is still not to be taken lightly. According to Hornaday,

> All of these films vary widely in artistic quality, mind-set and theological point of view, from the fiercely anti-secular defensive crouch of "God's Not Dead" to the less strident sincerity of *Miracles from Heaven*. But for all of their perceived differences, each of them hewed to common modes of the contemporary Christian filmmaking that, in the wake of *The Passion of the Christ*, has sought to exploit the market Mel Gibson so shrewdly identified by alternately patronizing, proselytizing or pandering to it ["The Rise"].

Paradoxically, that these narratives are allowed to exist is at once unusual, and almost inevitable. As with many popular cultural products, once a "new" avenue of consumable narrative is determined to be profitable, entire industries arise to create them. Like reality TV or movie sequels, Christian movies with and without Jesus as a protagonist have become a thriving genre for niche markets, which sometimes go mainstream.

In addition to large bore blockbusters, like *Noah* and small self-funded "Christian" movies, there have been some "arty" films such as *Last Days in the Desert,* written and directed by Rodrigo Garcia (son of renowned author Gabriel Garcia Marquez). Hornaday describes this kind of religiously themed movie as "Christian movies for the rest of us," suggesting that other movies on these themes are aimed only for a niche religiously minded audience.

Last Days in the Desert deals with some of the same material as *Last Temptation of Christ,* covering the period in the desert where Jesus (referred to in the film by the Hebrew *Yeshua*) grapples with Satan's temptation, but complicates the internal psychology of Jesus to suggest, among other things, a broader view of the relationship between fathers and sons more generally than the biblical source. In the film, Yeshua fasts and prays for a long time before he cries out, "Father, where are you?" and receives no response. The scene prefigures that of the cross, when Jesus questions God's abandonment. He soon befriends a family with a stern father and young son who are building a house on the edge of a craggy desert chasm. Overall, this is a much quieter and introspective film that either *Last Temptation* or *Passion*. According to *New York Times* film critic Stephen Holden,

> The characters' simmering passions never explode. *Last Days in the Desert* is also the opposite of a violent, bloodthirsty movie like *The Passion of the Christ*. A final, enigmatic sequence jumps ahead to show Jesus's final moments on the cross and his entombment. There are no choirs of angels or signs of celestial disruption. Yeshua is a man alone.

Holden sees the movie as focusing on neither "extended theological debates" or quotes from scripture: "There are no parables, words of wisdom or reflections on eternal life. Yeshua's relationship to God is personal and private." This depiction is one that simultaneously highlights the problematics of an incarnate God. Yeshua is human not only his relationship to other humans, but in his relationship to God, the father, as a human son, who might worry about abandonment, about the stern rule of the father that sets up impossible expectations for his children. The experience of the human Christ is emphasized as over and against either his divine nature or his unique relationship to God as his only begotten son. But, in this structure, Jesus is also unhuman, "a man alone," who is not quite one of us, but not quite divine.

For filmmakers, Jesus movies continue to represent a difficult minefield to navigate between blasphemy, ardent belief, and introspection. As a subject, Jesus, the man, is a frail figure, whose chief strength lies in his ability to sacrifice his human body for the sake of all who believe in him. He bleeds for us, but he is called upon to do it according to the plan of his exacting and unerring father. God the father suffers no such frailty; he is demanding, unyielding, unapproachable, and all-powerful, which allows for a much more scornful comic treatment than Jesus. In many movies, God, the father, is mocked as either a dithering old man or an overbearing tyrant, without as much concern about blasphemy.

But, Seriously, Folks…

Representations of God as a funny old man in movies may have begun with George Burns in *Oh, God!*, the tagline for which was "Anybody who could turn Lot's wife into a pillar of salt, incinerate Sodom and Gomorrah and make it rain for forty days and forty nights has got to be a fun guy." And perhaps because he was old enough to have attended Christ's Bar Mitzvah, Burns managed to look venerable, wise, and funny. Burns's rendition of God comes off as mildly humorous and sort of corny, but his wisdom and paternal concern comes through. God appears to be Jewish in *Oh, God!* where there is no mention of Christ. He nonetheless appears to be weakened in his human manifestation. His omnipotence seems represented only by some parlor tricks, appearing and disappearing from select faithful and saving the day at the last possible moment. In *Oh, God! Book II*, he rides a motorcycle with a sidecar, which he has just materialized, but starts out haltingly, as if he is just learning how to ride it. From a representational perspective, Burns is an unlikely choice to play the role. Throughout the three *Oh, God!* movies, it is very difficult not to imagine Burns sucking on an unlit cigar as he frailly totters around in quintessential Burnsian fashion.

Is God dead, as Nietzsche reports, or has he just become an old, broken-down vaudevillian? Or is this the same thing? Did God have to die to be reborn as a filmic comedian? At the movies God has become very funny, a transformation not restricted to him; many other celestial and infernal creatures have become humorous. In the Harold Ramis remake of the 1967 *Bedazzled*, a decidedly shapely Lucifer (though the Devil has always had the power to assume a pleasing shape) in the form of Elizabeth Hurley seduces Brendan Frazier into selling his soul for a girl. Ultimately, in *Bedazzled*, God and the Devil seem to be working together to keep humanity on the straight and narrow, as is true in *Little Nicky* where Harvey Keitel plays the role of Lucifer, having inherited the post from his father, Satan, played by Rodney Dangerfield. *Little Nicky* stars Adam Sandler as the ne'er-do-well son of Lucifer, who is charged with going to earth to capture his two older, meaner, eviler brothers and returning them to Hell before his father is destroyed. The two have jumped through the mouth of Hell thereby freezing it so that new souls cannot get in (in a sense Hell is freezing over). Not only is his father's life in jeopardy, but the balance between good and evil is threatened and therefore the fate of humanity is at risk. This sort of irreverent depiction of celestial and infernal beings is quite common in contemporary movies. This is not so much a desecration of God's holy nature, but a bringing it down to earth, an incarnation of sorts. God and his heavenly creatures are still holy, but are so in a much more human manner. In these instances humans are not elevated to a celestial plane by association with celestial beings, but rather celestial beings are diminished through contact with humanity.

Representations of God the father have undergone a revision similar to that of the New Testament. God in film—an essentially visual medium—must somehow be represented, a move that usually involves giving him human form. Yet, this humanizing of God, a type of Christian incarnation, goes in the opposite direction of Christ. In other words, God becomes more human than Christ. God shows humor, weakness, irritations, desire, while Christ is not allowed to demonstrate any of these human characteristics. Like American religion, films have un-deified God, and sacramentalized Christ as the one and only God. In this transformation, the films reflect the movement of American Christianity which has become more and more obsessed with the person of Jesus, but a person who paradoxically is revered for his divinity rather than his humanity.

Christianity's defining moves were to humanize God and to make a sacred event out of his death. God, in the person of Jesus Christ, dies to expiate the sins of mankind, but this requires an overwhelming sacrifice. Since God ultimately cannot truly die, the sacrifice is represented through suffering. It simply would not do to have Christ just die with full awareness that his death is but a temporary step; he must suffer for the sacrifice to count. The concept of Christ's passion is built up in the Middle Ages as a way to explain the manner by which Jesus redeems humanity. As we have been saying, American religion tends to eschew the creeds and doctrines of the Old World, but the traditions and stories persist. They are reworked, refashioned and re-imagined, but they remain nonetheless. The medieval convention of the suffering of Christ as the symbol of human salvation thus continues to be the central tradition of American Christianity.

It's Just a Flesh Wound

One of the central moments in the Gospels, for many Christians, is the point when an angel tells the women who have come to visit the tomb of Jesus that he is gone. At the core of Christianity, then, is a negative image; it begins with an empty tomb. This story is retold in churches every Easter and this moment was re-enacted in medieval Europe through liturgical theater which sought to "embody" the supreme sacrifice of Christ, precisely through emphasis on the absence of that body. The history of Christian thought is, in some ways, an attempt to reconcile this absence. From the Mass, where the priest, as Burcht Pranger says, "denies, however briefly, the loss of the body, restoring it to its former self" (182) in the communion bread to Gibson's *Passion*, which eucharistically attempts to re-present that body on film, Christians have created practices, rituals, and art, to convince them that the body is real, that it is not really "gone."

Film, in essence, can act as a form of transubstantiation that features a man-made act to bring viewers in touch with the body of Christ. It accomplishes this feat because of the perceptual registers upon which it functions. One may say that films offers the most naturalistic representation of reality available, but this not an uncomplicated arrangement. According to film theorist Christian Metz,

> More than the other arts, or in a more unique way, the cinema involves us in the imaginary: it drums up all perception, but to switch it immediately over into its own absence, which is nonetheless the only signifier present [802].

Film creates an illusion of reality by exposing us to multiple perceptual experiences simultaneously, but it is necessarily recognized as an illusion. Like the corpse absent from the tomb, film most accurately represents what is not there. When the massive cross Christ struggles to drag up to the Hill of Golgotha slams to the ground in *The Passion of the Christ*, the sound thunders in Dolby stereo making the audience jump, but this sound is an impossibility, an exaggeration that emphasizes and underscores the physicality of the represented world of the film. Like the scourged flesh of Christ, which similarly signals both the illusory quality of film and the "truth" of the suffering sacrifice, the absence of God becomes manifest through the tormented flesh. The more materially represented, the more carnal, the more like a savagely butchered slab of meat Christ is, the more actualized the sacrifice, the closer the deity comes to being human, and finally the further God is from being present. The representational mode itself becomes the thing it represents; film's absent presence becomes theology.

Contemporary Christian salvation theology focuses almost exclusively on the human suffering of Christ as redemptive. According to Billy Graham, "NO ONE IN HISTORY ever suffered more than Jesus Christ. The culmination of His suffering came on the cross of Calvary, the supreme symbol of both physical and spiritual suffering" (67). Where older films engage the jealous and cranky God of the Hebrew Bible, Gibson's *The Passion of the Christ* represents a signal engagement with the precepts of Christ as sacrifice. The focus on suffering both humanizes and mystifies the person/deity of Christ. On one hand, the brutal human suffering of the film elicits an empathic response from its audience. The level and kind of violence depicted in the film, however, create a distance between the pain that is imaginable or endurable by the audience and that possible by the sacrificial and divine Christ. Gibson's film, though on a very different register than, say, *Little Nicky*, could potentially be seen as blasphemous, because of the dehumanizing nature of this suffering. Several online Christian commentators have drawn attention to this aspect of Gibson's film. According to a Christian website:

> His endurance of the savage beatings may indeed be the world's greatest model of endurance and forgiveness, but that is not the Biblical message. The Scriptures proclaim that Christ Jesus' endurance of God's wrath against sin is the key element in the Gospel. It was His taking upon Himself God's wrath for our sins that provides atonement for us who believe that we are saved only by His sacrifice [Dunbar].

Christ is both more and less human, the incarnation more and less biological, the representation more and less real. The physicality of this movie attempts to represent a "real" that goes beyond the bounds of the everyday. Nothing in this film is mundane or common, or fades into the background. Rather than an attempt to reflect a naturalistic reality, the film makes every effort to capture a hyperrealism that imbues every ray of light with significance.

In its use of language and subtitles, *The Passion* also attempts a linguistic rather than a visual hyperrealism. The "documentary illusion created by modern subtitles under ancient languages thus simulates a voyage not so much to distant lands as to a distant era." This artistic choice, declares Jack Miles, "is a brilliant stroke" ("The Art of *The Passion*" 11). In presenting all the dialogue of the film in Latin and Aramaic the film tries to recover the Word as it existed even before the Bible. Although it would have been the language spoken by the common people of first century Judea, the Christian Bible was written in Greek, not in Aramaic. By using this language, Gibson interposes his film between the actual events and the gospel texts he claims to be following; that is, rather than a linguistic and representational translation of an extant text, this depiction attempts to recuperate an original text which, of course, does not exist. The film becomes a linguistic simulacrum attempting to mix the Gospels' authority with the primacy of the "original" spoken language.

Yet another hyperreality is created by the lush cinematography of the film, which aims for a painterly realism rather than a photographic or cinematic one; many of the screenshots evoke the work of Renaissance painters, in essence, recognizing the rescripting of previous centuries. As has been noted, the sequence toward the end of the film where Christ is removed from the cross ends with a tableau that resembles a number of paintings of the subject, particularly depositions of Christ by Carivaggio, Titian, Tintoretto, and Botticelli (Phelan). According to Jane Schaberg, in the tableau with "Mary his mother at his head, Mary Magdalene at his feet, John in the middle [as his] hand moves up the thigh of the corpse.... Psychoanalytical interpretations of infantile attachment and underlying homoeroticism are certainly in order" (73). These cinematic techniques obviously render unintended results for Gibson as he attempts to integrate major frames of Western culture into his vision of the sacred text. The technique is carried throughout the movie, as the use of light and shadow and color filters renders an atmosphere of otherworldly delicacy. In the midst of the great horror and torture, the viewer is always aware of the otherness of the scene.

The film takes great pains to represent at once this aesthetic painterly reality, while also conveying the minute details of scourging flesh. The body of Jesus is immolated through desperate violence, but bits of flesh and blood are followed lovingly by the camera's eye. Although the camera technique is pure Hollywood-stylized violence, it is fitting that the model for this exhaustive treatment of wounded flesh is the medieval passion play, wherein Christians of the Middle Ages could see for themselves the great suffering of their savior. It was important then, as it was for Gibson to create a spectacle to prick the conscience of the onlooker, to think on him who died on the cross for the sins of humanity. Gibson's success in this goal is clear from contemporary reactions to the movie of several prominent preachers and ministers:

> After a private showing, Billy Graham praised it. Mission America Coalition plans to use the movie for evangelism. Campus Crusade is promoting it. Rick Warren's Saddleback Church in southern California purchased 18,000 tickets. The Evangelical Free Church of Naperville, Illinois, purchased more than 1,000. Two members of Wheaton Bible Church in Wheaton, Illinois, have offered to buy out two screenings of the movie at a local theater [Cloud].

This response from American Protestant leaders echoed the reported support given by Pope John Paul II and the unnamed official who insisted that there would be conversions on the basis of the film, though, of course, there was no mention of whether these conversions will be specifically to Catholicism.

The overwhelming response of American Christians to the movie was positive. Most felt that it offered a very realistic presentation of the last twelve hours of the life of Christ, and others praised it for getting people talking about the issues even if its representation was a bit exaggerated. This response is staggering, particularly given the overwhelming predominance of Protestants and anti–Catholic sentiment among American Christians. To quote Paula Fredriksen, "Gibson has taken this now somewhat old-fashioned, quintessentially Roman Catholic fixation on blood and pain and sold it to millions of Sun Belt Protestants" (92).

But not all Protestants were convinced by Gibson's rendition. Some traditional Protestant conflicts arose regarding the possibility of representation of Christ at all. One issue raised by a book, *The Passion of Christ in Scripture and History*, by Samuele Bacchiocchi, published soon after the release of the movie, asked:

> Is it biblically correct for a movie artist to impersonate and dramatize the last twelve hours of Christ's suffering, by portraying His body splattered with blood on the way to Calvary? Can such dramatization be biblically justified? Or does it represent a sacrilegious act condemned by the Second Commandment? [Bacchiocchi].

This is a question rife with the controversies of the Reformation. It is a question raised by the Puritans regarding the staging of the Corpus Christi Cycles (last performed in York in 1472). The answer for Bacchiocchi is "absolutely not!" but the very question informs a certain approach to the issue of Christ's divine and human nature. From this perspective, Christ's divinity, his holiness, is so impeccable that to represent him even in the service of evangelizing is a sacrilegious act. Would this hold for other kinds of representations? Are paintings of Christ, such as Caravaggio's and Da Vinci's, after all, created by mere mortals, in their very nature idolatrous and sacrilegious?

While most American Christians, and indeed almost all those who enjoyed Gibson's film, would disagree with this position, the question still frames discomfort with representations of Christ. Andres Serrano's infamous photograph, "Piss Christ," for example, becomes sacrilegious for its mishandling of the sacred image. In this case, it is not the image itself or necessarily the subject, as the photograph merely shows a crucifix enhanced by a glowing liquid, in fact resembling stained glass. If Serrano had titled his photograph of a crucifix, say, "Golden Christ," there would have been no controversy surrounding it. Indeed another Serrano work, "Madonna and Child II," is described by April Watson, the Curatorial and Exhibition Assistant in the Department of Photographs at National Gallery of Art, in just these terms:

> The Madonna and Child appear in Serrano's photograph as a clouded yet radiant symbol of the Mater Amabilis, the maternal Virgin Mary embracing the Christ child. Submerged in a luminous amber liquid that diffuses light and softens details, the small figurine appears greatly enlarged, composed to emphasize the infant's gesture as he turns to his mother. Just left of center, a mucilaginous bubble connects the child's forehead to his mother's cheek, evoking a corporeal, in-utero connection [Watson].

In this case, as with the "Piss Christ" photograph, the title provides a frame for interpretation. If this photograph (which appears to use the same "medium" as "Piss Christ") had been called "Piss Virgin," the National Gallery would have been hard pressed to defend it, or, conversely, had Chris Ofili's painting "The Holy Virgin Mary" festooned with elephant dung been called "African Woman," it would not have elicited the responses like that of Dennis Heiner, a 72-year-old Christian who was so incensed at Ofili's painting that he threw white paint across it and proceeded to smear the paint over the canvas in the Brooklyn Museum (an act treated sympathetically in several New York City tabloids). Responses to artistic expression and representations of Jesus are inescapably bound to the social and cultural frames.[3]

Since American religion focuses its gaze on the person of Christ, American filmmakers must be careful not to transgress certain lines in their depictions, especially since they must appeal to a larger audience than contemporary visual art in order to survive. The scourging of Jesus' flesh in *The Passion* is substantiated by its *serious* treatment of the subject matter and the fact of the movie's purported scriptural accuracy; a condition that also explains Gibson's insistence on his scriptural sources. While a depiction of Christ still bears some scrutiny for believers, representations of God the father are not as assiduously analyzed. The Christ of film continuously bears resemblances to earlier renditions; several critics have noted that in choosing Jim Caviezel, Gibson was looking to enhance the likeness to the Shroud of Turin, for which the film makes a case in the final scenes. Conversely, God the father is non-essentially embodied in film. In older films, God is represented as a disembodied voice, a burning bush, swirling torments and roiling seas, and, in newer comedies depicting God, his "body" is unessential, even when materially represented.

Persecuting God

If cinematically acknowledging Christ's human body in a sexual way can be blasphemous (*Last Temptation of Christ*), and if to depict it being violently tortured and flayed can produce a spiritual or even sacred event, then what analogy is there to be found in filmic representations of God? God, as we have seen, can be represented in film as almost anyone without offense, but what if a film were to show God being violently beaten? God's body when not represented through Jesus is non-human, or merely occupies the human without being of human. *Dogma* illustrates this point through the non-essentialized body God occupies. In the beginning of the movie, God, played by Bud Cort, is (as in *Oh, God!*) a frail old man. After being beaten within an inch of his life by hockey stick-wielding teenagers, he lays powerless. This frail old man, now a resident of a South Jersey intensive care unit, on life-support and in a coma, is not God, but God trapped inside of a human. This body, within which God remains trapped, is very much the pivotal plot point of the movie. Because he cannot escape from the bounds of this now comatose human body, God cannot act to stop the two renegade angels from exploiting a scriptural "loophole" and walking through a church door, thus negating all of existence. God thus becomes frail and powerless through association with the human body, even as scripture retains its literal and ultimate authority.

In *Dogma*, God is embodied in two human forms: before becoming a woman, God is the old man who is hospitalized. In newer comedy movies about God the father, his body is inconsequential; it makes no difference who plays him and what resemblance the actor may have to earlier conceptions of God's image. In these movies, as in Aronofsky's *Noah*, God occupies a space of non-materiality. In the television series *Joan of Arcadia* (2003–2005), God appears to her in several forms, but always as regular people. In *Joan*, as with Abraham and Moses, it is God's voice (his text) that identifies him. While in *The Passion*, Jim Caviezel is clearly identifiable as Jesus as traditionally depicted in art, in comedies about God, the body is not the point. Counterintuitive as it may seem, the immutability of the body in depictions of Christ symbolize his divine nature, even as they focus on corpus. Comedic representations of supernatural beings now tend to be drawn in much more earthy tones.

Such is the case in *Dogma*. Matt Damon and Ben Affleck, who play fallen angels Loki and Bartleby, have been consigned not to hell but to Wisconsin, ever since Loki (who was the angel of death) put down the flaming sword after the destruction of Sodom and Gomorrah on Bartleby's advice. They come into the movie at an airport as Bartleby tells Loki that he has received news of a Catholic loophole that will allow them to return to heaven, although it will come at a great cost to humans: "Leave it to the Catholics to destroy all of existence," says the muse Serendipity (*Dogma*). In the first scene with the two fallen angels, we witness an exchange between Loki and a nun in which, after the deft literary criticism of the Lewis Carroll poem "The Walrus and the Carpenter" (quoted in our epigraph), Loki convinces her to use the money she has been collecting for her order to buy a dress and find a guy or a woman with whom to share life's precious moments. Loki's argument is based on a theological interpretation of the poem, which in the movie sounds erudite and thoroughly plausible.

On some level, this reading of the poem points back to a suspicion of intellectualism resident within American popular culture and religion. For Billy Graham, "the wisdom of this world, encouraged by Satan, is cynical of the Cross. The apostle Paul said, 'The message of the cross is foolishness to those who are perishing, but to us who are being saved it is the power of God'" (68). *Dogma* presents an ambiguous position to this sentiment, as Bartleby's response to Loki after he has played this cruel trick on the nun is to chide him:

> BARTLEBY: You know, here's what I don't get about you. You know for a fact that there is a God. You've been in His presence. He's spoken to you personally. Yet, I just heard you claim to be an atheist.
> LOKI: I just like to fuck with the clergy, man. I just love it. I love to keep those guys on their toes [*Dogma*].

This exchange reveals the predominance of a positivist understanding of God as against a theorizing that conceptualizes a more problematic relationship between creature and deity. While Bartleby emphasizes the absolute surety of God's existent, he also refers to God with the masculine pronoun although the movie will eventually determine that God is female. There is an obvious narrative-driven reason for this "slip," in that it would be too soon to reveal this fact now. However, the resulting contradiction yields up some interesting results in terms of the film's representation of God.

In the universe of the film, God's existence is guaranteed; there is no question. The film goes to great pains to emphasize this fact. One could, in fact argue that *Dogma* takes a much more positively determined view on the existence of God than *The Passion* or *Noah*, at least from the point of view of what is represented. In viewing *The Passion*, there is no character who can tell us with the level of assurance expressed here by Bartleby of the nature and ontology of God. From the perspective of any of the skeptical characters in the narrative, no convincing event really occurs. The resurrection which occurs at the end of the film does nothing to convince anyone of the divinity of Christ or his father, since it occurs "offstage," so to speak, with no one present to witness it. One must already be convinced in order to be won over by the events as depicted.

Dogma, obviously, takes a very different approach as it expends an inordinate amount of expository time and narrative energy espousing and discussing theology. From the Cardinal Glick's "Christianity Wow!" campaign, and the discussion of how exactly Loki and Bartleby intend to get back into heaven, to the explanation of the Golgotham (or shit-monster), the movie is obsessed with theological constructs and their explanation. At one point, as Bethany begins to have second thoughts about the heaven-ordered mission, she tells Rufus, the thirteenth apostle, "Yesterday, I wasn't even sure that God existed. Today, I'm up to my ass in Christian mythology." Rufus responds, "Let me let you in on some inside info, God hates it when people refer to it as 'mythology'" (*Dogma*).

In *Dogma*, God is a certainty; in *The Passion* the only certainty is his absence. Anyone in the audience of *The Passion* who is completely ignorant of the central tenet being depicted would not understand what is being witnessed. Nothing in the movie is explainable except within the context of faith. One must be a believer/unbeliever in order to give meaning to the events it depicts.[4] In this case, the experience must fit into a long history within which we may find a previous exposure to its central idea. We enter the theater already knowing what we are about to see, already aware of what is necessary for its understanding, the rendition is all that is new. The film focuses exclusively on the visceral, the flaying of skin, the tearing of flesh and the blood, all the blood. It is neither allegorical nor symbolic; we are to witness the actual, but it says nothing about the presence of God. The more the movie strives for cinematic realism, the more Mel Gibson's God is made absent.

Satan, Where Is Thy Sting?

Into this equation we may include the representation of Satan in the film. Hailed by many as the most innovative aesthetic and narratological move made in the movie, the role of Satan is played by Rosalinda Celentano, described by Jack Miles as a

gray-faced, hollow-eyed terrorist, speaking in a weirdly masculine or masculinized voice, as if delivering a death threat in a disguised voice ... the most insinuatingly sinister Satan ever on screen. Hers is, in truth, one of the most memorable performances in the film ["The Art of *The Passion*" 14].

There is no doubt that her performance is memorable. She slithers her way through the film with a menacing leer and the androgynous look (compared by Timothy Beal to Marilyn Manson), and manages in very short snippets to be nearly as disturbing as the relentless and brutal flogging that takes up most of the screen. But Celentano's screen time, which is not more than two minutes, features only one scene of dialogue, or, more accurately, twin monologues.

At the beginning of the movie, as Jesus is praying in the garden of Gethsemane, Satan appears as a hooded figure in the shadows. Although she looks
directly at the prostrated Jesus, there seems to be no direct engagement
between them; she speaks to him; he speaks in prayer only to God:

SATAN: Do you really believe that one man can bear the full burden of sin?
JC: Shelter me, oh Lord. I trust in You. In You I take refuge.
S: No one can carry this burden, I tell you. It is far too heavy. Saving their souls is too
costly. No one, ever. No. Never.
JC: Father, you can do all things. If it is possible let this chalice pass from me, but let Your
will be done. Not mine.
S: Who is your father? Who are you? [*The Passion*; capitalization as presented in subtitles].

Christ's words here are a composite from the Gospels, but in none of the
Gospels is there an encounter with Satan at Gethsemane. In this sequence
Satan does not, in fact, deliver a death threat; the death threat is from God,
and Satan's words are a temptation for Christ to forgo the cup of the new
covenant which is to be filled with his blood.

The scene ends with Satan unleashing an asp from below the hem of
her robe and Jesus stomping its head as sign that he is willing to accept his
fate. This is the only part of the scene that might be called an exchange. As
soon as he stomps the snake, Judas and the Temple guards appear to fulfill
his betrayal. All the other scenes that feature the Satan character are fleeting
and their symbolic meaning is elusive. In the most remarkable scene, Satan
glides along the crowd holding what appears to be a suckling baby. When the
baby turns toward the tortured Jesus, we see he is a grotesque, gargoyle-like
figure; the camera then shifts to the inconsolable Virgin Mary, who weeps.
The effect of the scene on the viewer, as it is with all the scenes featuring
Satan, is that there must be some symbolism at work. But, again, they are so
short-lived and cryptic that it is difficult to assign them meaning.

The appearance of the figure of Satan in a part of the story that is non-
scriptural becomes a distraction from the relentless torture, and may offer
the only real theological question of the film. Is Satan's suggestion that Christ's
suffering may be in vain the last temptation of Christ? The Gospels suggest
that the moment in the garden at Gethsemane is one of doubt. The synoptic
Gospels (Matthew, Luke and Mark) all have Jesus asking God if it is possible
not to go through with his plan in almost exactly the same language. But
John, whose gospel Gibson uses to establish the basic narrative structure of
the film, is silent on this point. Gethsemane becomes only the site of Judas's
betrayal and the capture of Jesus. Gibson's extra-scriptural choice, along with
his going back to the synoptic Gospels draws attention to a particular theology.

Christ's moment of doubt in the garden signifies a separation between
God's will and his. Jack Miles suggests that the film leans toward a theology

that requires both Satan and the resurrection in contrast to one in which Christ's suffering is meant, in and of itself, to expiate the sins of humanity. The function of Satan then becomes to obfuscate and confuse the very human Jesus in order to derail mankind's redemption. Miles also suggests that cruelly smiling figure implies a Satan who thinks s/he is winning the battle only to be sorely disappointed in the end when s/he is shown shrieking in some pit. If this were the case, why would Satan at Gethsemane attempt to talk Jesus out of his sacrifice? It is more reasonable to think that the smiling Satan and the symbolism of the infantile grotesque are meant to show the futility of the suffering.

The final scene of the movie gestures toward the resurrection through one quick sequence of jump cuts. We see the tomb from the inside with a stone rolling to close it, through dappled light and shadows we see a robe flutter and empty itself, and finally, for the first time, we see, in a close-up, Caviezel's handsome, well-groomed, unpummeled face. He quickly rises to his full height, and we glimpse the smooth naked well-toned body of the savior now unblemished by the scourging. Finally, we see his right hand, with a hole through which we can see his thigh; the screen fades to black. This montage should give us some pause. If Christ has been resurrected and if that resurrection is to be signaled by the appearance of a newly restored body, then why the hole? We must presume that not many hours from this moment, Jesus will appear to his disciples and Thomas will be given a chance to reassure his doubting heart by poking his fingers into his wounds.

As the film has focused throughout on the physicality of the suffering sacrifice, here it again focuses on a material rather than a spiritual renewal. The hole in the hand smacks of romantic essentialism which focuses the audience's reaction on one physical trait to identify the whole person. This is a serious enough flaw with mere mortals; when dealing with the very complex personhood of Jesus and his dual natures, it becomes dangerous. It is odd that Satan's last gambit in the garden appeals not to spiritual doubts, but to creaturely ones.

The scripture makes a point of the fact that as Jesus prays in deadly earnest, his disciples fall asleep. Jesus chides Peter, "What, could ye not watch with me one hour?" (Matthew 26:40 KJV); the sequence is repeated in Matthew and Mark. In Luke, an angel comes from heaven to strengthen the spiritual resolve of Jesus, but his disciples are only men and their sorrow and fear remains tied to the earthly material concerns. They fall asleep out of a bodily weariness connected to emotional stress and perhaps too much Passover wine. Satan's temptation seems puny and ineffectual in its corporeal focus, but serves to set the stage for a film that in its two hours of horrific torture and violence will test the human nature of Christ.

Not of This World

Where *The Passion* is bodily focused, *Dogma* is very careful to show the non-human qualities of the angels. In the scene at the airport, as Bartleby waits for Loki to finish talking to the nun, he is shown with two paper baskets of popcorn. As he eats the popcorn from one basket, he spits it out into the other. Later, when the Metatron (the voice of God) beams himself and Bethany to a Mexican restaurant for "really good" tequila, he makes a point of ordering two tequilas and an empty glass into which he will immediately spit out the drink. Before this, while in Bethany's bedroom, to assure her that he will not rape her, he reveals to her that he is "as anatomically impaired as a Ken doll," by exposing his absolutely smooth crotch. The depiction of these creatures shows a clear demarcation between the human and the heavenly, but also the authentic and the marketed. Christ's only appearance in the movie is as "The Buddy Christ," the bigger-than-life plastic sigil unveiled by Cardinal Glick to replace "the wholly depressing" crucifix as part of the "Catholicism Wow" campaign, a stinging parody of the personal Jesus of American Christianity delivered by the famously atheistic comedian George Carlin. *Dogma* has no truck with questions about the dual nature of Christ or the elemental makeup of heavenly creatures; these are closed topics, but other theological issues concerning God are very much open to discussion.

Movies about God by necessity must deal more closely with theology than those about Christ. Depictions of Christ allow very little flexibility of character, narrative, or motivation. God, on the other hand, appears in so many different ways throughout the Bible, and is not contained within narrative or character traits. Film must then select or create the rules to define God and his divinity, yet still keep it within an acceptable Judeo/Christian context—a process that while sometimes arbitrary is highly theological. In the expository scene where Bartleby explains the loophole to Loki, director Kevin Smith follows a long tradition of biblical exegesis by paying very careful attention to the accuracy of some doctrinal interpretation and giving no regard to others. Bartleby is quite correct in pointing Christ's problematic promise to Peter from Matthew 13:19: "I will give you the keys of the kingdom of heaven, and whatever you bind on earth will be bound in heaven, and whatever you loose on earth will be loosed in heaven" (NSRV). It was precisely this doctrine, when combined with plenary and papal indulgences, with which sixteenth-century Protestants, particularly Martin Luther, had so much trouble. The theory of transubstantiation, however, is not scriptural, for there is no mention in the Bible of any angel having the ability to transubstantiate to human form. This bifocal approach to biblical and doctrinal sources is carried through the whole movie, mirroring contemporary American Christianity which adopts its theology from a myriad of sources, scriptural and non-scriptural, traditional, hagiographic, and popular. In *Dogma*, sometimes these differences are a direct function of the plot such as the invention of the character of Serendipity, a muse who has come down to earth, with God's consent, to seek her creative fortune. In some cases, as in creating new characters such Rufus, the thirteenth apostle, played by Chris Rock, the movie just seems to be having fun with us (although the idea of a self-appointed apostle has an important precedent in the person of Paul).

This also seems true in the film's representation of God as a woman. The God we meet in the first scene of the movie is not actually God in its divine form. As it turns out, God is an avid Skeeball player who regularly takes human form in order to indulge its obsession with the game. The "real" image of God, which we see at the end of the film, is Alanis Morrisette. This conception of God as a member of a minority group is not restricted to this film. In *Holy Man*, Eddie Murphy plays a character named G, who, while not explicitly referred to as God, seems to have all the requisite qualities. In *Bedazzled*, Brendan Frazier as Elliot runs into God, who is a young black man, as a cellmate in prison. In both *Bruce Almighty* and *Evan Almighty*, God is played by Morgan Freeman. So what are we to make of this new vision of God who, like TV courtroom judges, seems always to be female and/or a minority?

Stewart Hoover, a scholar of religion and media, explains that contemporary media has moved much faster than churches to facilitate spirituality and religious expression in a changing American society. Hoover cites several factors affecting people's religious expression in America today, including a decline in institutional authority, the rise of personal autonomy in beliefs/seeking/questing and media functioning as a "marketplace of religious symbols, then, televangelism and religious broadcasting more generally remain significant elements of the landscape" providing a symbolic catalog which determines possible personal belief selections (Hoover 61). Stewart seems to be saying that more Americans get their churchin' from the mass media than from any other source. If this is true, the God with which these folks are establishing a personal relationship is a much more human and humorous God than the Hebrew Bible would indicate. This trend could point to a discomfort with the myopic interpretations that have been assigned to Christ's human side. The danger in monotheism (although it has always been difficult to claim Christianity as truly monotheistic) is that humans invest God with our own weaknesses and then in turn use him to justify their actions. Comedic and liberal depictions of God can be seen as a form of liberation theology through which minority groups break down the social and ideological restrictions and limitations imposed by a hegemonic divinity.

If film can serve as an important force within society it is because of its potential to reach large numbers of people. Paola Marrati explains that

Cinema, unlike theater, brings into play the link between humans and the world, because from the beginning cinema has been an art for the masses. This link between the masses and the world allows Christian and revolutionary faith to converge in cinema: faith in the transformation of the world by humans and faith in the discovery of a spiritual world inside humans [238].

Pierre Bourdieu might be helpful in placing this phenomenon within a context of a cultural economy. In his study, *The Field of Cultural Production*, Bourdieu theorizes the field of artistic production within the matrix of economic structures which function through the culture as a set of guidelines for various fields, creating "culturally symbolic capital." For Bourdieu:

The opposition between the "commercial" and the "non-commercial" reappears everywhere. It is the generative principle of most of the judgments which, in the theatre, cinema, painting or literature, claim to establish the frontier between what is and what is not art, i.e. in practice, between "bourgeois" art [82].

What is true for the field of art production is true for the religious belief, and reading these representations of God in film blends these two fields to allow us a broader view of the cultural condition of religion in America. The oppositions which exist between various "fractions" of society with regard to aesthetic principles in Bourdieu's formulation exist in the interaction of Hollywood film and independent filmmaking.

These oppositions include the concern with economic profit and commercial success of Hollywood productions and the disinterest on the part of independent filmmakers. However, both parts of this equation are at play in the construction of a cultural product. The myth (and for Bourdieu a rule of the marketplace) is that filmmakers interested in producing an artistic film must disavow all commercial interest. The method through which an artistic product is accorded symbolic cultural capital, according to Bourdieu, is determined in the culture through experts in the field. In American culture, and for the two films we are discussing, this means radically different sets of viewers. Mel Gibson, who used his own money to create what was seen in Hollywood as a devotional dog of a movie, generates symbolic cultural capital through an affinity with certain deeply held religious beliefs. Kevin Smith's first movie, *Clerks*, was an independent, ultra-low-budget movie which gained attention from the cultural elite and thus accreted financial and artistic capital for its director. Smith plays to the intellectual crowd, while Gibson eschews intellectualism and scholarship in favor of a devotional experience that resonates with and energizes evangelical fervor. These two forces are at odds in American culture and its symbolic capital is split down the middle, but each is a part of the vortices that are at play as popular culture and popular religion reflect and enact each other in the broader American culture.

Fin

Despite the Protestant insistence on language over image, Christianity has been communicated primarily through images, whether presented in stained glass, staged pageants, or painted canvases. Although Jesus says, "Blessed are those who have not seen and yet believe" (John 20:29), a more typically American aphorism would be that "seeing is believing." Filmic representations of Christ enact the tension between these two—presenting "realistic" imagery that challenges or enhances the viewer's feelings about Jesus, at the same time that film's fictionality dramatizes the absence of faith in what one sees.

We see in movies like *Dogma* and *The Passion*, different ways in which popular culture revisits theological issues that obsessed the early Christians. These issues, as they are played out on screen, are often—as is appropriate—deeply paradoxical. When film depictions of God and Jesus express confusion about the relationship between God and Jesus and the dual nature (human and divine) of Christ, they negotiate historical theological debates that are not central to most American Christians, but are yet always implied in the biblical narrative. In order to establish Christ's divinity, *The Passion* paradoxically focuses on his humanness. This is most disturbingly depicted through the splattering of realistic blood and flesh, but also in the always theologically troubling sentiments contained in "My Father, why hast thou forsaken me," a line that is, of course, biblical, but which is emphasized in the film. In *Dogma*, Rufus, the most doctrinal character in the film, says of God that "she's not really a woman, she's not really *anything*." He also tells Bethany that when he gets back to heaven he is going to tell the *Man* about her performance. Clearly here, God and Christ are not the same "person," and God does not have a physical essence which he/she/it can share with Jesus the "son." Unlike the Bible, or even the church fathers, who can remain ambiguous and contradictory, films that present a single, more linear narrative must make certain decisions about the overlap of God and Christ and about the physical relationship between man, God, and Jesus.

These arguments, which go back to the Arian heresy in the fourth century, focus on two irresolvable questions: How can an actual biological person be the Son of God and if he is, how is it possible for God to suffer? Arius, a fourth-century theologian, insisted that proposing that God suffers was blasphemy; therefore, Jesus had to be subordinate to God. The Church ultimately ruled Arius a heretic and declared Jesus to be divine, thereby saving the idea of the incarnation, which they deemed essential to salvation. Despite these declarations, made at the Council of Nicaea in 325, however, the dual nature of Christ necessarily remains slippery and ambiguous. Although these debates, which continued through the early Middle Ages into the modern era, are not an essential part of the discourse of American Religion, they remain hidden, unanswered, and often unasked questions that lie beneath the faith of believers, yet, as we have seen, negotiated within texts of popular culture.

It is perhaps film, with its perception of immediacy and its simultaneous presentations of real and unreal, presence and absence, which offers the best medium to traverse these complicated issues. The cinema, as film theorist Christian Metz writes,

"more perceptual" than certain arts according to the list of its sensory registers, is also "less perceptual" than others once the status of these perceptions is envisaged rather than their number or diversity; for its perceptions are all in a sense "false" [801–802].

So while Christians, Evangelical and Catholic, flocked to see *The Passion* to weep over the "real" experience it offered, they were also constantly aware that "Jesus" was an actor named Jim Caviezel who had recently played the love interest of Jennifer Lopez in *Angel Eyes*, and that the director was also Martin Riggs in the *Lethal Weapon* movies. As "realistic" as film can be, the transubstantiation is never complete, the blood of Christ is always a product of the makeup artist. The "unique position of film," as Metz says, "lies in this dual nature of its signifier: unaccustomed perceptual wealth, but at the same time stamped with unreality to an unusual degree" (802). In other words, viewers watching *The Passion* or *The Last Temptation of Christ* or *Dogma*, are forced not only to grapple with their perceptions of the contradictory and dual nature of Jesus Christ, but also with the paradoxical dual nature of film itself. The viewing of these films ultimately asks theological questions of what is real, what is god, what is human, and how we explain the central mysteries of faith and belief. These difficult questions, often lost in the direct expression of American Christian faith, are rediscovered in the juxtaposition of popular religion and popular culture that film offers. While some viewers of *The Passion* perhaps felt that this was the film that offered an answer, as we have seen, in many ways films like *Dogma* are more theologically sophisticated. The theology of popular culture needs them both. It is only in the full spectrum of films—from *King of Kings* to *The Life of Brian*, from *Oh, God!* to *The Last Temptation of Christ*, from *The Passion* to *Dogma*—that these impossible questions are fully addressed in American culture.

Although the success of Gibson's *Passion* was influential in creating a wave of religiously themed movies, the prediction of many that it would lead to a sequence of successful biblically inspired Hollywood films did not quite materialize. The success of more recent independent "Christian" films, which often take an apologist position, suggests other ways in which the success of Gibson's rescription of the passion continues to influences a niche market. However, the biblical blockbuster returned in 2014 with Darren Aronofsky's high budget version of the Noah story, starring Russell Crowe as Noah. While the film resists actual depictions of the divine, its explorations of prophecy, magic, evil, and vengeance, within what is a sort of a biblical Midrash or perhaps fan fiction, point to other big questions at the intersection of religion and film, like how do we distinguish the voice of God from madness, or why are the innocent punished?

In the film, Noah and his family live hidden away from the murderous descendants of Cain, who killed Noah's father and rule the whole of the Earth. Noah dreams of a great flood, and travels to see his grandfather, Methuselah, on the way adopting an injured and abandoned young girl named Ila, who will become Shem's wife. Methuselah (played by Anthony Hopkins) gives Noah a seed from the Garden of Eden and helps him realize his destiny to build the ark to survive the incoming flood. The film introduces the pseudo-biblical elements of a supervillain (Tubal-Cain), a barren woman (Ila), and a race of giant six-armed stone "Watchers" or fallen angels, kicked out of heaven and cursed by God for helping the post–Eden humans, who help Noah build the ark and fight off attacking evil villagers. Once aboard the ship, with the world and all humankind underwater, Noah assumes that God's ultimate plan is for them to be the last surviving humans (unlike the Bible there are not three fertile young wives aboard). When Ila miraculously conceives, he promises that he will murder her newborn child if it is a girl. When Ila gives birth to twin girls, Noah cannot bring himself to kill them and considers himself to have failed to fulfill his divinely ordained command. The ending returns to the more traditional biblical story as Ham leaves, Noah drinks himself into a naked stupor (Genesis 9:18–27), and then redeems himself in time to view God as a giant rainbow.

Although sections of the movie resemble previous biblical films, it also seems to hover between times and genres. It combines equal parts *Ten Commandments* and *Lord of the Rings*, with a little *Gladiator* and the *Transformers* thrown in. It seems to echo the post-apocalyptic world of *The Road* or the eco-disaster landscapes of *Waterworld* or *The Day After Tomorrow*, as much as a traditional biblical ones. Like Anthony Hopkins—whose acting as Methuselah echoes his role as Odin in the *Thor* movies—*Noah* seems to exist somewhere between the Bible, Greek mythology, science fiction, and the Marvel Comics universe.

The film received mixed but generally positive reviews; critics tended to find it flawed and uneven, but also praised it for taking chances, for its artistry, and for taking the story seriously as an exploration of ideas of guilt, evil, mercy, justice, and power. The main debate over the film occurred across the Christian community. Mainstream Christian organizations and publications tended toward the positive. For example, Alissa Wilkinson wrote in *Christianity Today* that Noah "takes a sober look at the evil in the human heart" and that it is "a movie worth watching." However, more evangelical churches and writers criticized the film for its inaccuracies, and for its non-canonical elements, for example, that God is referred to as the "Creator" throughout the film, or that animals are described as innocent and that Noah is a vegetarian. As a criticism of the movies shortcomings, evangelical churches across the county posted signs that read:

> Noah: In your Bibles now Genesis 5:32 through 9:29. Read the full unedited story in the inspired word of God, The Bible. No artistic license is needed or taken. You don't have to spend fourteen dollars and sit in darkness being deceived.

Of course, what is notable here are the characteristically American assumptions that the story as it appears in the Bible is "unedited" (when it is clearly the edited result of several versions of the flood myth), the idea that the Bible involves no "art," and that art is deception. These assumptions highlight some of the difficulties of making biblically based films, but some of these are also matters that are almost as likely to come up in any act of adaptation involving a cherished original; we find the same objections to cinematic versions of *Lord of the Rings* or *Harry Potter*.

Despite the freedom with which it adapts the biblical text, the film actually makes explicit some of the implicit questions of the biblical version. Is the world created for us or are we here to protect and care for it? What happens when what we think is right goes against what we think is moral? How do we determine innocence or guilt, and who gives us that power? When Noah receives his message in several ambiguous dream visions, he appears to misunderstand God's plan, assuming that God means to wipe humanity from the earth completely. This plot device leads to the central conflict in the film—Noah, as a type of Abrahamic anti-hero, feels obligated to kill the newborn twins—but it also introduces the very real possibility implied in multiple stories across the Bible and from Augustine to Oral Roberts that the words of God can be misunderstood, that we can be deceived in our belief.

While the story of Noah is one of the more familiar Bible stories, and has been depicted in countless toys and children's Bibles, it is one that has been resisted by Hollywood, very likely because it presents some serious ideological and ethical complications when it comes to fleshing out the bare bones narrative presented in Genesis. The story of Noah is, when you think about it, a deeply problematic story of divine self-doubt, righteous genocide, and survivor's guilt. Perhaps the central question of the Noah story, like *Battlestar Gallactica* or *The Walking Dead*, is whether humans even deserve to survive or not. The giant divine rainbow that appears at the end of the film feels hollow next to the potential for destruction and evil that we know survived the flood. In many ways these are complicated and deeply religious questions. Like *Dogma*, it is the elements of the film that most offended believers—

Noah's murderous anger and misjudgment, the ambiguous nature of God's commands, the indeterminate relationship of humans to the natural world, and the flexible approach to biblical narrative—that proved the more authentically "religious" negotiations among viewers and throughout the discussion surrounding the film. Although not often recognized as such, the debates that surrounded the film—beyond the arguments over what was "true"— rehearsed complicated questions of power, divine authority, and indeterminate narrative that are located within the very core of what religion and religious discourse have always been. The ever-changing American religion will be a reflection of and a reaction to these trends, and popular culture's gods of film will continue to be as multiple and complex as its relationships to religious expression, creating new texts which will be accepted as sacred and denounced as profane.

CHAPTER 6

Television Drama, Fan Communities, Vampires and Theology

Television may not only be usurping functions which once belonged to religion, but likewise restructuring the very shape of belief.—William Kuhns

"Note to self: Religion freaky"—Buffy Summers in *Buffy the Vampire Slayer*

Maybe Jesus was the first vampire. Man, he rose from the dead too, and he told people, "Hey y'all, drink my blood, it'll give you special powers."—Jason Stackhouse in *True Blood*

Televising the Absent Image of God

If—as we have been saying—popular culture and religion necessarily intersect, mirror, and influence each other, then the position of television in this relationship is central. Television (even as its definition and role changes) has arguably retained its status as the dominant medium of American popular culture for almost three quarters of a century. The relationship of television to the theological and the religious, like any popular text or artifact, can represent, reflect, alter, and mediate popular beliefs and practices. Although often criticized for its simplistic presentation of complex issues, television, like other texts and forms of popular culture, can also provide a more nuanced and speculative experience than is often realized. Although televangelism, religious programing, reality shows, and news and sports coverage all offer rich example of intersections of religion and popular culture, this chapter will focus on the rescripting potential of TV drama, particularly genres of the magical and fantastic. Television dramas or "small screen fictions" have the potential to create intense experiences of perceiving, questioning, and debating philosophical and religious issues outside of institutional control and traditional categories.

From the 1990s and into the early twenty first century there was a discernable and growing presence religious themes in prime-time drama, a shift that has been discussed in the mainstream press, in Christian publications, and in academic journals. These shows were both supportive and critical of traditional religious beliefs, and range from the saccharine sweet *Touched by an Angel* to the ironic *Joan of Arcadia* and the overly serious and critically panned mini-series *Revelations*. But this trend is also, less obviously and more interestingly, seen in fantasy and science-fiction series such as *The X-Files, Buffy the Vampire Slayer, Battlestar Galactica, True Blood, The Walking Dead,* and *The Leftovers*—shows that did not establish themselves clearly within any kind of religious orientation, and shows whose alternate realities allowed them to recreate religion in ways that imply important questions and comments on actual belief and practice. What is perhaps most noteworthy, for our purposes, is that many of these shows have also shown a specific interest in exploring ideas of religion, although often, plot-wise anyway, outside the boundaries of the specifically or normatively Abrahamic, human, or earthly.

While the "religion" portrayed in these shows is often superficially one-dimensional—religion is either good and God is benevolent, or religious rituals and texts are a mysterious link to magical and ancient sources of power long forgotten by mankind—further discussions of the shows, by both fans and scholars, often reveal more sophisticated explorations of theological issues and religious concepts. For example, while *Battlestar Gallactica* presented its competing religions (mono- versus polytheistic) in somewhat reductive ways, issues of canonicity, prophecy, scripture, humanity, and history were explored in ways that have much to say about how we understand our own framings of religion.

The current wave of popular shows featuring elements of the supernatural can be traced back to the success of *The X-Files* in the 1990s, which was a popular cultural phenomenon and trendsetter in addressing religious themes on serious prime-time television drama. The series (and its reboot in 2016) depicts agents in a special branch of the FBI that investigates incidents relating to the paranormal, the unexplainable, and the extraterrestrial. Although the later years of the show increasingly showed a more obvious religious presence—from backwoods Pentecostalism to Catholic exorcisms and satanic rituals—from the very beginning the series offered an intriguing and thought-provoking blend of the alien, supernatural, and the satanic that questioned what is real and what is imaginary and interrogated whether it is always possible or even preferable to make the distinction. The show's creator,

Chris Carter, says that the show "deals with faith, not religion with a capital 'R' or Catholicism with a capital 'C' ... the idea of faith is really the backbone of the entire series—faith in your own beliefs, ideas about the truth, and so it has religious undertones always" (qtd. in Peterson 195). The central conflict of the show is indeed belief—whether one could believe in the paranormal, whether it existed despite characters' skepticism, or whether it functioned because other characters wanted or needed to believe.

These issues of faith, practice, ritual, and text, all revolving around essentially unseen phenomena or evidence, naturally found their way into religious and theological territory. In the show, faith in God is juxtaposed and contrasted with faith in aliens, ritual is portrayed as both effective and superstitious, and reality and perception are always subject to revision. Paul Peterson calls *The X-Files* "one of the deepest and most sophisticated treatments of religious phenomena ever found on network television," especially pointing to how it "interweaves complex issues regarding institutionalized religion and practice" (181). Focusing on individual reactions of belief and skepticism, rather than on the paranormal itself, *The X-Files* examines the religious practices and psychology that exist between the popular and the dogmatic. And although we see the effects of paranormal activity, and occasionally get a glimpse of an alien or monster, the primary emphasis is on human imagination, not on the literal presence of monsters, gods, or aliens.

A characteristically American negotiating and interrogating of important moral and religious issues can be seen in dramas such as *The Sopranos*, *Breaking Bad*, *True Detective*, *Big Love*, *Deadwood*, *Mad Men* and *Six Feet Under*. For this chapter, however, we will be focusing on less "realistic" and more speculative dramas. By placing plot lines outside of accepted reality, speculative dramas of fantasy and science fiction encourage viewers to think outside of their received ideas. With this in mind, in pointing to the presence of religion in television we are intentionally not talking about more obvious examples such as *Seventh Heaven* or the History Channel miniseries *The Bible*. Rather, we look to the more hidden, subversive, and complex depictions of religion and theology within more secular seeming dramas. We are focused on television shows that make significant social, cultural, philosophical or theological interventions, and that, at the same time, are open, challenging, and interpretable texts that have attracted serious critical attention from scholars, critics, and fans. The later twentieth and early twenty first century saw a multitude of this kind of "quality" television. Looking at TV fantasy and science fiction programs rather than the perhaps more obvious subjects of religious programming or realistic dramas allows us to indirectly explore ways in which fictional narratives play a role in exploring and negotiating theological questions within popular culture and within fan culture.

Televised Religion: Fan Communities, Religious Discourse and Web 2.0

Watching television, so the story used to go, is a passive activity: one sits in a living room chair staring inactively at a screen uncritically absorbing the flow of images and information that are controlled by the network and its advertisers. Over the last twenty years or so, this perception has gradually changed; viewers, scholars, and, to a certain extent, the popular media, now take television and the participatory nature of the viewing experience more seriously. Although Jonathan Bignell's *An Introduction to Television Studies*, could still claim in 2004 that "television is most often watched as a sequence of programmes" (17), today this is no longer the experience of many viewers. Primarily because of new technologies, but also because of related shifts in attitudes, television is not limited to the "flow" that Raymond Williams influentially described in his 1975 book, *Television: Technology and Cultural Form.* Today's serious viewers can choose not to be subject to a flow of "uninterrupted, unpunctuated stream of programmes, advertisements, announcements and logos" (During 118), but to instead take charge of the programming. Viewers are more interactive and more in control, creating a viewing experience on their own terms, watching when and how they want, an experience broken up and augmented by multiple viewings, internet discussion, blog posts, podcasts, and DVD commentary. Through DVD's, DVR's, downloaded episodes, podcast commentaries, online blogs, wikis, and fan sites, viewers can now study every episode and every scene, review dialogue that they miss or find especially interesting or ambiguous, stop and examine an interesting image, skip over commercials, and discuss themes and minutiae immediately with like-minded viewers in on-line communities.

Yet, while academics and critics have begun to pay more attention to critical readings of "quality television," it is still common to hear educators and journalists refer pejoratively to television watching as a passive experience. The reality of the experience is making that claim less and less supportable. While much formal critical attention has been focused on technological, social, and aesthetic issues, digital technology and the internet have opened up possibilities for the study of the more comprehensive viewing experiences and multiple critical discussions. And while just a few years ago Henry Jenkins wrote that

> Media scholars have long sought to escape the stigma of fandom, often at the expense of masking or even killing what drew them to their topics in the first place; and fans have often been hypercritical of academics because of their sloppiness with the details that are so central to fan interpretation [3].

The last several years have seen an increase in discussion of "participatory fan communities," and scholars such as Matt Hills, showrunners like Russell

Davies, and critics like Emily Nussbaum continue to blur the traditional lines of fan/scholar/critic/director.

Now more than ever, it is necessary to study multiple spaces of discourse to understand the impact of television dramas. Fans produce their own content: creating blogs, posting original artwork, writing fan fiction, and remixing online content. Increasingly these creations are viewed and, in turn, engaged with by a public, and, in the case of television, this content has begun to cross over into the "canonical" material, even challenging the concept of what it is to be canonical. Fan material and fan platforms influence writing and casting decisions; they are used in promotional materials, and even placed into the actual shows and plotlines. In the twenty first century, large corporate forces continue to control TV production, but some of the interpretation and even the perceived texts have been at least partly distributed away from centralized institutional powers. In other words, fan communities are able to create a discourse and theoretical network on their own terms, based on rigorous and detailed viewing and creative experiences. ABC may control the content of their hit fantasy drama *Once Upon a Time*, but they have no control over the growing community of bloggers and fan fiction writers that are part of that show's appeal, and that through creating their own fictional content and critical platforms, ultimately, play a role in the reception and perception of the show and in the decisions of producers and showrunners. If we are to make statements about a show's "meaning," and particularly its religious meaning, surely we cannot deny that such meaning exists somewhere between fan, writer, critic, actor, and showrunner and the various texts that each produces. It is in the intersections of television drama, fan communities, amateur criticism, and scholarly activity that have grown up around selected television shows where we can best find examples of how popular culture has reinvented and rescripted traditional religious faith and activity.

There are several reasons why the medium of television offers such fertile ground for inspiring amateur and professional discourse about serious subjects like religion. Most obviously, the increasingly utilized serial dimensions (the construction of a continuous plot over multiple episodes) of television drama allows for complex discussions of ideas to be fleshed out and explored from multiple angles over many hours. As American film is driven more and more by the need for blockbuster success, it has more often been the small screen which, taking advantage of its longer plot lines and greater freedom to appeal to smaller audiences, has ventured more into subtle and ambiguous portrayals of complex or controversial subjects, and can maintain ambiguous narratives over multiple episodes without the pressure to be conclusive. Another important aspect of the fantasy or science fiction shows that we are considering is that they have been extensively studied and written about, both within fan communities and by television and literary scholars, resulting in an unprecedented body of analysis for television drama. Perhaps, because of a perceived need to establish shows as Christian or not, or religious or secular, the ways in which this phenomenon participates in popular religion have been under-explored and often overly simplified. Like any complex and interpretable text these shows cannot be reduced to a simple black and white perspective.

Our definitions and descriptions of television, like religion, have been so radically decentered that its very categorization is part of the difficulty of understanding its changing role. The TV no longer holds a central space in the American living room or weekly schedule. Viewing now just as likely happens on laptops, digital notepads, and phones, and on trains or in coffee shops and offices. Popular shows are not associated with specific days and times; instead, they are just as portable in time as they are in space. Even influential writing and discourse about television—scholarly and otherwise— now is just as often found on a blog or during a comic-con panel than in a book, a journal, or at an academic conference. As new technologies of distribution and dissemination emerge and, for many people, replace "linear TV" it becomes harder to group them all as "television." James Poniewozik asks in a 2015 *New York Times* piece, "What am I watching?" and "Is Netflix TV?" Poniewozik goes on to say, that these new forms are "becoming a distinct genre all their own, whose conventions and aesthetics we're just starting to figure out." While these changes appear to be related only to the mechanics of viewing and the presentation of televisual images, they also describe ideational and cognitive changes that ultimately influence not only how and what we watch, but also how we come to perceive and understand what we have watched.

Although fan communities have always found sophisticated ways to discuss their favorite shows, and while the rise of cultural and media studies in recent decades has encouraged the academic study of television, early academic studies of television concentrated more on the fans than the content they produced or even the shows themselves. Cultural studies theorist Simon During points out that because research into TV has traditionally concentrated on audience reception, "it is as if the programs themselves aren't worth taking as seriously as their impact on viewers [and] it has been impossible to concentrate on close readings of TV texts or to construct a TV canon" (114–115). More recently, however, television studies have seen an increased emphasis on close reading of specific programs as well as on the shifting relationship of the viewers to the show. Television dramas are now more firmly established as observable texts in themselves, as objects available for study. On the other hand, studies of the fans themselves have grown more sophisticated. As the viewing experience and the shows grow more complex, plural, and interactive, the texts that we study grow more slippery and ambiguous.

Compare, for example, someone watching *The X-Files* in the 1990s and watching *The Walking Dead* in 2016. *The X-Files* was one of the first shows on television to begin to link an internet presence with fans and with elements of the show itself. *New York Times* television writer Joyce Millman wrote in 2005 that it was the first show to find its audience growth tied to the growth of the internet," and fan ("X-philes") communities, fan fiction, and websites devoted to the show grew during the show's run. The show itself anticipated the future of television and featured internet driven plots as early as 1994, and, in a nod to its fan communities, named a minor character after a fan fiction writer who had died of cancer in 2001.[1] The show was also one of the first television shows to spawn a publishing industry of paperback novels and comic books. Yet, despite this plural presence, the show itself remained central to the discourse and the majority of viewers (despite the rise of video recording technology) would have experienced the show on their living room television set on Friday night at 9:00 p.m.

Fans of *The Walking Dead* in 2016, on the other hand, watch the show on a television, a computer, a notebook, or a smart phone, whenever and wherever they wish, and as many times as they want. There really is no such thing as "missing" an episode because there are multiple ways of accessing any past episode. If viewers do watch the show in "real" time—which can now take on almost a ritual like experience—they likely share comments with friends online (who may be virtual *Walking Dead* "friends" they have never actually met), they may participate in AMC's "Two Screen Experience" which allows them participatory activities such as polls with other fans, they will stop the show to repeat a line of dialogue or examine an image more closely, and they might also watch the *Talking Dead* afterward, a talk show featuring interviews, analysis, and highlights related to the just finished episode. After finishing the show they might immediately go to their favorite blogs to read analytical summaries of the episode and while there will likely leave their own comments on the blog. The conversation may debate an element of the plot ("Is Glenn really dead?") or a more abstract question ("Is there a moral difference between how we treat walkers and how we treat dangerous animals?). They may compare the episode to the original comics or the digital comics, they may choose to re-watch the black and white version, they may participate in a rewriting or remixing of the episode themselves, content which they will then share with their online community for further comment, creation, and editing.

This change, to what has been called "Web 2.0," has blurred the distinction between fan, critic, and scholar in ways that have created whole new discursive models for analysis. Web 2.0 is a somewhat contested term, but generally describes the move from static online consumption (merely reading websites), to dynamic interaction and regular user-generated content. Within television studies, this shift has been significant. Even a publication as associated with traditional static consumption as the *New York Times* now offers extensive fan-driven discussion of its regular television summaries in the online edition. As thinkers like Michel Foucault have reminded us, discourse does not simply describe, it also creates. As opposed to older models of viewers (passively observing and obediently buying products) or of "fans" (wearing Spock ears and living celibate lives in their parents' basements), today's participatory fan communities are more mainstream, a more sought after demographic to advertisers,[2] and create new discourses out of which texts and cultural movements emerge. These changes in the way TV is watched, written about, talked about, and interpreted represent major cultural shifts in the relationship of popular culture to popular religion.

Like much American Christianity, fan-based theorizing operates outside of institutional and legitimated modes of thought. "Fandom is one of those spaces where people are learning to live and collaborate within a knowledge community" (134), as Henry Jenkins writes. Although, as evidenced by the increasing numbers of conferences and publications, professional scholars are a part of this trend, it is primarily driven (economically and textually) by a highly literate general audience hungry to exercise its knowledge and ideas about their shared popular texts. Discussions about television drama in newspaper reviews, scholarly monographs, online journals, informational wikis, and comments section of blogs, represent new hybrid types of scholarship about complex texts. While theoretical books and articles about television shows are still predominantly written by professors, they are commonly read and commented on within the fan communities, and, increasingly, scholars draw on fan discussion platforms for their research, often quoting blogs with the same respect that they would quote an article from a refereed journal.[3] Despite the traditional separation between communities of "scholars" and "amateur critics," the importance of these groups as both consumers *and* producers of intellectual discourse and theorizing about television is now often acknowledged. In his book *Fan Culture*, self-identified fan/scholar Matt Hills makes the case that many fans are very good critics and very good theorists, and, in *Street Smarts and Critical Theory: Listening to the Vernacular*, Thomas McLaughlin "sees fan communities as among the most active sites of vernacular theory-making" (3), and insists that "vernacular culture produces its own theoretical practices and it is time for academic theory to celebrate their achievements and recognize its own connections to the vernacular" (30). While there is a tradition within leftist thought of recognizing non-academic theorizing—from Antonio Gramsci's "organic intellectual" to Theodor Adorno's "homespun philosophy"—the rise of internet culture has elevated the potential for vernacular theory and its incorporation into a larger discourse to an unprecedented level.

Therefore, while academics have not fully accepted "the idea that there was any legitimacy in seeing how fans actually theorize their own practices" (Jenkins 13), a new wave of scholarship points to ways in which this bias is shifting. A relationship that was once defined by disdain, then cautious suspicion, has lately become an increasingly cooperative if still sometimes tenuous bond. Within certain spaces, virtual and actual, the gap between fan and scholar has almost closed. As Jenkins writes, "fans are central to how culture operates. The concept of the active audience, so controversial two decades ago, is now taken for granted by everyone involved in and around the media industry" (1). Jenkins and others in the new wave of cultural studies resist the idea that "fandom [is] created entirely from the top down by the studio's marketing efforts" (2), instead pointing to the sophisticated and creative power exhibited by fans. It is now either impossible or ignorant for a scholar working on popular genres such as film, video games, or television to ignore the vast contributions by fans in analyzing, categorizing, and organizing textual material, and for their contribution in creating content or in crowdfunding the material.

This new intellectual activity is not without an important religious element. The explosion of participation in this kind of dialogical textual production based on interpretation of common text through websites and online discussion groups has become a type of *Midrash*—the Jewish form of commenting on or interpreting scripture. What is typically American about these discussions is the emphasis on individual interpretation, but what is similar to Jewish interpretation is its willingness to incorporate and accept multiple interpretations. As opposed to the Greek/Christian tendency to search for unity, to gather various meanings into a *one*, the Jewish and rabbinic tendency, by contrast, is "towards differentiation, metaphorical, multiplicity, multiple meanings" (Handelman 33). In *Midrash and Literature*, Geoffrey Hartman writes of the close relationship between Jewish Scripture and "literature" and between literary and rabbinical hermeneutics:

> The problem we face, strangely enough, is not that we cannot define Scripture but that having gradually redefined fiction in the light of Scripture we now find it hard to distinguish between them. We see both within a global definition of what textuality is; and the same merging occurs as we recover a knowledge of midrash, so that literary criticism and midrashic modes begin to blend into each other [12].

For Hartman and Handelman, studying the structure and practice of traditional Jewish hermeneutics reveals modes of understanding contemporary textual analysis. For our purposes, we can use Midrash as a model to compare fan-based theorizing of religious issues through their viewing of television texts.

These forms of theorizing go outside of the characteristically accepted American ways of discussing popular religion, but at the same time are reflective of American tendencies to continually re-invent new religious and theological experiences. As we have said before, American religious practices, both popular and institutional, tend to emphasize the practical and the experiential over the dialectical and philosophical. Believers are more likely to talk about their personal relationship with Christ than debate his dual nature or the ontological status of his divinity. Yet these questions are inherent within any form of Christianity and often surface where they are not expected or invited. In fan discussions of television drama there are spaces where these traditional theological discussions take place—albeit often in secular terms. For example, conversations around the show *Battlestar Galactica* (2004–2009) and its complex depiction of the interaction between humans and their rebellious creation, the "Cylons," have focused on the existence of a human "soul," whether what we call a soul can exist outside of a biological person, and what it means to call something "human." (This argument is further complicated by the fact that the Cylon's religion is apparently monotheistic while the humans worship multiple gods.) These discussions—enacted within the context of the show, within fan communities, and in scholarly collections and journals—follow along the lines of theological and philosophical discourse that ranges from early Christian debates over accepting gentiles to nineteenth century arguments over the existence of an African's soul to twenty first century theorizing of the posthuman. Many other recent television shows have provided sophisticated texts for discussing this same issue: *The Walking Dead, IZombie, Dollhouse, Sense8,* and the BBC's *Doctor Who* are all partly based on the tensions over defining just what is and isn't human in a world in which the borders have shifted. Most importantly, these dense and complex debates are exactly what does not exist in the vast majority of American religious traditions and are taking place in and around the increasingly related platforms of the internet and television.

Buffy the Vampire Slayer *as Religious Text*

In any successful monster text—from *Beowulf* to *Dracula* to the stories of demons we will see in Chapter 7—the horror and suspense blends with issues of defining the human, recognizing the Other, and grappling with issues of good and evil, right and wrong, the efficacy of ritual and the sources of power. It is only logical that at the turn of the twenty first century, fundamentalism, holy war, and the possibility of evil within us reemerged as important topics of discussion, that the defining monster narratives would reflect these issues. Many of the shows that opened up some of the most rewarding discourse on religion were shows that had no obvious divine presence and rarely even mentioned God or traditional religion. The rest of this chapter will focus on two long running shows—*Buffy the Vampire Slayer* (1997–2003) and *True Blood* (2008–2014) whose depiction of vampires in the modern world offered fans and scholars rich material for metaphor and analysis.

In choosing to examine *Buffy*, we are selecting a show that has been the site of a rich and complex intersection of primary texts, scholarly attention, fan discussions, and a long afterlife in graphic novels and fan fiction.[4] From its humble beginnings as a mid-season replacement on what had been constructed as a "teen" network (the "WB"), the show rapidly gained the admiration and attention of fans and then scholars. From 1997–2003, through seven seasons and 144 episodes, *Buffy* garnered a reputation as a well-written and complex show that tracked a core group of characters through everyday trials as well as in combat against vampires, monsters, and demons. Praised by critics and fans for its sophisticated use of symbolism and metaphor, its linguistic playfulness, and for its complex development of ethical, religious, and philosophical issues, the series developed a passionate following among popular youth culture, the media, and professors of literature, philosophy, and cultural studies. Through published articles, blogs, websites, college courses, conferences and conventions, *Buffy* watchers discussed and continue to discuss the ontology of the soul, the possibility or impossibility of free will, the ambiguous definitions of absolute good and evil, the negativity of heaven, the contradictory present/absent existence of God, and the canonicity of extra textual material. It is through this interplay that the show becomes a multivalent text that persists as a space of theological debate, a process that rescripts the canonical location of these discussions.

The premise of the series is that Buffy Summers, the chosen Slayer of vampires, is the latest in a long line of young female heroes who battle the "forces of darkness." She and her friends live in the town of Sunnydale, a fictional southern California town situated on a "Hellmouth," or a "mystical center of convergence." The Hellmouth allows all sorts of demons and vampires to pass through and also serves as a constant reminder that growing up is literally hell. The later seasons of the shows, while maintaining the balance of humor and drama that characterized the early seasons, followed Buffy and her friends into college and the workforce, saw them confront the deaths of loved ones, addictions, and sexual confusion, and grew increasingly dark and narratively and psychologically complex.

The creator and primary writer of the show, a then little known Joss Whedon, was a self-described "angry atheist" who referred to God as a "Sky Bully" and claimed that one of his themes in the show is that God does not exist and will never come down from on high to make things better (DVD commentary to "The Body"). These comments drew a lot of attention, both critical and popular, but did not prevent Christian interpretations of the show. In a review on the Christian website HollywoodJesus.com, Maurice Broaddus claimed that although Joss Whedon was a "self-proclaimed atheist," he was also the "perfect case study for the fact that God is 'hardwired' in men's hearts" (HollywoodJesus.com). Although his statement may seem myopic, it is also an example of a vernacular theory that is close to the influential position of philosophers like Jean-Luc Nancy who claim that despite what secular Westerners may assert, we are still "bound within the very fabric of Christianity," and that *"all* our thinking, our very being is Christian through and through" (115). While some fans reduce the show's "meaning" to what Whedon says it means, this characterization of *Buffy* as a "Christian" show, despite the claims of its creator, reveals a sophisticated separation of text from author. This separation of creator from text, not often recognized outside of intellectual discourse, is almost a necessity if we think of *Buffy* as a rescripted sacred text.

There were and still are, of course, numerous websites that comment on and contribute to this dialogue, sites that focus on specific elements of the show (*Buffy* and philosophy), specific themes (lesbianism, Wicca), or their favorite character, or on fan fiction. On the fan website Soulfulspike.com, a blog describes one fan's experience attending all the *Buffy* panels and papers at the national conference of the American Popular Culture Association. She describes each of the panels and her overall conference experience including her informal conversations with *"Buffy* scholars."

> We had a great convo last night about *Buffy* and *Angel*—completely outside the panel room. It was like a face-to-face posting! We talked about evangelism, good vs. evil, and how Buffy was actually religious. Joss as atheist and hidden deist was discussed, complete with references and was just great fun! [Soulfulspike.com].

As well as indicating the blurring of fan and scholar theorizing, perhaps what is most interesting about this post is its praising of a conversation as coming up to the level of virtual communication ("like a face-to-face posting!"). She is impressed that a real life conversation is as interesting as an on-line one, the standard of interesting dialogue is set by internet interaction; the virtual communities and discussion become the real and the canonical.

Another perspective on virtual theorizing is offered by discussions about *Buffy* and religion that appear on Christian websites such as artsandfaith.com where, while the show's "immoralities" are noted, many postings "admit" being fans of the show and claim that the show "sure has a healthy following in Christian communities" (artsandfaith.com). While most of these sites establish a superficial pro- or con- position towards *Buffy,* a closer look often reveals that the discussion within Christian viewing communities goes beyond an identification of the show as either Christian or not, or moral or not. On Christiananswers.net *Buffy* gets an "A" for "Avoid" rating, and a post claims that the show is a "direct offense to God and his commandments." If one takes the time to read other posts, however, the decision to "avoid," even on this fundamentalist site, is not so clear. Posts claim that *Buffy* is a "PG rated C.S. Lewis book with a twist," that it shows a "remarkably sophisticated emphasis on ethical characterization," and "one of the things I like most about Buffy is that nothing is ever simple and clear-cut." It is this ambiguity that leads to deeper theological discussion, as one commenter uses *Buffy* to ask

> how much can an angel be allowed to struggle with God's will before he/she turns into a full-fledged demon—are the angels allowed times of trial, times of temptation, or do they instantly become "always bad" the moment they have doubt about their vocation?

These questions, addressing the ontology of good, evil, angels and the role of faith and doubt, while they are ones Augustine and Milton grappled with, are not typically discussed within the structures of much American Christianity. The prominence of these kind of discussions surrounding *Buffy* prompted the Christian humor magazine, *The Door*, to select *Buffy* as their 2002 "Theologian of the Year" calling it a "modern-day morality play" that deals with topics like "evil, redemption, resurrection, sex, guilt, existential angst, selflessness and sacrifice, religion and the occult, often all before the first commercial break."

Much of the pro–*Buffy* discourse within Christianity parallels the thinking of Jana Riess, whose book, *What Would Buffy Do? The Vampire Slayer as Spiritual Guide*, claims that "just as God is nowhere mentioned in the book of Esther, God is merely implicit in the Buffyverse, present every time the characters put their own lives on the line to save others." However, like so-called "biblical" archeology, the purpose of the search greatly determines the findings, and in the same way that many scholars[5] would disagree with Riess's interpretation of the book of Esther, finding it instead a literally Godless book, interpretations of the presence of God in *Buffy* never remain stable.

Fans and scholars writing about religious themes in *Buffy* tend to focus on several common touchstones: the use of holy water and crosses, the demons' reverence for relics, the battle between good and evil, and the various mystical rituals that echo Judeo-Christian traditions. Much of their writing attempts to associate *Buffy* with specific fields of philosophy and critical theory and to contain, categorize, or totalize the show as a work of religious art, or as a work that demonstrates a determinate religion or religious-ethical content. Fans and scholars have found in *Buffy* analogies with diverse strands of Christianity or have seen it as a model for ethical behavior, a "practical theology," or a "domestic church."[6] The characters of Buffy and the "good" vampires Angel and Spike are often seen as figures of Christ who descend to hell and back and sacrifice themselves for a greater good.

A more skeptical interpretation, although still oriented towards deterministic religious traditions, is offered by Lynn Schofield Clark in her book *From Angels to Aliens*, where she points to how media in general and *Buffy* in particular capture and encourage the tendency of many young people to accept religious figures and themes while distrusting traditional institutions. *Buffy* and the spin-off series *Angel*, like *The X-Files*, offer viewers a model for religious experience. In her book, Clark suggests that *Buffy* echoes "the current contradiction among young people who claim to believe fervently in God yet have rather lukewarm feelings about organized religion" (47). For Clark, *Buffy* is an example of "some of the ways in which religion is approached in contemporary teen culture," particularly in how it debates definitions of good and evil, and depicts the "dark side of evangelism" (47).

But however one reads these aspects of *Buffy*, there is no disputing that the show both employs and distances itself from traditional religious practices and beliefs. Throughout the series there is an unstated but constantly dramatized tension between the existence and non-existence of superior or supernatural power for good. Although its emphasis on complex ethical issues necessarily resonates with our culture's mingling of ethics with religion, it rarely if ever proposes a divine solution to these issues. And if its demons, monsters, and hell dimensions suggest a reflection and parody of Judeo-Christian mythology, then the absence of a divine presence and the characters' general indifference to religion is also a common theme throughout the series. Although *Buffy* may use, refer to, and suggest religious systems, ideas, rituals, and symbols, it rarely endorses them, explicitly or implicitly. While critics and fans often discuss the good versus evil orientation of the show, there is never any statement of absolute meaning or divinity (good or bad) that is not ultimately opened to questioning and subversion.

The Radical Theology of Buffy

What invites and frustrates religious and theological interpretation of *Buffy* is that it both is and is not religious. It is both of these things because it presents religion not only as traditional trappings and as simulacra, but because sometimes these trappings do seem to carry some power. It is dismissive of all of the central issues of religion (a divine creator, free will, good and evil) and yet is obsessed with these very issues. It is at once free play and the real desire for meaning; it relishes in its irony and yet invites viewers to seek some kind of center. By closely reading a few scenes within the show itself we can demonstrate how the actual text plays a role in contributing to a complex theological discourse, one that permits and relies upon the contradictions and paradoxes that necessarily exist on *Buffy* and in our own popular and religious cultures.

This complex and subversive nature is established in the very first episode of the series ("Welcome to the Hellmouth"), when Buffy's first major physical fight finds her battling a super vampire named Luke in a mausoleum in a cemetery. As the vampire fights Buffy, he grandly prophesizes the coming "ascension" of the "Master" vampire in the style of the King James Bible:

> But on the third day of the newest light will come the Harvest. When the blood of men will flow as wine.
> When the master will walk among them once more. The earth will belong to the old ones. And Hell itself will come to town ["Welcome to the Hellmouth"].

As he ostentatiously intones the coming hell, Luke throws Buffy into an empty coffin and, as she cowers, Luke closes his speech with a dramatic "Amen," and leaps on top of Buffy as the episode ends. The scene continues in the opening of the next episode where Buffy is saved from death by the cross around her neck, as Luke recoils upon seeing it, giving Buffy her chance to escape.

This initial confrontation is an early example of the ways in which the show's recurring battle scenes will represent shifting psychological and conceptual conflicts, keeping the action fresh and interesting. It also raises philosophical issues that will be explored throughout the series and that incited debate within fan and academic communities. Where does the power in Buffy's initial confrontation with Luke lie? Luke is powerful because he is a vampire, a hybrid species that is part human and part demon, and because he is connected to the "Master," an ancient vampire entombed beneath a church with connections deep in a mythical past before humans swarmed the earth "like a plague of boils." Buffy is powerful because she is the "slayer," a seemingly human creature imbued with a mysterious power and responsibility given to her through an ancient and apostolic process that will only gradually become less murky as the seasons progress. Each source of power draws from signifiers and symbols, from religious traditions and folklore: the church, the cross, the vampire, and blood.

Yet each of these sources of power comes with subversive questions as well. The cross Buffy wears around her neck in the first battle of the show is a powerful repellent of vampires seemingly because it is connected to ancient traditions. But this very cross has just been given to her by a vampire who was evil until a Gypsy "curse" gave him a soul, and whether the power of the cross should be seen as a Christian or a folkloric tradition is ambiguous. In this opening scene, then, the cross, the word "Amen," and conflicting pagan, folkloric, and Christian mythical and mystical forces, each embody some sort of power. But what are the actual sources of these powers? To put this question in philosophical or theological terms: Do any of these powers have a true *essence*? Each of these elements on their own represents not an essence or even an autonomous object but simulacra. They can only be read as they relate to each other. A cross means nothing until it repels a vampire. A soul is meaningless until it is absent. How are we to read this complex web of forces?

They must be read *as* a web and not as essential or autonomous powers, a reading that mirrors many current perceptions of contemporary culture. Within *Buffy*, if we take any of these threads of power out of context, it is easy to overstate the connections and the coherence of the show's relationship to traditional or determinate theology. Instead of stating that Buffy's cross *is* a Christian based power, or that a vampire *is* a symbol of Satanic evil, we see that in each case it is the intertwined complexity of competing powers which produce meaning. Each force (iconic, mythical, and mystical) depends on the other, supports the other, and exists dialectically and symbiotically. In the fight scene from "Welcome to the Hellmouth," if we take only Buffy's cross, for example, without the vampire's "amen," we misrepresent the complexity with which religion exists in the show, and by extension, in our culture. As the multiple interpretations of the show indicate, we are not allowed to associate Buffy purely with a (Christian) Good and the vampire with an (Satanic) Evil. The most interesting modern literary representations of religion—in Nietzsche, Borges, or Proust—present religion in a way that does not allow it to be totalized or explained and avoids the either/or logic of traditional criticism; they force us to be creative. Like these texts, *Buffy* neither has nor gives an answer to any of the large questions it continually implies. Like other texts, sacred or secular, the importance of *Buffy's* relationship to religion lies in the difficulty of the *act* of its interpretation.

The symbols and rituals of *Buffy* are perhaps the clearest pointers to traditional religions and have been a focus of both fans and scholars looking for religious significance in the show. Crosses, holy water, holy relics, and churches all play a role in the world of *Buffy*, leading many to characterize the show as Christian. Yet over the course of the series, these echoes of traditional religion consistently exist outside of any determinate religious, theological, ethical, or social institutions. Although crosses and holy water seem to be on the side of "good," the religious and magical aspects of ritual belong mostly to the monsters and vampires. And crucifixes, crosses, and holy water all lessen in importance throughout the run of the show, as vampires come to see them as merely annoying irritants, more like allergens than anything else. While they seem to "contain" power, the mystical objects on Buffy ultimately suggest instability. In the same way that God, religion, and evil are perhaps best seen not as *things* but as *actions*, the objects are defined by what they do rather than what they are, and since that is so variable their effect is one of destabilization. They are not connected in any way to an absolute power, but only to physical power. Nor do they appear to be linked to any possible transcendent good or evil. They are interruptions of the real empirical world, and yet part of it. A cross has unexplainable power, and yet is ultimately just another weapon in Buffy's trunk of stakes, swords, and knives.

One of the few references in the show to the actual Bible casts a line from Isaiah, "and a child shall lead them," as a prophecy about a young pow-erful vampire, the Master's anointed one ("Prophecy Girl"). Vampires adapt the language and style of evangelical preachers, they follow a "Master," an "anointed" one, and a "vessel," and they facilitate eucharistic resurrections. A vampire exhorts a group of other vampires using the style of an evangelical preacher: "We have lost our way. We have lost the night. But despair is for the living. Where they are weak, we will be strong. ... Within three days a new hope will arise. We will put our faith in him. He will show us the way" ("When She Was Bad"). Just as vampires get to affect biblical language, the most religiously influenced moments of ritual and speech tend to come from monsters and demons.

While demons and vampires seem to be drawn to the rituals, languages, symbols, and the epistemology of traditional religion, Buffy and her friends are not. Although it would seem out of place to have Buffy, her watcher Giles, or her best friend Willow refer to the Christian origins of the cross, vampires joke about it, such as when a vampire comments that "I haven't had this much fun since the crucifixion" ("School Hard"). Willow, who is Jewish, does have a moment of humor when she is placing crosses around her house to protect her from vampires, but has to hide them from her father at the same time. For humans it is only in irony that religious objects signify traditional mean-ings. In other words, vampires enact the dark negative side of traditional Christianity in contrast to the Christianity that often appears as essentially powerless on the show.

While the issue of whether *Buffy* is a "Christian" show or not has been endlessly debated, it seems clear that Wendy Anderson is correct in pointing out that the "religions of the Buffyverse are overwhelmingly demonic" (214). But, more importantly, what does it *do* when traditional religious symbols and ritual are diminished, found powerless, or are connected to evil? In indirectly asking this question, *Buffy* points to important discussions in both contemporary philosophy and popular culture. Can we make a separa-tion between good and evil? Are they necessarily inter-reliant? Are we fated to keep thinking through the same patterns of religion even if we believe they are empty? Is to think the divine always also to think the mon-strous?

This blurring of the monstrous and the divine is built into the very fabric and mythical ground of the show which involves an obvious reversal of the Judeo-Christian Garden of Eden myth. As Giles explains,

This world is older than any of you know. Contrary to popular mythology, it did not begin as a paradise. For untold eons, demons walked the Earth, and made it their home—their Hell. But in time they lost their purchase on this reality, and the way was made for mortal animals, for Man. All that remains of the Old Ones are vestiges, certain magics, certain creatures" ["Welcome to the Hellmouth"].

Many of the Judeo-Christian resonances of *Buffy* reflect the vampire's connections to this primal time of pure evil.

Yet, while fans delight in its analysis, within the context of cultural criticism there is not much to be gained by delving into and analyzing *Buffy's* mythology *as* a mythology. Every fantasy or science fiction text creates its own rules, its own boundaries of realism and possibility, but myth is revealing when it is myth, it can have no author—and that takes thousands of years. What *is* revealing is how fictional and fabricated myth is perceived and received by the viewing audience and fan communities, in other words, how they or we react to created myth. For example, when Angel, the "vampire with a soul," is returned to Sunnydale after Buffy kills him, we can try to explain it through an analysis of the cosmology of the show. But the most we can discern is that Angel may or may not have been returned from Hell by the "First Evil" to kill Buffy (or perhaps for some other reason). Yet what is important is not *how* it happened, but whether viewers found it convincing. Does the "Buffyverse" seem like a world where this event can happen? Had Angel been lifted out of Hell by angelic creatures from heaven, it would have seemed ridiculous to a regular viewer of the show. But to be hurled naked onto the earth, shivering and feral, returned perhaps by forces of good and perhaps by forces of evil, to take many episodes slowly returning to the Angel we had previously known, does, within the context of the series, seem an authentic action, and fans readily accepted it. Only within moral ambiguity and cosmic complexity does *Buffy's* mythology "work."

Although Angel is not returned by any obvious heavenly forces, the mythology of a "heaven" did appear (shockingly, for many fans) in Season Six. In the final episode of the fifth season, Buffy, in an act that many saw as Christian or at least Christ-like, had hurled herself to her death in order to save the world from the chaos of a hell dimension. In the beginning of the next season, after Buffy has been returned from the dead by a black magic ritual enacted by Willow, she reveals that she thinks she has been in "heaven" and feels torn away by her friends.

> I was happy. Wherever I … was…. I was happy. At peace. I knew that everyone I cared about was all right. I knew it. Time … didn't mean anything … nothing had form but I was still me, you know? And I was warm and I was loved and I was finished. Complete. I don't understand about theology or dimensions, or any of it really, but I think I was in heaven ["After Life"].

For many fans, Buffy's heaven, in ways that were hard to define, did not feel like part of an "authentic" *Buffy* mythology; it was too literal, too absolute. Although Buffy's is not a classic definition of a Christian heaven, she does present a heaven that many Christian believers recognize. Yet, the statement "I was in heaven" rests uncomfortably within the context of the supernatural world of the show. Like Buffy, we could accept that we don't understand the different "dimensions," but we weren't expecting Buffy to ponder "theology." But as the season progressed viewers had reason to doubt the existence of her "heaven" as a theologically and divinely created paradise. Her friend's question, "do you think she was walking on clouds, wearing Birkenstocks and playing a harp?" ridicules the thought of a traditional Christian heaven. Buffy herself never thanks or credits a divine presence or plan for her Heaven, nor does she seem to change her agnostic orientation. It comes to seem not a Christian heaven at all, but an absence, an almost nothingness. In fact, in Season Six the few flashes we get of the old happy, joking Buffy are when she is invisible ("Gone") or when she temporarily has amnesia and is unaware of who she is ("Tabula Rasa"). These two glimpses of a joyful Buffy both relate to a suggestion of the nothingness of a heaven where she was "happy." Buffy is happy when she is *not*, a realization that leads to a contradictory mythology that viewers could accept, debate, and discuss.

The mythology of *Buffy* is more accurately anti-myth—not an affirmation of older systems of thought—but a continual challenging of them, not stories that explain and comfort us with certainty, but stories that pull the ground out from under our understanding. We can especially see this kind of subversiveness in the tendency to focus on "mythical" elements that don't and can't make sense, where the correspondences don't match up: Slayer lore and the First Evil are examples of myth-like creations that never quite make sense and raise questions about their own creation. It is these kinds of unexplainable constructions that, like the Bible itself—the paradigmatic example of anti-myth according to scholars such as Herbert Schnedau—contribute to the creation of interpretive communities that endlessly research and debate meaning, but that ultimately produce only questions.

The Abrahamic God is rarely mentioned on the show and when directly asked if there is any evidence of God's existence, Buffy herself responds, "nothing solid" ("Talking with Dead People"). Buffy's answer to this question of ultimate presence is more revealing than the show's writers were (probably) aware. Her two words—nothing and solid—express the two polarities around which concepts of God are based. This need for solidity in an answer to questions of indeterminate nature is characteristic of traditional interpretation—readings that presume stable meanings, origins, and autonomous existence. The word "nothing" as the opposite of something solid, is both an expression of atheism and also a favorite way of mystics, Jewish and Christian, to refer to a divine figure that is impossible to characterize or imagine. Buffy's answer, "nothing solid," expresses not only the show's ambivalence towards religion, but also, through the word solid, suggests the importance of literal presence—the need for something solid that occupies space and can be located and framed by both character and viewers. It is in the very tension between the two opposing words that the "theology" of *Buffy the Vampire Slayer* and of American popular culture is located.[7]

Theologically and otherwise, the show resists categorization and static meaning throughout, and, especially in its later years, introduces subversive elements onto the conceptual universe of the earlier seasons. The series is an instructive text on the interaction of American popular culture and popular religion in that it presents religious and theological themes in ways that refuse to provide comfort and stability. It is an example of a text of popular culture that refuses to fit into the convenient categories usually assigned such texts, demonstrating in its undefinablity a complex depiction of the different sides and shades of belief and unbelief, of human and nonhuman, and of the importance of finding ways to understand these issues.

Buffy's existential questions: "Why am I here?" and "What is my purpose?" are never answered, and in fact are established as unanswerable questions, especially in the show's final two seasons. The controversial Season Six followed Buffy's sacrificial death and centered on her struggle to accept being alive, her destructive sexual relationship with a vampire, and her best friend Willow's continued self-destructive slide into dark magic. In reviewing the earlier seasons, it is hard to avoid thinking that they inevitably aim towards the darkness and near-nihilism of Season Six. From almost the beginning of the show we know that Buffy must die young, that there is no apparent transcendent Good, and that Good and Evil are slippery terms. But it isn't until Season Six that the show and its viewers truly faced the darkness they had created.[8]

Willow, who brought Buffy back from the grave, sums up the darkness of these later episodes, when she confronts Buffy.

> You're trying to sell me on the world? ... This world? ... I know you were happier when you were in the ground. The only time you were ever at peace in your whole life is when you were dead ["Two to Go"].

Although the end of the sixth season and then the final Season Seven offer a sort of redemption, it is one that doesn't deny any of the emptiness and pessimism. Buffy and her friends find that they *can* go on, but only with the realization that life has no point, that there is no transcendent good, no ruling hand of providence, and no promised end. Buffy realizes that life is essentially irrational, painful, and meaningless, but that there are reasons to go on living, there are things in the world to be appreciated and enjoyed.

By breaking free of traditional forms of good vs. evil, mythology, and theology *Buffy* creates a worldview that, while it may not be Christian, also is not un–Christian (although it may occasionally be anti–Christian). The final episode ends on a shot of Buffy half smiling, half squinting into a brightly lit if ambiguous future. The last line—spoken by her sister—is, appropriately, a question: "What are we going to do now?" No longer featuring Buffy as the Chosen One, having defeated the god-like disruption of the First and destroyed the Hellmouth, the show neither denies nor affirms any religion; yet despite the end of the series it remains an important part of American popular culture and popular religion. As is even more clear now than when the series concluded, *Buffy* represented a model for a new kind of television and a new kind of scholarship. Made possible by a combination of new information technology, and a characteristically American creative process that allows the rescription of new monsters and mythology as well as the serious discussion of their role in our culture, *Buffy* epitomizes a new kind of forum for discourse, a new blending of vernacular theory with academic theory, and a subversive and constructive force within American popular religion.

Vampires and the Real Presence: Blood, Bodies and Absence in True Blood

The success of *Buffy the Vampire Slayer* was predictably followed by a series of popular vampire television shows and films, among them the *Twilight* films (2008–2012) and TV's *The Vampire Diaries* (2009–2017). In 2008 HBO premiered its award winning contribution to the genre with *True Blood* (2008–2014), an adaptation of a series of popular vampire novels by Charlaine Harris. The main premise of the show is that vampires have always existed secretly alongside humans and that the recent invention of a synthetic blood ("Tru Blood") allows vampires to exist without feeding off humans, and therefore "come out of the coffin" and live openly among people. As the series progresses, other supernatural creatures are introduced, including faeries, werewolves, witches, and shapeshifters. The main character of the series is Sookie Stackhouse, a telepathic waitress in a small Louisiana town, later revealed to be a human-faerie hybrid.

Religion is a primary and complicated theme at the core of what makes *True Blood* fascinating and important. Although religion is more visible as a cultural background in *True Blood*, the show, like *Buffy*, presents its most interesting religious themes outside the church or Christian belief. The "religion" of *True Blood* is not so much in the rural Louisiana churches, but is instead found in acts of sacramentalism, of ritual, and of transcendence through sex, violence, desire, and drugs. These acts of religion, then, are found in the very elements of the show to which many American religious organizations most objected. These "religious" elements are usually seen as outside of normative Christian experience, but the show suggests that these opposing elements are perhaps not so opposite. *True Blood*'s brilliance is in showing that, although mainstream religious institutions rarely acknowledge it, the fear of and desire for sex, death, blood, salvation, and immortality are closely and inextricably linked with our religious feelings. Like the vampires in *True Blood*, these desires have accompanied sacred rituals and sacraments for centuries, hidden in the shadows of traditional worship and married to the fears, anxieties, and nightmares that will continue to make us religious long after the original beliefs and stories have changed.

True Blood mirrors the messy, violent, and conflicted ways that various Christianities have traversed contradictory ideas of body, pain, evil, death, creation, and immortality. Religious studies scholar Leonard Primiano writes that *True Blood* "presents a rich, disturbing, ironical, critical, depressing fantasia on American religion in general—both in its institutional expressional and also in its lived, hybrid, vernacular expressions" (42). The different presentations and definitions of "religion" as they appear in *True Blood* open up into a larger discussion of what religion is, where it comes from, and how it changes. Historian Jon Butler argues that we should expand our definition of American religion to include popular practices of magic, astrology, and occultism. By showing how these have always been part of American religion, Butler demonstrates that many seemingly fringe elements of contemporary belief should actually be seen as part of a long and characteristically American tradition. But even more than an exploration of these elements of American religion, *True Blood* can be seen as a demonstration of the bloody and exciting confusion that always accompanies a major epistemological shift in belief. Beneath the surface of *True Blood* there is an underlying subversive structure that reveals what it means when a belief system suddenly changes.

The opening credits of *True Blood* offer an indication of the blend of religious themes that the show addresses and gives us a strategy for viewing and thinking about them. The opening sequence begins underwater: Like a creature rising from the primordial depths, or perhaps a dead fish floating to the top, the camera surfaces to reveal dark swamps, run-down liquor stores, crosses and cemeteries, a churchgoer "slain in the spirit," provocative dancing, threatening snakes, a Venus fly trap, a toddler-aged Ku Klux Klan member, black and white footage of civil rights riots, young boys messily eating blood red berries, and a river baptism. The sequence weaves these images together with quick flashes of naked flesh and is accompanied by the bluesy suggestive song "Bad Things." The first images set the location: scenes of the swamp, an abandoned car, a dilapidated building on the bayou, small houses lined up in little rows. But the first words of the song, accompanied by barely visible clips of entangled naked bodies, shift the sequence into a world of sin and salvation, of ecstasy and orgasm, and of blood and decay. There is nothing fantastic or supernatural about any of these images. The only direct reference to vampires in the credits is a sign saying "God hates fangs," which is, of course, a heavy handed reference to the Westboro Baptist Church and their claim that "God hates fags." But the conflation of sex and religion and of transcendence and death sets up a paradigm through which we can read the human/vampire intersection throughout the show.

Despite the complex presentation of religion in the opening credits, most actual Christianity, as presented in the episodes of *True Blood*, is one-dimensional and unproblematized. Whether it is the good-versus-evil view of the anti-vampire, Fellowship of the Sun, evangelical church, the there-is-a-purpose-for-everything religion of Sookie's gentle and wise Grandmother, or Sookie's open-minded God of forgiveness, religious beliefs of the characters are rarely treated with any complexity. Sookie may have objections to her friend Tara's use of the "J word," but when she is attracted to a vampire and overhears thoughts like "What kind of a good Christian girl would even look at a vampire" ("Strange Love" 1.1), she doesn't pray about it, she doesn't think through any possible religious or theological consequences, and she doesn't ponder the eternal soul or ontology of the vampire. Instead she merely says "I don't think Jesus would mind, if somebody was a vampire." Sookie's Jesus and her God, while assumed presences by the human characters in the show, serve to support her preconceived morality rather than form or challenge her worldview.

In the DVD commentary, *True Blood* creator Alan Ball claims that the opening credit sequence is supposed to "set the world" for the show by creating a "strange mix of religious fervor and getting drunk and … how they both sort of are two sides of the same coin … some sort of transcendent experience." But the sequence depicts more than just alternative forms of human release; it offers a theory of understanding these actions. Although the images are in themselves striking, the impact is mostly in the juxtaposition and imagined connections between images: a woman writhing provocatively in a bedroom is juxtaposed with a rattlesnake that coils and strikes; the face of a young boy in KKK attire cuts to a middle-aged man on a porch; and dirty dancing, religious ecstasy, and biological images of birth and decay are woven together throughout the sequence. In some ways, the opening credits offer a primer on how to view the show, teaching us to pay attention not only to the complexity of images but also to juxtapositions and transitions, and to read the space between images, the implied, the unsaid, the contradictory.

While the most obvious themes of the opening are the blurring of sacred and profane and the predatory character of man and nature, when we add the music and the premise of the series, it presents an even more complicated message, which insists that we make sense of these paratactic images, while continuing to deny us closure. Primiano suggests that the credit sequence implies a question: "If vampires have enough self-control to resist the lure of human blood, should humans possess sufficient self-control to resist organized religion?" (49). But it can also be seen to say just the opposite—to point at primal urges within humans that are necessarily and inescapably built into their religions, rituals, beliefs, and practices. The opening credits create a slow crescendo through music and images that reaches its peak in a final full immersion adult baptism scene. In a nighttime shot, two men lower a woman into the water; as the song and the credits come to an end, she flails about, seemingly in a type of ecstasy, but just before the shot cuts away it is more suggestive of her trying to escape. As the woman splashes her way (blissfully? desperately?) towards us, it is ambiguous whether we are to feel a cathartic release or a sense of suffocation, the credits (and religious ritual) pulling us back underwater where the sequence began.

The opening credits, like baptism, ask us to ponder the importance of the body to the soul, the material to the spiritual. The body is, on the one hand, the source of our certainty, the proof that we are real. On the other hand, it is the cause of our fall, the location of our sinful impulses and violent transgressions. *True Blood*'s emphasis on the human body forces us to confront our assumption about these issues. Throughout the series we are continually shown naked, suffering, contorted, bleeding, and headless bodies; we see close ups of flesh that we barely recognize; we hear the amplified sounds of wounds and of piercing and sucking. When vampires are killed they explode into sticky globs of blood and flesh that must be mopped up and wiped off. Unlike *Buffy the Vampire Slayer,* where dying vampires disappear neatly into dust, the *True Blood* vampire is physically broken down into tendons and globules. What is the power that does this? Is it indeed, as the show's the Reverend Steve Newlin says, evidence of the power of God? Or do these gory deaths show just the opposite, emphasizing the physical not the supernatural natures of vampires, life, and death?

The Event of the Vampire

If the final image of the opening credits leaves us vaguely uncomfortable, then the music and lyrics add to that feeling. The first line of the song, "When you came in, the air went out," paired with the simultaneous flashes of entangled naked bodies, introduces an element of hidden or repressed sexuality. The line itself seems to refer to human sexual attraction; perhaps we think of Sookie's reaction when the vampire Bill first walks into the bar where she works. "The air went out" seems a clear metaphor for a situation that radically changes, whether through overwhelming attraction or a world in which monsters are real. This moment for Sookie is a true "event" in the philosophical sense, when one's sense of reality is changed and a new truth can be perceived.

The "event," as philosophers such as Alan Badiou theorize it, is a moment of rupture in which ontology is changed, a moment that introduces possibilities beyond ordinary calculations. An event, Badiou argues, is "totally abnormal": *none* of its elements are represented in the 'state of the situation,' and something new has entered that belongs to the situation, but that that exists outside of it (Badiou 2005). The entrance of the vampire—Bill into the bar, vampires into the realm of reality, and *True Blood* into our living rooms— can be seen as a type of event. A new truth is witnessed; the rules of life and death, of history, how we imagine the present and how we construct the past are never the same again. Paradigmatic examples of such events might be the Lisbon earthquake, the French Revolution, or the entrance of Christ into human history. While most older religions celebrated cycles of life and death, Christianity insisted that one specific historical intervention was the turning point in all of human history—Christ rose from the grave, the cycle of life and death reversed, and nothing would ever be the same again. The bodily resurrection of Christ seems to suggest that Christians valued the body and saw it as inseparable from the soul. But, on the other hand, many Christians from the beginning devalued or even claimed disgust at the human body. But if such actions as sex and birth are so disgusting, then where does Christ come from? What is it that we worship on the cross? What happened in Bethlehem or on Golgotha that is worth remembering or reenacting?

For philosopher Slavoj Žižek, the lasting significance of the crucifixion is not that it symbolizes suffering or the resurrection. Instead, the crucifixion represents an event in human history when we realized that God is truly dead, that we are now on our own. This moment on the cross, demonstrates "God's weakness," and, as Žižek writes, "only in Christianity … does god himself turn momentarily into an atheist" (96). For Žižek, "only atheists can truly believe (101)," which is another way of saying that Christ is only significant in the meaninglessness of his death, and that for Christianity to remain meaningful we must continue to *not* believe, we must continue to re-experience the death of the transcendent God that the moment on the cross demonstrated. *True Blood*, like much of Žižek's philosophy—and like many of the popular culture texts we discuss—offers a negation of Christianity that yet remains Christian. Vampires offer a proof of the weakness of God and Jesus, whose supposed immortality, if true, is not unique. After vampires, Christ's intervention in history is rendered less of an event.

Žižek, borrowing from Hegel, characterizes Christ as "monstrous" and "inappropriate" in order to emphasize the role of Jesus as Other. The vampire, like Jesus, represents a monstrous and not-quite human figure that alters how humans see themselves. If Jesus was monstrous because he was God in finite flesh, then the vampires on *True Blood*, as humans in infinite flesh, are similarly monstrous. The human, as Badiou points out in *Being and Event*, is a "being which prefers to represent itself within finitude, whose sign is death"

(149). For finite humans, since the infinite is assumed to be beyond understanding, it is associated with the divine. Within this context, both Jesus and vampires represent a new possibility, a theoretical and theological trope, and a type of thought experiment that changes the ways humans imagine history, time, and themselves. In other words, what happens in *True Blood* resembles the uncertain shifts in thinking among the early Christians. Faced with an impossible theological conundrum, the great church councils of the fourth century ultimately created a greater one, deciding that Christ was both and equally man and God. Badiou labels this contradiction a *limit*; in other words, two opposing terms and concepts are somehow allowed to coexist—a new logic of being has been created, and both God and the world are different after this encounter. For these early Christians, humans become more like the divine and Gods are more like humans; by the same logic, in *True Blood*, the vampires are more human and the humans more vampiric. They are both changed to the very core of their being, in that they do not exist as they previously did.

Another major debate among early Christians was whether God or a god had really physically come to them here on earth—essentially a question of transcendence versus immanence. Yet a god who becomes flesh risks becoming less magical not more. On *True Blood*, paradoxically it is the vampire—a previously supernatural fantasy—that forces humans towards a disenchanted world. When Bill says that Holy Water is "just water," and a Crucifix only "geometry," his comments apply to humans as well as vampires. In the First Season episode "Cold Ground," Bill is asked to speak of his experiences as an actual veteran of the civil war. Speaking in a church, Bill represents a form of "real presence," and of an absolute material continuity with an imagined past, concepts central to Christianity but also to the American South. Before Bill comes out to speak, two local attendees attempt to remove a large brass cross from the altar, fearing (mistakenly) that it will harm Bill. Interestingly here, this cross, which cannot be moved, and Bill both represent a mastery over death and an assumed continuity to a glorious past. Bill reassures the church audience that, "we vampires are not minions of the devil. We can stand before a cross or a Bible or in a church just as readily as any other creature of God." Like Žižek's reading of the crucifixion as a site of the end of a god rather than the beginning, both Bill and the cross signify a world that now exists in the absence of God. The show seems to suggest that while some kind of god is always desired but never present, vampires—like Christ and early Christianities—represent a break, a chance to rethink our narratives of life and death, and beginnings and endings. In other words, humans see in vampires both a Christ-like intervention into ontological categories of being, *and* they see evidence of the absence of their old transcendent God. Like Christ, vampires challenge, subvert, and exemplify the contradictions inherent in a divine figure that is somehow transcendent (a god beyond categories) and immanent (present in flesh and blood).

At the end of the "Cold Ground" episode, Sookie performs three related ritualistic acts as a way of healing after the murder of her beloved grandmother; each act echoes Christian ritual yet is enacted in a world of an absent God. After leaving the funeral, where, overwhelmed with telepathically overhearing the judgmental thoughts of people, she yelled at everyone to "shut the fuck up," Sookie finds Bill's grave. This silent moment forces us to fill in the blanks—perhaps, like Sookie, doubting the role of death, gods, and Christian burials. What was her grandmother's funeral commemorating if Sookie is dating the man whose grave she now looks at? What do all the crosses around her at this moment represent? Does this grave, like the cross, represent an ending and a beginning? Sookie knows that no body lies beneath that stone—but then Christianity, too, begins with an empty grave. It's not that graves and crosses have lost their meaning, but their meaning is now something different.

Upon arriving home, Sookie, in a fan-favorite scene, slowly and ritualistically eats the last pie that her grandmother had cooked with a hymn playing softly as background music. As the music continues ("Take me home, Lord, take me home"), the camera cuts to extreme close-ups of the pie, both emphasizing and defamiliarizing its materiality. As Primiano writes, the scene creates a "new religious iconography" and resembles the "reverence and dignity of the reception of the eucharist at a funeral" (52). But, taking our cue from the credit sequence, if we view the show through juxtapositions and gaps, meaning is always plural and unstable. The images of Sookie are complicated in this scene by cuts to other characters. We briefly see Sookie's boss and friend Sam hooking up with her friend Tara in a hotel room, where Sam says to Tara that he wants "something real" in his life. We then cut back to the empty pie pan and to Sookie looking in the mirror. The non-verbalized visual comment is that Sookie, too, is acting out of a desire for "something real" which adds to the resonance of the Eucharist, a ritual that Catholic theology sees as producing the "Real Presence" of Jesus Christ. Without changing expression, Sookie almost ritualistically lets her hair down and changes into a white dress as if preparing for a wedding or a sacrifice. She calmly looks out the window waiting for the sun to set and then runs barefoot across a blue tinted misty field to her first sexual encounter with Bill. In the final scenes of the episode, she kisses his fangs and then offers her throat for him to bite; "I want you to," she says. Sookie here is body and blood—and pecan pie. As he drinks from her, the final shot is an extreme close-up of skin, blood, teeth, and tongue—linking the image to the close-up of the pie and presenting both as religious iconography: a eucharistic replacement that conflates life and death, human and monster, the saved and the damned.

The opening teaser to the very next episode, "Burning House of Love," opens with the same shot that concluded the previous episode: Bill's mouth and fangs and Sookie's skin and blood. The scene then depicts the more traditional sexual penetration as Sookie moans with pleasure. This conflation of bodies, blood, ritual, sex, danger, and ecstasy is an echo of the opening credit sequence that this scene leads directly into. After the credits, Bill retires alone to his resting place beneath the floor, emphasizing the difference between Sookie and Bill, between human and vampire. This cuts directly to a shot of Tara's alcoholic and evangelical mother Lettie Mae's coffee cup (which is spiked with vodka, another eucharistic substitute) and we hear a Christian radio station playing in the background: "what does it mean to accept Jesus as your personal savior?" What *does* it mean? Has that meaning now changed? In this episode, we see each character searching for and questioning the sense of the "real" that is at the center of the eucharistic performances. The previous episode's re-presentation of the eucharist has opened the door to rethinking the relationship between life and death and human and divine. Throughout this episode, which continues to play with the perception of good and evil and complexities of reality and appearance, different characters seek forms of fulfillment, transcendence or escape through a force that is simultaneously sexual, physical, ritualistic, and dangerous: Lettie Mae seeks money for an exorcism, even offering the banker sex in exchange for a loan; Sookie's brother, Jason craves "V" (the powerfully hallucinogenic and addictive vampire blood); Sookie continues to desire sex with Bill. When Jason and his new girlfriend Amy take V together, she makes the implicit explicit by saying "you just know this is what Holy Communion is symbolic of." What forms of transcendence are real in this episode? What forms of power are based in something outside of the human imagination? V? Sex? Exorcism? Money? Magic? Bill says to Sookie "we're all kept alive by magic ... my magic is just a little different than yours" ("Mine" 1.3). Within Christian traditions, "magic" is associated with forms of creation: the world from nothing, blood from wine. But what is the magic that animates Bill? Or Sookie? Or any of us?

When Jessica, a newly created vampire (and a very recent Christian human), asks her "maker," Bill, "are you a Christian?" he responds, "I was." How should we read his answer? All of the human characters in *True Blood* seem to be Christian in some sense or another, yet Bill has either chosen not to be or he cannot be a Christian anymore. Is it because he realizes that Christianity is not "true" and can then no longer be a Christian? Or, as an immortal, does he no longer need to be? If he ceased to be Christian upon rising from the grave, it is in effect his accepting his fallen status—an essentially Christian and Catholic move (if always a problematic one). If he is evil, what is it that is evil about him? How he is made evil? Like many Christians throughout history, must Bill accept that our evil nature does not depend on effort, thought, or action, but that we must yet accept our responsibility for it? Does Bill metaphorically represent what happens when the resurrected Christ continues to believe God has forsaken him?

While the Jesus that Sookie imagines is the friendly and present Jesus of American religion—the "loving, open-minded Christ, who himself knows something about existence after death" (Primiano 44)—the figure that really changes her conception of being in the world is Bill. Bill and the knowledge of vampires change reality and the experience of being for Sookie in ways that can be compared to a religious experience. Within the implied ideology of *True Blood* the vampire is not a negation of Christianity[9]; instead the vampire's intervention into humanity reveals and participates in the contradictions and aporias that are part of Christianity itself. Most traditional definitions of religion—by both those who claim to be religious and those who deny it—portray religion as a force against chaos, as a harmonious "light against the darkness" in the words of *True Blood's* Fellowship of the Sun, or as giving 'order and meaning' and providing "happiness and emotional security" in the words of a religious studies scholar (Lippy 2). However, the nature of Christianity is built around unstable ideas and irresolvable contradictions, and religious thought and events are just as often harbingers of chaos. In some ways, shows like *Buffy the Vampire Slayer* and *True Blood* present a model of how this works. Like the intervention of Christ into history, they force us to shift how we think about the borders of the human and the divine, the categories of life and death, and the desire for the presence of a God who continues to express only divine absence.

Conclusion

True Blood and *Buffy*—as do shows like *The X-Files, Battlestar Gallactica, Dollhouse,* and *The Leftovers*—create strange fantastic creatures and worlds that encourage viewers to challenge their own idea of authority, history, scripture, and humanity in our time and place. The vampires, zombies, aliens, slayers, and cyborgs of television offer a new perspective on the theological questions surrounding these issues. Recent thinkers have pointed to the importance of popular narrative like television in communicating and negotiating important contemporary religious issues. Theologian Elaine Graham, for example, points to the centrality of narrative in general, and texts of popular culture in particular, as "supplying Western culture with exemplary and normative representations of what humanity might become" (221). It is in their negotiating of issues such as these that television drama and the surrounding discourse can play an important role. Television drama allows viewers to discuss central topics within their religious experience that are rarely brought into question. A show like *Battlestar Galactica*, with its complex depiction of the human-created creatures Cylons, or *Buffy the Vampire Slayer* and its ambiguous ontology of a vampire-with-a-soul, can explore these very issues, encouraging energetic debate and commentary outside of religious limitations. Few Christians, for example, are willing or encouraged to publicly question what it means to "believe," but within the context of *The X-Files*, *Battlestar Galactica*, or *The Walking Dead* this becomes a central debate. Because these theological and philosophical issues exist in an unreal setting, viewers are often destabilized from their core beliefs and may be surprised to find the positions that they are taking, a space of confusion that can be the beginning of speculative thought.

From the first episode of *Buffy* in 1997 to the final episode of *True Blood* in 2014, the methods and texts through which viewers navigated these issues have changed radically. Although the surprise explosion of academic scholarship surrounding *Buffy* was unprecedented and helped redirect scholars' attention toward the content of television drama, it is the rise of alternative discourse within previously unimagined platforms that most connects these shows to a true rescription of American religion and sacred scripture. From the fan/scholar model of sites like *Slayage* to the explorations of fan fiction, to the creativity of Comic Con and the blurred lines of critic/creator/participant, these new platforms of discourse match the freedom of interpretation and the flexibility of authority and of religious ritual that is the often unacknowledged lived experience of Americans both inside and outside of confessional faith traditions.

CHAPTER 7

Monsters, Demons and Spiritual Warfare

Beyond Good and Evil

And I stood upon the sand of the sea, and saw a beast rise up out of the sea, having seven heads and ten horns, and upon his heads the name of blasphemy. And the beast which I saw was like unto a leopard, and his feet were as the feet of a bear, and his mouth as the mouth of a lion: and the dragon gave him his power, and his seat, and great authority.
—Book of Revelation 13:1–2

As Christians, we need to understand the realm of the satanic supernatural because it does exist and we are participants of the battle.
—Bob Larson, radio show host

Dreams and beasts are two keys by which we are to find out the secrets of our nature ... they are our test objects.—Ralph Waldo Emerson

Perhaps it is time to ask the question that always arises when the monster is discussed seriously: Do monsters really exist? Surely they must, for if they did not, how could we?
—Jeffrey Jerome Cohen

Monsters and Demons

In our previous chapter, we looked at how the vampires and demons on *Buffy the Vampire Slayer* and *True Blood* challenge ideas of stable belief systems, absolute recognition of good versus evil, and established ideas of the human soul. Ultimately, *Buffy* and *True Blood*'s complex depictions of the fight against evil in an indefinite world of ambiguity are examples of how popular narratives can demonstrate the difficulty, even the impossibility, of ascribing "essence" to anything, whether it is the Christian cross, the reality of a vampire, the idea of divine good or absolute evil, or even the concept of religion itself. In its portrayal of these ambiguities, the shows help us to recognize an important function of monsters and demons throughout history. It is their contradictory representations of essence that make monsters and demons such elusive and liminal figures, and each age needs to recreate them in the process of assessing its own boundaries—the boundaries that in turn help define who we are. In other words, because each age and each culture redefines the borders of what is considered right and wrong, sacred and profane, humane and monstrous, the monsters and demons become symbols of where these lines are drawn.

What makes monsters important and interesting is not only that they help humans define themselves, but that they also make this definition more difficult. In her work on the monstrous and the human, Elaine Graham claims that indeed "definitive accounts of human nature may be better arrived at not through a description of essences, but via the delineation of boundaries" (11). For Graham, "monsters have a double function … simultaneously marking the boundaries between the normal and the pathological but also exposing the fragility of the very taken-for-grantedness of such categories" (39). Although the monsters and vampires of film and television are obviously fictional, they are in dialogue with the monsters or demons that come from the world of folk and popular religion and myth. Like their counterparts in literature, film, and television, monsters and demons in popular religion have also played the role of denying essence, blurring boundaries, and ultimately questioning what it means to be human.

Although the monster is a part of a necessary process of continual human self-definition, monsters also have a darker and more perplexing function. While monsters and demons have always been important figures in popular culture and popular religion, in the contemporary world it is rare to acknowledge, in the manifestations of these dark and contradictory spaces, the existence of "real" monsters. We like to think of monsters as symbols and metaphors, as figures for film and television, and as existing fully in the realm of the imaginary. However, few cultures have been able to remain free of the fear of actual monsters, and there has been, within much of popular Christianity, a strong resurgence of interest in actual and physical demons. As shows like *Buffy* or *Supernatural* seem to take the *literal* role of demons less seriously, at the same time we have books, tracts, sermons, and radio shows proclaiming a real demon presence of which most of us are supposedly unaware.

In addition the discourses of the monstrous and evil have increasingly become pat of how we process our anxieties over climate change, terrorism, laboratory viruses, and intelligent machines. In this chapter we will look at how demons are currently constructed and represented within a religious context, and then at the perhaps equally "real" monsters of popular culture and modern life.

Monster Philosophy and the Construction of Evil

One way to begin to explain the variety of monster narrative within any culture is to ponder what the culture's relationship is to the concept of evil. Monsters and evil, are, by definition, on the borders of the normative, the acceptable, and the human, and although a definition of what constitutes an evil act of being is perhaps also by definition elusive, what we can examine is the rhetorical act of labeling. What happens when we speak or use the word "evil" today? What does it mean to call someone or something a "monster"? Is there a difference between the use of the word in a fictional context versus the "real" world (however complicated that distinction may be)? These are different questions than the classical ones of theodicy: why is there evil in the world when God is omnipotent and benevolent? What are the origins of evil? What are the consequences of evil? To ask what the word "evil" does, while related to traditional inquiries of theology and philosophy, is essentially a different question; it is a question of cultural studies, and maybe one of lived religion. Not only what do people mean by "evil," but what do people say that they don't mean? What is it people hear? Does using the word "evil" change the ethical, moral and social guidelines? These questions, like most questions about evil or monsters, resist answers. However, any level of understanding relies on seeing popular culture and popular entertainment as at least a way to question that gap between philosophical and popular religious and cultural discourses. The effects of the word and concept of evil are complex webs, formed by what people see on television, in theaters, what they read in newspapers, books, and comics, hear in sermons, presidential debates, or conversations, and what they play on their PlayStations, Xboxes, and iPhones.

Philosophical texts analyzing modern notions of evil point out that historically it has been formulated as the theodicic problem of a world full of suffering. For Augustine the answer is that there is no innocent suffering, it is the *deserved* suffering of our fallen condition. Until very recently this was the standard interpretation of the Book of Job—he was not thought of as an innocent suffering randomly at the wiles of God, but as a human sinner who deserved to suffer. Around the eighteenth century the word "evil" was used to refer to both acts of human cruelty and more natural instances of human suffering. As famously discussed in *Candide*, the Lisbon earthquake is an example of a natural evil.[1] More recently, philosophers and theorists have pointed to a gap between academic and popular conceptions of evil. While philosophy, for the most part, has abandoned the discourse of theodicy (and for much of the twentieth century even the problem of evil itself),[2] popular reaction to traumatic events such as 9/11, the Newtown school shootings, or the Paris attacks of 2015, signals a return to traditional questions of theodicy—asking how it is that a good God can allow horrible events to happen to a Christian people, or how a normal neighbor can suddenly turn into a murdering monster.

A more current philosophical question of post-theodicy might be how do we think about evil if we no longer have confidence in traditional explanations, if there is no way to "justify" evil, and it is impossible to reconcile ourselves to the existence of evil? The framework for this question, however, lies outside of most American popular culture and its popular religion, both of which still insist on concepts of theodicy, divine justice, and pure evil. The cultural questions of this chapter are, then, how do we think about evil within this perceived gap between the philosophical and the popular? And is there an assumption of essentialism about evil? Is it still assumed to be punishment for something? According to philosopher Richard Bernstein, "there is a disparity between the intense moral passion that we feel in condemning something as evil and our ability to give a conceptual account of what we mean by evil" (ix). The immediate and palpable feelings elicited by perceived monstrous acts of evil belie the difficulty of forming an elaborated, philosophically nuanced position. In the wake of the injurious effects of perceived evil, "conceptual accounts" give no comfort; and the populace turns toward a concrete, hardline model to make their revulsion clear. The concretized concept of evil is thus used in contemporary culture and has immediate consequences in the realm of the ethical and the political, and in the day-to-day behavior of people. By labeling something or someone as evil or a monster we change our standards of what action is appropriate; we change the rules.

Contemporary conceptions of evil are shaped, in large part, by resonances of Nazi Germany and the Holocaust: an event of "absolute wrongdoing that leaves no room for account or expiation" (Neiman 3). For philosopher Susan Neiman, evil is something that does not fit into our context of experience; it "threatens the trust in the world that we need to orient ourselves with" (8–9). Jean Lyotard compares Auschwitz to an "earthquake that destroys not only lives and buildings but also the instruments used to measure the earthquake itself" (qtd. in Neiman 251). Within contemporary American popular culture, many see the attacks of September 11 as most forcefully responsible for reintroducing the concept of evil back into our mental landscape. The attacks were fully disruptive acts that may fit philosophical, theological and popular definitions of what constitutes evil.

Most characterizations of the events appeared to revert to earlier concepts of theodicy. George W. Bush's comments that "there are evil people in this world," and that "we will rid the world of evil-doers," along with similar characterizations in the media, figure a Manichean world of Good versus Evil in which each force occupies a separate political sphere, the self-described "Goodness" of America assuring a clear demarcation of the parameters of the two. Other perspectives were provided by the sermons and statements of well-known Christian fundamentalists such as Franklin Graham and Jerry Falwell. Falwell asserted that we were being punished for our sins (echoing the Augustinian view) and, on the other hand, Graham's October 2001 statement on *NBC Nightly News* that Islam "is a very evil and wicked religion" reflects a deep-rooted suspicious characterization of the Other in American popular culture and religion. In each of these interpretations the position of the United States as the intended object of evil requires a butting up against old theological and philosophical arguments as explanations. Even more important, from our current perspective, is to try to understand how our cultural consciousness has been changed by contemporary concepts of evil, and how the changes to our cultural consciousness affect both popular culture and popular religion in America.

Two paths of understanding play a constant part in framing and containing cultural perceptions of monsters and evil. On one side, there is the purely theological frame, which plays out in identifying evil as "pure evil" and associating it with an ultimate demonic force or identifying suffering from evil as being in some way deserved. We see both of these rhetorical strands surrounding 9/11, most publicly in Falwell's and Graham's explanations. The other frame for evil is the more nihilistic and postmodern thinking that questions the validity of evil altogether, which emphasizes the difficulty of determining what is good or bad, evil or not.

Although these points of view could be identified as marginal, they change what lies within the mainstream. Again, it is not what evil is, but how people perceive it that is significant, and there are serious ethical problems with following these paths of thought. To either dismiss the Holocaust or the 9/11 and Paris attacks as no different than other crimes or to see them as uniquely and essentially diabolical are both ways of dismissing the significance of the event by putting them into traditional conceptual resources for coping with evil. To marginalize the disruptiveness and the senselessness of an event places it within something that can be understood and dealt with through traditional means—it domesticates evil. Yet, "radical" or "pure evil" can never be completely domesticated because domestic "evil" is always already part of the culture and thus can never be read except as a violation or disruption of the norms to which it is always subject. Pure evil is always an outside force, whether from just outside the culture or from a supernatural realm, which seeks to disrupt the social stability of the culture.

This structure, which externalizes the origin of evil, perpetuates a situation where the "all too familiar popular rhetoric of *evil* that becomes fashionable at such critical moments obscures and blocks serious thinking about the meaning of evil. *Evil* is used to silence thinking and to demonize what we refuse to understand" (Bernstein x). To give something an essentialist definition of evil removes humanity from its responsibility, or, in other words, if the Nazis or bin Laden or the Paris shooters are monster or devils, then their actions reveal nothing about us. *We are not them.* What these depictions of evil have in common is the attempt to construct a narrative to make sense of the unknown—a narrative that all too often reflects what Edward Said has called "a cartoon-like world where Popeye and Bluto bash each other mercilessly, with one always more virtuous pugilist getting the upper hand over his adversary" ("Clash of Ignorance"). The attempt to materialize a concept through language can be traced to the power of words, the idea that the occurrence of a term in one's own language ensures that it refers to something with a real presence, a real signified that thus has the power to create a reality. By materializing evil, the United States can demonstrate the ability to control reality and therefore adjudicate a moral system within which American culture can continue to put forward a notion of its own exceptionalism.

While material conceptions attempt to encapsulate the term, philosophical theorizing about evil—like contemporary theories of lived religion—focus not on what it *is*, but what it *does*. In other words, evil, like religion, has no essence, it has to be actively created and recreated. The significance of an evil, as Neiman suggests "something that shatters our trust in the world"—is more in the effect than in the cause or even in the act itself. Thus what evil does has more to do with public perception than intellectual ratiocinations, and popular culture is where theories of evil are worked out in the public consciousness. While texts of popular culture often identify evil as an essential thing—as in the most obvious portrayals of evil in popular culture such as the good versus evil structure of, say, a Steven Segal movie— other popular culture texts do allow a more thoughtful or more nuanced account. The *Star Wars* movies, for instance, have created a more complex and problematic characterization of Darth Vader (or his grandson Kylo Ren in the 2015 *The Force Awakens*) than what had originally been presented as pure evil, and the movie *Noah* (as we saw in Chapter 5) forces us to imagine a gentle vegetarian Noah committing an evil genocidal act. The zombie narratives in the graphic novels and television series of *The Walking Dead* give us an even more complex relationship of the human to the monster, acknowledging their dark destructive symbiotic relationship. In some cases, by seeing evil as more nuanced and objective, popular culture—at least sometimes—

demonstrates that theorizing about evil is not just an isolated esoteric pursuit of philosophers, but one that can be employed usefully in understanding our responses to concepts of evil, as well as the relationship between the ethical, the religious, and the political, and ideas of the Other.

Gods and Monsters

Many thinkers, including those oriented towards a religious tradition, acknowledge that the monstrous or the demonic and the divine can be indistinguishable. The moral and theological ambiguity of monsters can be found in the Bible, whose monsters are notoriously hard to define and interpret. Timothy Beal points to the figure of the Leviathan, mentioned in Genesis, Job, Isaiah, and Psalms, as a contradictory being who is sometimes depicted as part of God's plan (Psalm 104) and sometimes as an opponent to it (Psalm 74),[3] a description that may just as easily apply to Satan. For Beal, "Biblical monsters bear no single meaning, no overt unity or wholeness. They are theologically unwholesome ... [and] stand for the haunting sense of precariousness and uncertainty that looms along the edges of the world, the edges of society, the edges of consciousness and the edges of religious understanding and faith" (57). This double and contradictory movement of being part of and opposed to the ordained structure or known patterns is found throughout the Christian depiction of the devil, as well. Radicalized from his Jewish roots[4] by being recast as a snake in the Garden and as the wild terrifying beasts in Book of Revelation, Satan has also been continually domesticated into whatever social or ethnic groups are thought to be currently threatening the perceived Christian unity (Africans, Jews, communists, abortion doctors, Muslims, etc.). American Christians, therefore, have made Satan both more and less human, both a multi-headed dragon and your next door neighbor.

These two polarities of Satan represent two philosophical or psychological positions when discussing monsters or demons. One is to see them as the "demons within us," the aggressive dark side all humans must face, an essentially psychological approach, that says to understand monsters is to actually understand the turmoil that is within us. According to Stanley Cavell, "if something is monstrous, and we do not believe that there are monsters, then only the human is a candidate for the monstrous" (418), and for Stephen May, "all supposed talk of the other is really projection. Aliens are metaphors for ourselves" (41). To understand the monster, whether imagined by an individual or a society, for these pragmatic thinkers is to perform a psychological act, even a psychoanalytical one. Within Freudian thought, monsters *and* God represent something internal and psychological, and their tendency to return is just a part of our psychological repression of them: "the monstrous is a revelation not of the wholly other but of a repressed otherness within the self" (qtd. in Kearney 35). Monsters and gods cannot exist, they must be created by human psyche.

The opposing paradigm to the monster within the self is found in analyses of demons and monsters as "other," where the focus is on them as an unknowable and exterior entity. From this perspective, they represent the unthinkable—in the shadows and the abyss, on the fringes of the imagination and the dream world; the demon is something outside of us, so absolutely other as to be inconceivable. Demons, then, are paradoxically interpreted as both the other *and* the self—both inside and out. They are the strangers we can never hope to understand, or they are the dark recesses of our souls that we will never reach. Freud's important essay "The Uncanny" explores this paradox as its central thesis. For Freud the uncanny experience, while one of strangeness and terror, has to be one that is both familiar and unfamiliar (*heimlich* and *unheimlich*) or, if you will, both self and other.

These two opposing interpretations of monsters, as either ultimately internal or as the ever mysterious Other, have parallels in theology, religious history, and biblical narrative. As we have been emphasizing throughout, God has always been simultaneously presented in two opposing and seemingly incompatible ways: as a force that makes all meaning possible, and as that which is always impossibly beyond understanding. Biblically, we can see these two interpretations of monsters combined in the story of Jacob wrestling with an unknown figure, seemingly a dark demonic figure from his inner dream world that is turned into a god or angel by the light of day. In the story, as Jacob sleeps alone, a figure materializes and fights with him throughout the night. His adversary strikes or touches his hip, putting it out of joint. At this point Jacob appears to be winning the battle, and his opponent asks to be let go because the sun is rising. (Like many monsters, it appears he can only exist at night.) Jacob's opponent is (literally and figuratively) difficult to pin down. Man? Demon? Angel? God? The figure seems to come in a dream and then injure and bless Jacob. Not only does this figure go from inner demon to unknown other, it moves from monster to god. This slipperiness in determining and defining the difference between God and monster is part of the experience of the Bible, and is recreated in the contemporary American reconstruction of supernatural experience.

These various interpretations of a famous biblical "monster" bring us back to our question: are monsters and gods (or God) some sort of indefinable "other" that surpasses all efforts of interpretation and representation, or are they inner demons waiting to be understood and tamed? Although many thinkers continue to see monsters as only projections of the inner psyche, the trend in much current philosophical thought is to see gods and monsters as representing an unreachable other, outside of the realm of human understanding. This point of view is, in some ways, close to our current generation of Christians waging war against demons. The desire and attempts to reach across this abyss, to communicate or understand these radical figures of alterity are seen in the experience of art and of prayer. As philosopher John Caputo describes it, this unknown, this "impossible, unimaginable, unforeseeable, un-believable, absolute surprise" (73), *can* be seen as a god, but only by a true leap of faith, an act of total irrationality. This leap, making the blind and terrifying connection between self and absolute other, implies that, even within Christianity, God is an unknowable and monstrous figure. Religious thinkers, like the Talmudic scholar and philosopher Emmanuel Levinas, also emphasize relating to the other *as* other (rather than reducing the other to recognizable form) which keeps God indeterminate and ineffable, but also keeps monsters in the dark and under the bed, invisible, but unquestionably *there*. One must then open oneself up to the possibility of the impossible Other—be it God, or monster, or alien—in an attempt to see, interpret, or understand this moment of alterity. These contradictory readings continue to attract thinkers and creatives, and to inform the plots of TV shows, films, comic books, and video games.

The Return of the Demon

In the first part of the twentieth century, most scholars predicted the gradual growth of secularism and the decline of what many saw as superstitious beliefs. It seemed that post-enlightenment twentieth-century religion had separated itself from ancient and medieval beliefs in demons and monsters. In 1951, a scholar of religion reflected this prevailing view:

> For the most part, orthodox religious groups are emphasizing the importance of character development and there are fewer references to theological abstractions. We no longer believe that our misfortunes are due to malevolent spirits or that our neighbors are practicing Satanism. Except in remote communities, demonology and witchcraft survive only as lore, and the spirits and goblins of the past are remembered only at Halloween festivals [qtd. in Clark 35].

To many observers, twentieth century American religion seemed to be finally following Europe in dismissing such apparitions as superstitious. Although popular culture was full of images of monsters and demons, they were conspicuously absent from religious narratives. The monsters of film and media in the '50s, and '60s were either obviously fictitious—although often interpreted as manifestations of Cold War paranoia—or explained scientifically (usually either extraterrestrials or mutants from the effects of radiation). Most importantly, these monsters were almost always vulnerable to either military or scientific assault—they were natural and of the world, susceptible to the same kind of forces that created them.

However, as any classic film buff knows, part of what defines a monster is its tendency and ability to return from the dead, and by the 1980s and 1990s monsters in the form of satanic demons had returned to popular culture and to popular religion. Within American culture, following the 1970s when such popular movies as *The Exorcist, The Omen,* and *Rosemary's Baby* appeared, there seemed to be a shift within the beliefs of popular religion, and a renewed belief in, fear of, and fascination with satanic demons. It would be reductive to insist on a simple causality between the trend in film and the ensuing wave within popular religion. Popular culture, as we insist throughout this book, reflects, alters, and mediates the belief systems of the society at large, and to try to trace a single line of influence is to be blind to all sides of this complex relationship. Perhaps belief in demons had always been there, and practices like exorcism had never gone away, but it now moved close enough to the mainstream to begin to be noticed and imitated. Whatever the complexities of the web of cause and effect, the 1970s also saw some of the first popular and influential theological works on demons since the sixteenth century; for example, Don Basham's *Deliver Us from Evil* (1972) and Merrill Unger's *What Demons Can Do to Saints* (1977).

A perhaps related, if somewhat benign, phenomenon can be found in the fascination with and acceptance of the presence of angels. Recently the angel has become more real than metaphor. As literal belief in angels has risen (77 percent of American in a 2011 poll), the angel itself has been domesticated and its impact diluted. No longer the ambiguous, seemingly ambivalent creatures that the apostle Paul had such distrust for, the current angel figure looks like a Christmas tree decoration and exists to aid and comfort. In television shows like *Touched by an Angel* or in drugstore Christian paperbacks, their "otherness" has lessened; they are not god-like, not frightening, but more human in appearance and demeanor. They are sweet, pretty, generally female, and no longer retain their shock value. Demons, however, remained outside, untamed, and not much discussed in any mainstream circles. The descriptions of demons stress their distance from humanity; they are clearly not human or anthropomorphized. In their marginality, they maintained the influential "outsider" power to influence, shock, and haunt which angels used to have. Demons' relationship to angels can perhaps be described like this: If angels exist then so do demons; since angels have been so thoroughly domesticated, demons must take over the dark void left in their vacancy. Returning from the dead, resonating with descriptions from the Hebrew Bible, the Book of Revelation, and *Beowulf,* demons crawled out of the past to resurface in both popular culture and popular religion.

But although the added ingredients from Hollywood and television changed their look, demons are not really, nor have they ever been, fiction, nor can they be comfortably limited to ancient superstition. The struggle with satanic demons manifests itself in many ways ranging from the familiar demon possession to the more dramatic battles against "territorial spirits," that characterize modern practices of "spiritual warfare," or the idea of a battle against preternatural evil forces. The figure of the demon, like any monster, has roots in both ancient legends and in contemporary anxieties. "The monster haunts; it does not simply bring past and present together, but destroys the boundary that demanded the twinned foreclosure" (Cohen x), and these boundaries are precisely the ones that texts of popular religion question and threaten. Demons are both ancient and modern. Millions believe in them; unseen by most of us, they perch precariously on the edge of imagination, threatening and entertaining, demanding our attention. Whether we see them as dangerous or humorous, despite their absence in critical literature, contemporary demons are an imaginative force within society and popular culture.

The Art of Spiritual Warfare

Spiritual warfare is the most dramatic Christian interaction with demons, the most organized, and the most ingrained in forms of popular culture and popular religion. It goes beyond ideas of demon possession and posits the existence of an ongoing "war" between Christian warriors and armies of evil satanic demons; a war in which it is necessary for legions of Christian soldiers to become involved. This movement is one that is largely created by a subculture of writers, preachers, and "civilians" who are dedicated to fighting and proclaiming the war through an underground of written books, tracts, websites, and pamphlets. For non-believers or skeptics such claims pose philosophical problems. How "real" are these beliefs? What does it mean to call them real, or to call them beliefs?

We can interpret this movement in several traditional ways. We can point to how the ongoing battle with demons demonstrates a need to demonize the Other and the unknown in an attempt to distance the idea of evil. We can point to how it also shows a need to internalize and create imaginative outlets for these impulses. But spiritual warfare presents more difficult interpretive challenges. Although such a cosmic worldview is commonly ignored, dismissed, or ridiculed by non-believers of more mainstream Christians, we can theorize this popular movement within the larger context of American ideology. We will suggest that however marginal it may seem, spiritual warfare and its participants engage in a contradictory epistemology that is central to understanding American popular religion in general.

The spiritual warfare movement is traditionally traced to various evangelical Christian groups that arose out of Pentecostal congregations and religious leaders in California in the 1970s and 1980s. These movements, including most visibly Rector Dennis Bennett in the 1960s and the popular Vineyard movement in the 1980s, typically stressed emotional contact with the Holy Spirit and emphasized biblical prophecy based on a very specific way of reading certain biblical passages pulled from the Hebrew and Christian Bible. The combination of these two characteristics—individual emotional response to unseen power and radically new ways of offering dramatic literal prediction based on individual ahistorical Bible reading—is profoundly American, and led, in some cases, to a resurgence in the role and presence of demons.

The spiritual warfare movement is full of contradictions and paradoxes, but as we have often pointed to in this book, contradictions and paradoxes do not necessarily weaken theological or religious movements, and, in fact, are often central to invigorating their presence. Viewed psychologically from the outside, spiritual warfare can appear to be part of a contradictory need to seek separation from others at the same time trying to establish like-minded communities. It also reflects an urge toward a definitive explanation of what it means to be human while simultaneously questioning this very definition. Throughout American popular religion these contradictions coexist within common imaginative images and tropes, none more complex and powerful than the war against the demons of spiritual warfare.

As marginal as the belief in an actual war with demons may seem to many outside of select groups of Christians, we can see it as much more revealing of broad popular movements in imagination and epistemology. The need of many Christians to believe in this cosmic battle, in the narratives of it, and in the necessity of our participation in it, as well as the needs of others to dismiss such things as metaphors or as superstition, are all positions along a continuum of the human imagination; they are not isolated or strictly separate positions, as, in fact, each helps to define the other. Belief and disbelief in full-scale war with demons work together in a dialectic that can help explain imaginative leaps that are both literal and metaphorical (such as the willingness to demonize the Islamic world in both the twelfth and the twenty first century, or the continued practice of exorcism).

By seeing these demons as decentered, unstable, and marginal figures that are yet significant for understanding larger cultural trends, essentially our theoretical approach is part of a process of examining the margins to understand better the mainstream. This is a familiar strategy in recent cultural theory, and one often associated with the influential philosopher and historian Michel Foucault, who based much of his work on refusing to acknowledge the essence of normative humanism. His work focused instead on the liminal, the abject, and the almost human—the borders and limit points of what we accept as "humanity." Foucault understood cultures, in the words of critic Edward Said, as a "struggle between, on the one hand, the marginal, the transgressive, the different, and on the other, the acceptable, the normal, the generally social, or same" (*After Foucault* 3). Foucault's main point was that out of this struggle come our governing institutions, and that therefore it is necessary to examine the lesser "others" in order to understand the powerful and dominant.

This way of understanding power and knowledge is central to our arguments in this chapter. We can only understand American Christianity if we look at its marginalized texts and practices, areas of Christianity that mainstream denominations and institutions often try to deny or downplay. We can then take the further step of examining the margins of popular religion; demons and spiritual warfare are major points of tension existing in these liminal spaces. In focusing on this tension we can hope to understand the edges and the mainstream, which are both necessary parts of each other, points along the continuum, and in interpreting spiritual warfare we find our patterns of understanding resemble those inside and outside of belief systems. Claiming that spiritual warfare is not biblically based is an act that can only be done from *within* Christianity ("That's not *my* Christianity"), an argument that always subverts itself—like Nietzsche's image of logic as a snake eating its own tail (*Birth of Tragedy*). Furthermore, the emphasis on the act of marginalization is one that is consciously enacted within the primary texts of spiritual warfare. Texts urging concerted action against demons, for example, constantly point to the more "normal" and acceptable churches that fail to realize and confront the demonic presence which is accurately perceived by the more devout and more "biblically-based" little churches.

Because the idea of spiritual warfare is both an ancient and a relatively recent phenomenon, there are many ways to begin to interpret and discuss demons. How have they changed throughout history? Where do they come from? What is their relationship to God? To us? What decisions—theological, social, political, psychological, and aesthetic—are involved in their creation? As demons seem to increase their underground status as forces to be feared, they continue to be ignored in academia and mainstream media. This separation of demons from intellectually respected discourses is, of course, also a modern phenomenon (and, as we will see, some writers in the spiritual warfare tradition try to affect the language of academic discourse). Plato and Socrates could think about demons. Augustine and Aquinas could. Martin Luther felt he was constantly threatened by Satan and his minions. Yet despite their disappearance from philosophical texts, demons still have the power to surprise us, to remain concealed but present. Foucault famously asks, "what does it mean no longer being able to think a certain thought?" (50). Can we, in twenty first century academia, still think about demons? How do we speak of demons? Can we speak of their resurgence or "return," in the same way that scholars have recently begun to talk about religion and God?

Contemporary and popular demons clearly reflect a characteristically American flavor. American religion has deviated from its European models in its emphasizing feeling over theology, conversion over education, and the material Christ over the rest of the Trinity. Christ is not a mysterious figure, or an emblem of suffering, but is a kind, flesh and blood (and usually a very good looking) human being. The imaginative evolution of demons from Plato, Augustine and Milton to their material existence in contemporary America parallels this evolution of Christ. In contemporary American religion, demons and Christ have moved from mystery to material.

The Christian creation of this new version of a war with demons partakes in a paradox that we have been discussing throughout this book. At the same time much American Christianity has insisted on the Bible as the *only* path to holiness and only source of absolute truth, it also has been open to the creation of new religions, new sacred texts, new versions of Christ, and therefore new devils, new demons, and new cosmic realities. If American Christians are responsible for their own salvation, their own biblical interpretation, and their own personal relationship with Christ, at the same time they are encouraged to believe literally in the Word, then the openness to such beliefs as demons (often, as we will see, rooted in books) is not surprising. The combination of imagination and literal acceptance can be seen manifesting itself in an interpretation of life's struggles within a popular and fundamentalist epistemology as a war with demons.

Spiritual Warfare: Reading Is Believing

From Homer's singing of the shades of the underworld to medieval fears of the unbaptized returning as vampires, popular folk stories of the monstrous and the demonic have developed out of the religiously mysterious, invisible, and unexplainable, and then, in turn, influenced the beliefs and practices of popular religion.[5] If it is true, as a scholar of the Book of Revelation writes, that the "human imagination has always been controlled by certain basic images, in which man's own nature, his relation to his fellows, and his dependence upon the divine power find expression" (Farrer 13), then perhaps this monstrous aspect of imagination—depicted in medieval Europe by paintings of the Apocalypse and stone renderings of gargoyles—is most closely seen today in Christian paperback guidebooks and fantasy novels, folk art, and internet sites.

Perhaps the two most important texts of spiritual warfare in the late twentieth century were C. Peter Wagner's *Warfare Prayer*, a guide to learning "what it takes to step out against the demonic realm … as an informed and prepared warrior," and Frank Peretti's *This Present Darkness*, an extremely influential and popular novel about a "hideous New Age plot to subjugate the townspeople, and eventually the entire human race." These two books are read by common groups of people, are often referred to in tracts on how best to oppose demons, and draw on the same biblical and cultural material—they both serve as alternative scriptures to large populations of believers. Although grounded in select biblical passages, the importance of these alternative texts to these interpretive communities points to how spiritual warfare is truly part of the "rescription of the sacred" in some forms of popular religion. The *Handbook of Spiritual Warfare* states, "Cosmic dualism is a reality: spiritual warfare exists in heaven. Earthly dualism is a reality: spiritual warfare rages on earth" (13). The book points to the novels of Peretti as offering a view of this truth: "For excellent popular presentations of this dimension of reality see Frank Peretti's excellent books, *This Present Darkness* … and *Piercing the Darkness*" (522). What is significant here is how the *Handbook* characterizes the novel's role in understanding a "reality." Its existence as a novel (i.e. "fiction") is only important in that it helps make it "popular"—in other words it is primarily a way of presenting truth in a more entertaining (and effective) format. There is no acknowledging here the importance of its "fictionality," only its presentation of a "reality."

Popular guidebooks on demons ask us to believe literally in the words of a non-biblical text and a world of the unseen. To an outsider, there is much in these writings that sounds like it comes from a movie or a television show like *Supernatural*. Wagner's *Warfare Prayer* describes a specific location that has struggled with demons and claims that a physical rift in the earth allows demons to come in and take control of the city (Wagner 37). The author calls it the "Devil's Corner," whereas *Buffy* calls it the "Hellmouth," but it is essentially the same thing: a physical hole in the ground through which various hellish creatures can climb into the light of day—or, more metaphorically, a rift in our common (and necessarily fragile) understanding of reality that allows our darkest fears to become real, to be present, to become flesh.

These writings about demons and spiritual warfare by what are considered by many to be marginal American theologians have both thrown up and torn down boundaries—they have re-imagined old world demonology and created a vision of the cosmos embraced by millions of followers. While the tendency for many is to push aside these books as hopelessly out of touch with mainstream culture, religion, and modern knowledge, there are ways of thinking about these beliefs that place them in the context of American religious thought. Wagner and Peretti's demons are part of a way of thinking that includes the demons in *The Exorcist*, *Buffy*, or *Supernatural*, but their works are also related to growing presence of exorcisms around the country. And as marginal as many may want to see them, these writings about demons are also part of an eccentric and creative American religious tradition that includes Ralph Waldo Emerson and Joseph Smith.

As we have said, the combination of an insistence on biblical inerrancy and the right to personal interpretation of the Bible has its consequences, and spiritual warfare is only the extreme end of a spectrum that includes Smith, Emerson, the authors of the U.S. Constitution, and former Supreme Court Justice Antonin Scalia. Both Emerson and Smith looked to find an American philosophy outside of intellectual European traditions they perceived to be out of touch with American religious experience. The American stress on feeling and experience permeates writing on spiritual warfare, and it leads to narrow-minded misreading of other religious traditions.[6]

In Peretti's novel and Wagner's book, demonic power and Christian characteristics are given to other religious traditions and folklore; both authors seem incapable of seeing religion in any other way than as providing a power that can be felt and seen. Meditation and yoga become ways to literally communicate with Satan's forces; Krishna and Buddha are satanic figures. Any claim to peacefulness, whether Christian, Buddhist, or environmental, is misguided and deceived, part of an "evil con game" (Peretti 303). Prayer, as well, is a physical force without any dialectical processes, and is often described in military terms: A cover of bullets for Peretti or a coat of armor for Christ in Wagner. Spiritual warriors, too, distrust the language of "intellectuals" or as one Amazon.com reviewer said, reacting to criticism of Peretti, "search your feelings, take a day and relax from all this 'theology' stuff, whatever that is." Modern demons exist outside of any complex theology, and are real, physical, and monstrous. Borrowing freely from Hollywood, these demons are really ugly, appear to have nothing to do with angels, have their own mythologies, and float from Southern Baptist magazines to fantasy novels. From the point of view of believers, we are not supposed to try to understand them or to ponder their origins or purpose, just know they are there.

Major figures in the movement of spiritual warfare—pastors, novelists, radio celebrities and authors—are deeply indebted to each other and often cite each other as examples and support of their arguments. The center of their works is often the actual descriptions of demon figures. These descriptions are quite detailed and presented as objective fact. For example, Wagner describes a demon from the South American jungle, which, although it appears to be a round brass ring is actually a "water devil" that takes this form in order to roll tire-like under its own power. Racing undetected through the dark jungle this evil demon attacks the bodies and minds of Christian missionaries. According to Wagner, there are only a few ways to stop this fiend; its power can be neutralized by "striking the ring with a machete, putting blood on it or throwing a banana leaf in its path" (73–74). In his novel, Peretti describes one of the demons leading the invasion to take over a town; this demon had "arms and legs, but seemed to move without them.... Its leering, bulbous eyes reflected the stark blue light of the full moon with their own jaundiced glow. The gnarled head protruded from hunched shoulders, and wisps of rancid red breath seethed in labored hisses through rows of jagged fangs" (Peretti 11). Although Peretti sets his demons within a fictional context, Wagner and others cite his novels as aids to sensing the reality of the demon threat. In only the second sentence of his book, Wagner credits Peretti's books as "stimulating" audience interest in the supernatural and in Christian spiritual warfare. Peretti's novel, *This Present Darkness*, published in 1984, made a huge impact on groups of evangelical Christians and pentecostals who began calling themselves the "Third Wave," and even came to call the novel their "Bible."[7]

Wagner, a retired Fuller Theological Seminary professor, has been a leading figure in the spiritual warfare movement for decades, publishing many books and lecturing on the importance of spiritual warfare against demons. Although his books insist on the reality of a large-scale cosmic conflict, he often takes a more personal and pragmatic view than the fantastical fiction of Peretti. Spiritual warfare is important, Wagner insists, because it can aid evangelical efforts. A "divine alarm" has alerted him to what he calls the "greatest forward thrust of world evangelization in 2,000 years of Christian history." A more effective strategy than traditional evangelization, according to him, is to attack the controlling demons first, then to evangelize an area (26–27), and he recounts missionaries that had achieved no conversions who suddenly became dramatically more successful after applying spiritual warfare techniques. In his books, anecdotal accounts show how warfare prayer in action encourages evangelical success by demonstrating the power of Jesus over the demons (or by fixing dental problems and causing, in one case, a dwarf to grow 15 inches [28]).

Wagner explains that we are surrounded by multiple evil demons because "Satan can be in only one place at one time" and must "delegate the responsibility" by maintaining a "hierarchy of demonic forces to carry out his purpose" (63). For Wagner, the existence of these literal and corporeal demons is an obvious and verifiable fact that is the most pressing issue contemporary Christians face. Wagner's assumed audience is evangelical Protestant Christians, although he acknowledges that such a literal idea of a war may be new to some of his readers even within this community. Anything or anyone outside of a Protestant Christian tradition is assumed to either be demonic or to be incapable of seeing the dire reality of our position.

In his introduction to *Warfare Prayer*, Wagner attempts to position the book as a learned document, a "survey" of the field, complete with footnotes and an index, which draws from "theologians, biblical scholars, current authors and practitioners" (12). Although he worries that his work may sound like a "scholarly treatise," he also claims it to be "full of lively stories and anecdotes from the United States and other parts of the world" (13). His book, like Peretti's, constantly establishes the binary positions of us vs. them, here vs. there, and authentic vs. intellectual. One of the primary themes of the book is to establish demons as territorial, to show through readings of the Old and New Testament and through anecdotes that "certain supernatural spiritual beings have dominion over geo-political spheres" (92). This is one of the basic tenets of the discourse surrounding spiritual warfare—it locates the enemy, allows battle lines to be drawn, and designates the turf to be fought over.

Although evangelical action and dialogue based around literal armies of demonic activity has, at least anecdotally, declined in the first decades of the twenty first century, it is still a powerful presence within minority movements and organizations. Wagner remains an influential figure and has emerged as a leader in an international "apostolic and prophetic" movement that he has dubbed the New Apostolic Reformation (NAR). In a 2011 interview, Wagner claimed that there was a serious problem with "demonic control over Congress," and admitted that that "we don't believe we can kill demons and sometimes we don't believe we can completely get 'em out, get 'em away from a city, but we can reduce their power" (3 October 2011, *Fresh Air*, NPR.org). While Peretti's novels are not as influential as they once were, the massively popular *Left Behind* books (1995–2007), feature multiple demons.

Another major figure in the movement, Bob Larson, a radio celebrity and a sort of maverick exorcist (who now performs exorcisms over Skype), holds spectacular mass "deliverance rallies" where he directly confronts people and their demons, sometimes even striking them with his Bible to drive the demons out (Tennent 6). This literal use of the Word as a weapon is revealing of popular religion's relationship to the Bible. The demons are created by acts of writing; it is literature (words) that give them an ontological status. Whether these words are claimed to stem from visions, oral history, or eyewitness accounts or whether they are written as fiction/fantasy is not important. As we have seen throughout this book, reading, from paperbacks to roadside handwritten signs to chat rooms, is of primary importance and is where popular American religion escapes the denominations, where it slips out from institutional control, and where it truly finds a voice. Whatever else they are, demons (and angels, gods, Christ, even "man" and "history") are imaginative *literary* constructs; they are textual and intertextual creations formed in association with written texts and books.

The fear of demons demonstrates the "textual" nature of American religion in many ways. Actual practices of spiritual warfare—and Christian rejections of them—can be traced directly back to texts and not events. What makes these works popular and influential? What do they lead readers to believe and to do? What does it reveal to examine the texts within the context of popular culture and popular religions' texts of rescription—to look at how they are read and what they do? The words of Wagner and Peretti are obviously intended for a select audience. What can those of us outside of this audience learn from them? How marginal are these texts and what power does this marginality give them? In what ways do they participate in rescripting the sacred in America? Although most Americans are perhaps unaware of the movement of spiritual warfare, these questions lie at the heart of the American popular and spiritual consciousness, and are becoming increasingly more relevant to an understanding of our popular religious culture as a whole.

So what do we do with today's demon believers and today's spiritual warriors? Do we relegate them to the margins: a trace of leftover superstition? Do we accept demons and aliens as a growing presence and warn others of the dangers? Do we understand them as part of some overall human or national psychology? Can we truly dismiss demon belief, as Carl Sagan did, as just a "shared delusion based on common brain wiring and chemistry?" (124). And how does the enlightened "we" in this case escape the wiring or the chemistry? Although spiritual warfare is rarely addressed in the mainstream press, an article in *New States and Society* on spiritual warfare commented rather obviously that it is a "dangerous form of fundamentalism that can lead to paranoia" (19). While on some level it is easy to agree with these comments, to stop our investigation here limits our understanding of human thought. By putting ourselves on the unmoving platform of reason, logic, and science, and holding demons at arm's length, we simplify and reduce a major psychological force. Despite the attempts of Peretti and Wagner on the one hand, and scientists like Carl Sagan on the other, to define ways to defeat or disprove them, demons are loose, uncontrolled, imaginative entities. Constructed of fragments of history, dreams, theories, and religions, they can't be contained. They are kept alive by both faith and doubt, located between existence and non-existence. The whole enterprise is, in other words, thoroughly modern and even postmodern, existing without a true origin, sustaining itself through its own self-reflexivity. The demon world, not quite modern, not quite real, stuck between madness and poetry, lost in the discontinuity of history, is dangerous and fascinating, contradictory and creative.

In the same way that readers of Bruce Barton's 1920s Jesus novel, *The Man Nobody Knows*, claimed that it presented a more *real* Christ, readers of spiritual warfare texts often claim to find in the fiction of Frank Peretti or the *Left Behind* novels what they claim to be a more "real" depiction of the battle against demons. Reader reviews of the *Left Behind* books are full of statements such as "it explains scripture we have trouble understanding," or "they really do make the book of Revelation come alive in a way I can picture" (Amazon.com). Although these comments do not explicitly say so, what they imply is that these fictions are more "real" even than the Bible, perhaps because these fictions are more closely in line with their worldview. This privileging of "fictional" and literary texts is a point of view shared by literary theorists who claim that "narrative" often can posit "reality" more effectively than factual history or reporting. Because of this, we can look closely at what the literary language offers that creates the ontology of the demon. The ontology of spiritual warfare is unstable—not written down as a doctrine or a manifesto. The subject of study—to use an analogy from music—is more like interpreting jazz, where to try to fix the music in the same way we do the written texts of classical music is to ignore the improvisational aspect that is the essence of the art. Yet to understand this non-doctrinal basis in evil demons is also, paradoxically, to understand demons as solid and *actual*. This dialectic of improvisation and solidity is another model of our central theme, that American popular religion and popular culture is created by this tension between an absolute, unchanging belief and the freedom of creation. It is an improvised jazz solo over a steady bass line, held together by a faith in the unity of the narrative.

Fiction often creates or substantiates its own kind of reality; for Foucault, the sixteenth-century novel *Don Quixote* captures the complex relationship books and reading can have on a culture's epistemology. Like today's demon battler, Cervantes's famous "knight" launches himself into a life of battle and chivalry based on his readings of adventures of the lives of Christian warriors. Like Don Quixote, fundamentalist Christians "write themselves into a book"; their sense of being consists of stories that have already been written down. While their "book" has expanded beyond the Bible, beyond books even, into a multi-voiced and multi-medium web of texts, like Don Quixote, they must also "furnish proof" that these texts are telling the truth. Like Don Quixote, stuck between two worlds, they leave one world of the book behind, only to face a new textual world—a world still dependent upon the word as a source of meaning, but one in which the "Book" has been replaced by drugstore paperbacks, websites, and religious tracts. Readers of Peretti and Wagner see the world as it is described in these books; then, like Foucault's Quixote, they "read the world in order to prove their books" (48). Yet, as Foucault also says, in the modern world, the written word and things no longer resemble each other. For him, the person seeing a pure resemblance is either in a world of "madness and imagination" or in a world that takes a poet to rediscover (49). This site is where popular culture and popular religion engage in creating reality out of imagination or imagination out of reality.

From the Unreal to the Undead

As has often been pointed out, post 9/11 American culture saw an explosion of monster films, television shows, books, and comics, most obviously in the variety of vampire stories. However, as vampires became more and more popular, they also got less and less dangerous and threatening, a trend probably best exemplified in the *Twilight* books and movies. After this post–*Buffy* domestication of the vampire—handsome monogamous vampire husbands that glitter in the sun, vampires going to medical school—the turn to zombies in search of authentic fear and cultural disruption was a logical one. Without rehearsing the history of zombies, it is still useful to remember that it was essentially George Romero's 1968 film *Night of the Living Dead* that introduced that idea of a mass contagion and of what a TV broadcast in the film labels an "epidemic of mass murder." Romero's creation effectively channeled anxieties about escalating violence and became a metaphor of our dangerous world. Since *Night* and subsequent Romero films, through the post 9/11 *28 Days Later* and the humanist *World War Z* (which takes a position of human ethical exceptionalism), to *The Walking Dead* and its copies and spin offs, critics (and fans) have claimed zombie films as uniquely suited to give a political and social critique of contemporary society. *The Walking Dead* was published as an ongoing comic series beginning in 2003 by Robert Kirkman and then launched as an AMC TV series on Halloween 2010. The zombies of the *Walking Dead* television show and graphic novels are only one of the many examples of the popularity of a more apocalyptic monster in the twenty first century. Unlike the Cold War monsters who are vulnerable to military might and scientifically created viruses, or the satanic demons who can be cast out through prayer and exorcism, the zombies of *The Walking Dead* appear to be an unending and irresolvable problem, a new reality in a world without a happy ending. As James Reitter explains, "the zombie is arguably the most popular monster figure of the last 30 years" (100), and in the twenty first century, the zombie has taken over movies, video games, and—of course—television. Like all monsters, zombies are also "an embodiment of a certain cultural moment" (Cohen 4). The zombie figure embodies the fear of death by presenting an alternate distortion of eternal life. For Reitter "the zombie figure, more than any other, represents death—not as something inevitable, but suddenly pursuant and predatory" (103).

The idea of eternal life after physical death is almost inevitably linked to religion, but what happens when everyone's body lives eternally regardless of their beliefs? And what then happens to beliefs rooted in the eternal survival of the body and soul? As *The Walking Dead* offered a complete distortion of what it means to die—reminding us of just what was at stake in the idea of zombie apocalypse on the human level—the answer to these questions becomes increasingly unclear. This new kind of zombie narrative—in the words of Kirkman, a "zombie that never ends"—is significant in many ways, perhaps most significantly in its existence across multiple media and planes. The idea of a zombie narrative that "never ends" adds an element not really felt before—that of a continuous post-apocalyptic universe in which any kind of ending or closure seems impossible. Zombies are killed, safe spaces are found or carved out, but there is never any doubt that these moments are but temporary respites from the oncoming and never ending death to come.

As has been pointed to multiple times by critics and fans, the single most significant line and idea in *The Walking Dead*—announced in volume three of the graphic novel series and in the final episode of season two on TV and on multiple t-shirts and bumper stickers since—is "we're all infected." In other words, not only those bit by zombies would turn, but that this fate now awaited everyone after death. This twist on the traditional zombie narrative casts a nihilistic and more Calvinist view to the experience, almost taking hope out of the equation. While readings of monsters often focus on the idea of the Other, the truly monstrous makes us reflect and fear who *we* really are. In *The Walking Dead*, "we," are unambiguously also the zombies. Post 9/11 zombie narratives like *The Walking Dead*, as Kyle Bishop writes, "have flipped the original allegory: humans are truly monstrous" (73–74). The further a reader or viewer gets into the story, the clearer it becomes that humans and zombies are not enemies or at war but are symbiotically bound together.

The televised version of *The Walking Dead* and its extreme violence introduced all sorts of ethical and religious conflicts within characters, but also within fans of the show. Like characters on the show, fans perhaps search for ways to distract themselves from the violence and darkness of watching the show, often turning to humor or camp. As zombie themed Halloween costumes, Hollywood movies, Humans vs. Zombies contests, "kill of the week" discussions, and video games all demonstrate, killing zombies can be fun. But, as the show also continually reminds us, the same weapons that kill zombies also kill humans. One of the guns used to kill first graders in the Connecticut Newtown School shooting had been previously and humorously praised in an article in *Guns and Ammo* as one of the "8 Best Guns for the Zombie Apocalypse" (11). With this in mind, it is almost impossible to watch the opening episode where the first zombie killed—shot at point blank range by the main protagonist—is a small child.

Although *The Walking Dead* can be, and is, appreciated from both sides of the political spectrum, it is easy to see it as suggesting that "we have become chaotic creatures of selfishness, violence, and unchecked aggression who do more damage to ourselves and the world around us than any reanimated corpse ever could" (Bishop 74). To sum up our main point in this chapter we quote Marina Levina and Kiem-My T. Bui who write, "monstrosity has transcended its status as a metaphor and has indeed become a necessary condition of our existence in the twenty-first century" (2). Or, to put it another way, the demons that some Christians fight against, the plotting terrorists that politicians warn us about, and the zombies in a *Walking Dead* graphic novel are all equally "real" in American Culture.

Narratives like *The Walking Dead* can help us see a type of slippage between the human and monster and between good and evil. As Nietzsche famously wrote in *Beyond Good and Evil*, "Beware that, when fighting monsters, you yourself do not become a monster ... for when you gaze long into the abyss. The abyss gazes also into you" (Aphorism 146). In our real world, when we label the 9/11 terrorists and ISIS members or the Paris shooters as monsters or as evil, the implicit assumption is that they are not human, that their evil is not us. But part of what happens is exactly the opposite; in attempting to define ourselves as other to evil monsters, we pull ourselves into the continuum and onto the same slippery slope between the monstrous and the humane that is dramatized in *The Walking Dead*; we become the same unfeeling violent creatures that haunt our dreams. When 2016 presidential candidate Donald Trump got cheers for calling starving Syrian refugees "snakes" and claiming that he could look into the eyes of a Syrian refugee child and say "you can't come here," it is an example of how "we" can become that which we claim as evil; we are the walking dead.

Any monster, as Jeffrey Cohen, says, is on the border of the possible/impossible, and is both feared and desired, and stands at the threshold of becoming. These monsters, whether divine, science fiction, or radically other, "ask us to reevaluate our cultural assumptions about race, gender, sexuality.... *They ask us why we have created them*" (20; emphasis added). Like the drawings of sea monsters on medieval maps, they are poised on the margins of the known world—haunting our dreams, books, schools, churches, and politics.

CHAPTER 8

Religion, Video Games, Evil and the Real

Fret not thyself because of evildoers, neither be thou envious against the workers of iniquity. For they shall soon be cut down like the grass, and wither as the green herb. Trust in the lord, and do good.
—Psalms 37:1–3

Let the evildoer still do evil, and the filthy still be filthy, and the right-eous still do right, and the holy still be holy. See, I am coming soon; my reward is with me, to repay according to everyone's work.
—Revelation 22:11

War. War never changes. Since the dawn of human kind, when our ancestors first discovered the killing power of rock and bone, blood has been spilled in the name of everything: from God to justice to simple, psychotic rage.
—*Fallout 3* (Introduction Scene)

Rescripting the Visual

If the knock on television watching has been that it is a passive activity through which one is exposed to a seemingly endless "flow" of images without much room for thought, consideration, or action, video games have the opposite problem. Where watching television has been understood as an unengaged activity, the level of engagement the player has with the narrative of a video game renders this experience simultaneously more "realistic" and more dangerous to both society and the player. Critics often read the player's interactivity with games as dangerous because the player is drawn in by it to the point where the verisimilitude of the game overwhelms the concerns of real life. Since viewers and players experience television and video games through similar and now often the same devices, it is significant that conservative

193

critics have framed their dangers in such contradictory ways. These different perceptions of the ill effects of television and video games seem paradoxical, but they represent two sides of the same coin. In each case the worry is that video representation (through either unconscious passivity in the one or fanatical hyper-interactivity in the other) will so sway users of these cultural products that they will disregard the moorings of the real world and become either non-productive members of society, or worse: menacing to that society.

These concerns are a part of a worldview that understands representation as dangerous because it can become indistinguishable from the real. Concerns about the dangers of representation go back at least as far as Plato, who saw artistic representation as an obstructing perception of the ideal forms. When these concerns are read through the lens of contemporary popular religion, several avenues of inquiry open up and may be determined along at least two different axes. First, how are moral issues determined in games that can be called "secular," or how does playing a violent game affect the player's moral compass? Second, what are the effects of representing religious material in the contested space of a video game; is this space sanctified by virtue of sacred material or is it a profanation of the sacred texts? Third, in what ways can we see video games as part of a larger shift in such essentially theological ideas as that of the "real," or the "human," and can their study contribute to a deeper understanding of shifting constructions of meaning?

Concerns about the effects of video games are often raised, not only in terms of the potential actions of distracted players, but in terms of the moral paradigms these cultural products might embody. Passive TV watching may lead to acceptance of dangerous, transgressive, and a-normative ideas embedded in television shows, but for video games, it is the deep involvement of the players with the game that represents the biggest worry. From a religious perspective in particular, violent games are often attacked because they are seen as teaching moral lessons that are in conflict with the accepted religious moral principles. One famous example is the depiction of prostitution in the *Grand Theft Auto* series. One Michigan pastor warned players not to play the 2013 installment in the series: *GTA 5*, by indicating some of the immoral actions a player may engage in, "this includes soliciting prostitutes, driving them to a discreet location, and engaging in sexual activity with them. Then a player can make the choice to let them go or chase them down, run them over, murder them and take their money back" (Pastor Zoerhof). Questions of morality may be central to criticism of video games both as they apply to individual players—who may act out on the basis of a "warped morality"— and much more often by how the games' popularity might cumulatively influence American values for the worse. This is what is often described as the "coarsening of American values." After warning adolescents and adults never to play the game, Pastor Zoerhof admitted that he himself had never played. He also represents the other most common moralist reactions to the influence of video games, as he focuses on the notion of graphic realism of the game as problematic: "*GTA 5* is too real. The graphics of *GTA 5* are incredible. That's the worst part. *GTA 5* is too life like. It creates a false sense of reality for anyone playing. Players can interact in violent, morally bankrupt life scenarios without any sense of consequence."

Zoerhof points to the game's sense of "real" as the important issue ("the worst part"). For many critics, the realism of the games coupled with their perceived "immorality" makes the game dangerous for both individual players and society at large. But while it is certainly true that the *GTA* game series offers players a possibility of engaging in morally corrupt actions, it should also be mentioned that the example Zoerhof cites is entirely optional and not part of any of the main missions or narrative; the game's immersive environment also allows a player to *not* engage in those actions. Another important point to make here about this scenario is that, as in real life, *GTA* makes this action possible, but not consequence free. The game features "wanted level" meter, which keeps track of every time a player gets caught breaking the law. The higher the wanted level goes, the more intensely police will chase the player and the more difficult it becomes to progress through the game. As in real life, when players are observed by police participating in activities like these, they will be chased caught and arrested. It is also possible for a player to drive a taxi, an ambulance, or to do other "meaningful work" instead of doing the criminal missions or take part in immoral activities. This possibility lets the player maintain a great deal of moral agency.[1]

Cultural preoccupation with their moral implications insures that as cultural products video games become significant sites for exploring tensions between religious attitudes and popular mass culture, but because of their relatively recent development and the industry's appetite for narrative content, as well as their interactive nature, video games represent a flexible generic structure. This flexible structure can respond more quickly than other entertainment products to shifts in cultural tastes and rationalizations, and thus sometimes reify models of political rhetoric often as quickly as they emerge out of the wider culture, while creating interactive stories that more quickly incorporate those rhetorical models into their meaning-making systems. As such, video games participate in the kind of rescripting process we have been discussing throughout this book. As Heidi Campbell and Gregory Grieve write, "digital games have both intentionally and unintentionally become spaces to grapple with complex cultural histories, existential meanings, and religious narratives" (17).

Analyzing video games thus becomes a path to understanding the link between our rapidly expanding technological and digital world and the primeval impulse to create meaning in our lives through telling and perceiving stories. Popular religion, like all popular culture, has been changed by the more participatory nature of its practitioners and the radically more digitized world in which they practice. These spaces of interaction are clearly central to understanding religion, which has always occupied a place between storytelling and the technology used to tell these stories. One need only think about the role writing and reading had on the development of ancient Judaism and early Christianity or the role of moveable type on the Reformation. The mode and medium through which a story is told—oral tradition, sacred scroll, or Kindle—determines the possibility of variances within the story. Scripture can now be hyper-linked, searched, downloaded, tweeted, streamed, remixed, and mashed-up. If writing and printing created a culture in which the idea of a sacred text was one of an unchanging, determinate and mechanically reproducible text, could a digital game-based culture built around interaction and performativity lead to a more flexible sense of understanding scripture and religious practice?

Paradoxically, one of the most salient facts about the way in which video games represent reality is the verisimilitude often attributed to them, which when connected to their interactivity, leads many in the culture to retain suspicious attitudes towards them. This is not a new concern in relation to products of popular culture; we could find contemporaneous arguments for protection from every new conceptual and technological development in popular representations, from Victorian novels, to nickelodeons, to silent films, to IMAX and 3D TV. Each development that allows for closer approximation to photorealism immediately creates its discontents in the culture, who warn that the immersive qualities of the play, the novel, the "idiot box," the comic book, etc., will "rot your brain," and/or lead to immoral behavior and even cultural annihilation. But, for video games there is the additional feature which allows viewer participation in the narrative world of the text in unprecedented ways.

The development of technology has more recently allowed video games to mimic real life events even more instantaneously.[2] The speed with which events can move from experience to representation is not restricted to their treatment in video game form. The media, in all its iterations, makes it possible for events to be transformed into narrative as attitudes to those events are taking shape, which means that how we ultimately come to understand a particular event is often already shaped by its narrativization. When an event occurs now, it can be reported instantly and within twelve hours is already well on its way to being historicized. What is happening—due to technological and social developments—is that the time between event and history is getting shorter, and thus events become material for fictional representation almost concurrent to their incidence. For example, less than a week after Beyoncé performed her new song "Formation" at the Super Bowl 50 halftime show, it had been attacked by conservative media outlets and pundits—like former New York City mayor Rudy Giuliani—as "a slap in the face to law enforcement" that "glorifies the Black Panthers," referred to as a "hate group." It was also discussed on Salon.com as "Beyoncé's coming-of-age race story and as a "now-iconic video" (Ward). The whole scandal, including conservative overreaction, was captured hilariously by *Saturday Night Live's* brilliant parody "The Day Beyoncé Turned Black." The whole affair was old news within two weeks, its competing historical narratives already fading into the background.

Since video images of events occurring around the world can now be easily and quickly manipulated, those same images can quickly be incorporated into the latest video game. This immediacy gives the game an air of authority that renders it virtually indistinguishable from the real. While this may be a genuine concern, what is fascinating is how video game detractors have chosen to make distinctions in defense of some games and against others based more on ideology than the logic of the "too real" argument. When it comes to moral issues, for example, games that are considered evil are often decried for their violence or the a-normative behavior of the characters. However, there are some paradoxical elements to this argument that point up the interactions between American religion and video games.

In this chapter, we want to argue that video games exemplify a paradoxical cultural product that performs a number of rescriptions of the type we have been examining. First, because of their flexibility they can take up the socio-political rhetoric of the nation in response to real danger. Second, because they are necessarily "of the culture," they reaffirm values and notions maintained by the culture even as (or perhaps because) they attempt to appear to be subversive. Third, the technology that allows for graphic representation, while affording interactivity, is concerning because it blurs the line of the "real," a distinction that has been important to the history of religion and offers philosophical challenges in the twenty first century. Because of their interactivity, video games (particularly massive multiplayer online role-playing games or MMORPGs) occupy a unique place in the development of social media.

Participation in fan culture through online gaming communities, which in some sense go beyond what happens with television shows, poses yet another instance of blurring the lines between reality and representation, while making players co-creators of content. Finally, overarching these ideas are questions of moral or ethical concerns when games are produced specifically to reestablish the same idealized American morality which conveys the usual prejudices and flaws always already present in the culture.

Rescripting Virtual Evil

Because video games are often called into question for their moral content, they represent a unique site for interrogating moral questions and particularly in their understanding and deployment of evil as construct. The concept of evil as tangible gives us a great example to talk through moral questions and their elucidation within video games, and the reaction to them. Concepts of evil come not only from religious paradigms, but are continually reconstituted as part of our shifting paradigm of what religion is; that is, even within religious practice the idea of evil is a shifting signifier that incorporates ideas from the wide culture. How we understand evil is a big part of the issues that are usually raised against video games, and defining evil is a major part of how religious groups understand their own spiritual identity.

Some events are so massive in terms of cultural impact that they exert a great deal of gravitational pull. Because it has come to be such a defining moment for early twenty first century American culture—especially in relation to an examination of the nature of evil and notions of morality—the American reaction to the 9/11 attacks, have become a touchstone for cultural products ever since. The rhetoric deployed by political leaders at the time was mostly focused on a view of evil as a concrete force at work in the universe, rather than a complex philosophical abstraction. While this political rhetoric in response to the attacks focused on the idea that terrorism emerges from a single motivation (evil-for-evil-sake), religious responses to the attacks often took on apocalyptic overtones, like Jerry Falwell's suggestion that the attacks were allowed to happen by God as punishment for American "secularist" culture:

> The pagans and the abortionists and the feminists and the gays and the lesbians who are actively trying to make that an alternative lifestyle, the ACLU, People for the American Way—all of them who have tried to secularize America.... I point the finger in their face and say "you helped this happen" [Ambinder].

Because of their nimbleness, and in some cases low production costs, video games were among the earliest cultural products to reify the reaction to the attacks that saw the causes of terrorism as "pure evil" (a position which continues to be held by a prevailing segment of the American population). However, some religious responses participate in a different system of evil than the political rhetoric, and American religious attitudes are somewhat fluid and much more nuanced than Falwell and others would suggest.

Reading the 9/11 attacks as just the work of "evildoers," rather than deserved punishment for abandoning God, was the most common initial religious responses, which after some time became hardened into a prevailing attitude in the culture. Even more than a decade later, some of the Islamophobic postures expressed around the culture echo the sentiments expressed by Franklin Graham (son of the celebrated Evangelical preacher Billy Graham) in the immediate aftermath that "Islam is a very evil and wicked religion."[3] Franklin Graham argued against allowing Muslims to enter the country, suggesting that they should be encamped like the Japanese-Americans were during World War II, an attitude that persisted into the 2016 presidential campaign and Donald Trump. The attacks, then, can be either the work of evildoers who do evil-for-evil sake (the result of their "evil religion"), or the deserved punishment for our own evil. The first is wildly more common and leads to the ensuing notion that we must fight against evil and utterly defeat it.

Within the context of American popular religion, intervention against evil is clear and unambiguous and usually cast in militaristic terms—despite the advice of Psalm 37. Human agents of evil are both similar and dissimilar to the demonic agents we encountered in Chapter 7. In the context of the "war on terror," war against actual human beings is described in metaphorical terms as a war against evil, whereas in spiritual warfare it is couched in the language of a very carnal, militaristic, and ultimately worldly conflict. There, military terms stand as metaphors for spiritual concerns; but, in the case of the war on terror, evil (as a spiritual concern) gives purpose to very real militaristic actions through which the forces of evil must be fought and defeated in a righteous war that will eventually eradicate evil. This view participates in a system within which evil is imagined not only as a motivating force but as an explanatory one as well. Evil people are evil because they *do* evil; and, they do evil because they *are* evil. This solipsistic construction presents not only an ahistorical view of the motivations for violent acts against the U.S., but also generate a simplistic "black and white" moral structure which presents American interests as always informed by the "good" and its enemies as inherently evil.

This construction of evil typically pervades in the production and consumption of cultural products, including television shows, movies, music, and, of course, video games. TV shows focused on terrorism, homeland security, and sleeper cells have become a mainstay of this kind of reaction. With their "ripped-from-the-headlines" ethos, these shows create a seamless relationship between events (as they unfold in the world) and their narrativized worlds, while, to some extent, informing their viewer's judgment of what is at stake in the "real" world. Representations of Jihadist motivations as simply eruptions of evil in TV shows like *24*, *Homeland* and *Quantico* reveal how prevalent political rhetoric gets played out in cultural productions, while— as we argue in Chapter 6—other more nuanced and complex TV reactions to evil are presented in less direct ways in shows like: *Battlestar Galactica*, *Buffy*, *The Leftovers*, and *The Walking Dead*.

The development of video games in response to these rhetorical stances

demonstrates how they deal with moral questions that develop as a consequence of rhetorical discourse and helps us understand religious interactions
with video games. Mainstream video games, like Hollywood films, are, of
course, always intertwined with a culture's preoccupations of the time. Especially large budget games necessarily need to appeal to large masses of people,
and therefore tap into the fears, anxieties, and hopes of the specific time and
place. In the world of video games, what has developed in the years since the
attacks is a complex matrix of reactions with multiple strands that shares the
diversity of television approaches but is by nature more participatory. Video
games work in similar but in some cases more accelerated ways than TV. In
the early days after the attacks, "small games" developed, whose primary
objective was to depict retaliatory violence against the Islamists. There were,
for example, simple games in which the object was to either torture or kill
Osama bin Laden, or his followers. Small online games, designed to be played
only online in one sitting, go right to the point; they do not bother with elaborate rhetorical devices or metaphor. In one such game, called "War on Terror," the player was represented by a pair of arms, and a cartoon version
Osama bin Laden stood by passively, like other "small games" we will discuss
later, this game helps to simplify notions of evil and the Other to its barest
essentials. The object of the game was to punch bin Laden repeatedly until
he fell down dead. He offered no resistance and groaned pathetically as he
was repeatedly battered. Other social issues can be treated similarly; after
recent debates about illegal immigration, several games have emerged—
hosted primarily by white supremacist websites; for example, "A white
supremacist addressed the immigration issue by creating the interactive game
'Border Patrol.'" The object of this free online game is to shoot racist carica-
tures of Mexicans as they attempt to cross the U.S. border (Johnson 210).
Because of the low costs (both financial and labor) of producing them, these
games were able to take part in the crudest and most vilifying representations
of the "enemy," which were then read as "radical Islamists," and demonstrate
the simplest equation of evil.

Larger more expensive games by necessity offer a more nuanced representation of these forces. This is principally true about large-scale multi-level
games and particularly established franchise games like *Call of Duty 4: Modern Warfare* and *Soldier of Fortune*. Development costs for games of this size
and complexity make it improbable that they would be as crude or as blunt
as smaller single action games. Video game representations of evil can range
from the very concrete to the very abstract, in terms of their portrayal of
world events. The relationship, in this context, between American religious
doctrine and its cultural products is paradoxically problematic, and yet may
point to ways in which it is changing in the new generation. On the one hand,
religious concern for the moral hazard posed by popular cultural products

in general (but video games in particular) is demonstrated by groups like Focus on the Family, who regularly review and disparage violent games. On the other hand, the power and popularity of this form of entertainment makes it difficult for conservative religious groups to ignore, which often causes them to actually participate in making their own.

Tragedy Plus Time

The immediacy with which certain events become available as subject matter for video gaming creates a paradox of realism. According to Alison McMahan, in the *Video Game Theory Reader,* "realism" in gaming "is subdivided into social realism and perceptual realism. 'Social realism' is the extent to which a media portrayal is plausible or 'true to life' in that it reflects events that do or could occur in the non-mediated world.'" On the other hand, perceptual realism is what is usually vaguely meant by "realism" or "photorealism"—how much the environment looks and sounds like the real world (75). Any attempt to make the world of the game resemble the world of the game player is limited by what is available for depiction, not just from a perceptual (i.e. from a visual or other sense) standpoint, but from a socially acceptable one as well.

If we are considering evil and what it does, then there is a perceptual—and thus a representational—problem with depiction that organizes itself around issues of the real and the simulacrum. Games and other popular entertainment could not show the result of the actions of the "evildoers" at the time. Games like *9/11 Survivor* and *New York Defender*—created as artistic statements on the events by a French digital artist—were critically attacked as insensitive when they depicted the events themselves in the immediate aftermath. At the time, the socially available representation of the event was from a retaliatory stance; it is okay to show the capture of Saddam in his "spider hole," but graphic, even if animated, pictures of 9/11 victims jumping through gaping holes in the towers incited public outrage and calls for censorship. The response by major media corporations to delay the release of anything loosely connected to the events shows their awareness of problems of public perception.

It was impossible, at the time of the attacks, to release games with any graphic depiction of the events or any related material. Games that included shots of the buildings or focused on terrorist attacks or included identifiable shots of New York or Washington could not have been released at the time, not because the technology was not available, but because it appeared to their makers that such a game would be unpalatable to American consumers. So that, while technologically it would have been very easy to depict these events with great photorealism, it would have been culturally or socially "unrealistic" (or crass) to do so at the time, even as the "actual" footage was being shown again and again on television in news programs and documentaries and on the covers of magazines, newspapers, etc.

It is not, however, the recent memory of the events that determines public reaction. The rhetoric of evil put forward in reaction to the perceived threat takes some time to resonate with the public. Once this is achieved in the public sphere, often through saturation in the media, game-developers begin to produce games in an effort to maintain relevance. In 2004, for example, two separate game developers released *The Hunt for Bin Laden* and *Quest for Saddam*. Each of these games took up the rhetorical stance within a moral universe in which evil is literally tangible. Bin Laden and Hussein become the faces of a pure unadulterated evil, needless of nuanced explanations or evidence; they are cardboard villains, whose sole motivation is to do Evil. Once enough time has gone by, game developers are given free range in the culture to create games which take up the deployed rhetorical stances allowing a reified vision of American exceptionalism as a beacon of freedom and the uncomplicated evil of its enemies. However, a game that questions this cultural perception would be much more difficult to produce. Put more simply: a crude game that demonstrates the accepted view of evildoers can be produced right away and may generally be seen as perhaps capturing an unsophisticated jingoist ethos; a game that artistically depict the actual event cannot be created for some time. But large military games that depict the eventual retaliation and "justice" can be produced as soon as technologically possible. Several of these games take up the challenge of enacting the construct of evil as representative of U.S. enemies. In *Desert Storm II*,[4] a small unit of Special Forces sets out to capture Baghdad at the end of the first Gulf War. This title illustrates the frustrations felt by certain segments of American society at the irresolution of that war. The first volume of this game was released shortly after the first gulf war; its development, however, was begun almost concurrently with the buildup to that war.

As with many of these games, the American force, and thereby the player's avatar, is portrayed as small and relatively powerless against insurmountable odds. In each case, the large, overwhelming number of the actual U.S. force present in Iraq and its oppressive nature is played down in favor of an underdog status. It is easy to see the strategic nature of this narrative move in designing a video game. It is important for a player to perceive the struggle within the game as worthy and the resistance difficult to overcome; this gives a game the entertainment a player seeks. However, as we said earlier, there is rhetorical maneuver in place here as well. In the games that feature such a move, patriotic notions of Freedom, Liberty and basic American Goodness (all capital letters) are juxtaposed with the irretrievable evil of the opposition. It is telling that there are many games that feature terrorism, and most strive for realism and naturalism; however, none engage seriously with the issues of the situation, or engage with the reasons or motivations for terrorist activities, but instead choose to read those motivations as inherent to either the religion, culture, or mindset of the Islamic world. The geopolitical conditions are thus always rendered simplistically dichotomous and therefore in accordance with the basic equation of American goodness, usually cast in religious and patriotic terms.

Despite the moral implications raised by the player's actions, war-themed games depict the U.S. versus them ideology made prevalent in the culture by the political rhetoric in response to attacks. The game *Freedom Fighters* offers an alternate reality in which the United States has lost the Cold War and the communists have come to finish the job. Ironically, the Soviets claim to be "liberating the people of the U.S. from an oppressive regime" (*Freedom Fighters* game box). The player becomes involved with the guerrilla army fighting back against the Soviet occupation forces. The game uses something called "Charisma system"; as the player performs heroic acts s/he will garner more and more followers. This function is similar to the underlying logic of the Christian fantasy game *Left Behind: Eternal Forces*, which we will discuss in a moment, except that the inspiration here is political rather than spiritual.

The moral risk of violence in a game is often determined by who the enemy is; in *Tom Clancy's Splinter Cell*, which features missions defined by levels of "stealth," there is one domestic mission in which the player infiltrates CIA headquarters. This mission requires complete stealth and absolutely no killing; if any agent dies, the game is over. This prohibition is not extended to foreigners. So-called "fifth level freedom" missions against foreign nationals are carried out without concern for guilt or innocence; anyone who represents an obstacle to the goal of the mission may be "eliminated." Games like *Rainbow Six*, *Ghost Recon*, or *Socom: Navy Seals* all operate along the similar lines, with the player taking on the role of warrior against the forces of evil, always figured as the enemies of America.

These are large, expensive games which require a massive capital investment to develop and rely on large distribution to be financially viable. They are, therefore, very careful to observe a position sympathetic to cultural standards and thus they participate in the system of metaphor and rhetorical strategy available within the broader culture. These games show a kind of unity with political rhetoric, popular opinion, and cultural production. In every case, the argument that "evil" is a simple, clear cut, identifiable force that is by definition opposed to the desires of America is part of the narrative of the war-themed games, which mirror a straightforward relationship to evil in popular religion. Yet even as we say this, we cannot lose sight of the fact that there are always tensions within cultural products, and cultural hege-mony is never absolute. The designers and developers of these games manip-ulate the reality of the game world to adhere to rhetorical stances that are already present in the culture, placed there by political leaders, media and genuine belief in the righteousness of America, etc., but as cultural products they must—by necessity—contain all the contradictions, ruptures and erup-tions to which a large complex society is always heir. Players call out to get involved in the war against evil; *Splinter Cell's* slogan, "Freedom isn't Free," reveals this kind of unity of thought. We are to imagine ourselves taking part in the fight against evil and paying a real price for it, beyond the forty or fifty bucks the games costs, but it is always at some remove.

The inherent contradiction or tension in this chapter involves three notions: that video games are *only* reflections of cultural traditions; that they can be a subversive or challenging force in conflict with those traditions; and, that they are more reflective of newer "postmodern" ways of thinking about narrative and reality, which allows us to read through them to a more complex formulation of the values and ideas at stake in political and religious rhetoric of the culture. We would like to define our subject within these tensions, so as to deepen our understandings of how cultural negotiations ultimately play out. Observing any one of these mechanisms in isolation would give us a simplistic and skewed perspective on the relationship among religious prac-tices, political rhetoric, and cultural productions, somewhat in line with how a one-dimensional view of evil as tangible necessarily diminishes its very rich and complex ontology.

Wargames

War themed video games commonly take a mostly patriotic tone; Amer-ican war games have usually been historical or fantasy-based. As noted, typ-ical narratives involve a small American force engaging a large foreign force. This structure serves both the ludic and nationalistic objectives of the games. After all, playing as a large army against a small force would not make for rewarding gameplay, though it might be more representative of actual con-ditions on the ground. On the other hand, casting the U.S. military as the underdog, while less reflective of reality, improves the gameplay and avoids the potential for the U.S. appearing to be bullies. These conditions are not restricted to the world of video games, rhetorical strategies deployed mostly (but not exclusively) by the Right figure the largest military power on the planet as somehow both invincible and vulnerable.

Video games within the war themed genre have employed plotlines that logically follow from the acceptance of the discourse of evil as the result of evildoers. Recently these games often involve military action against Islamic terrorists. One of those games is *Soldier of Fortune*, "best known for its graphic depictions of firearms dismembering the human body. This graphic violence is the game's main gimmick" (Gamespot.com). As the title indicates, the player's character in this game is a mercenary: "John Mullins, a 'consultant' hired by the U.S. government to do the jobs that they cannot do as a country." "Your mission," as described on the side of the box,

> is clear: survive. Track your prey across the globe in a series of secret missions to take down a fanatical terrorist organization ... before it takes you down. Welcome to the secret world of mercenary combat. Your mission: hunt down four stolen nukes and then stop the terrorist group that was responsible for the theft before they can pull off their master plan. The safety of the world is in your hands [*Soldier of Fortune Gold*, box].

The mercenary scenario of the game participates in this common structure of military games. There are some clear gameplay advantages to this configuration. As a mercenary, the player's avatar is both able to occupy the underdog position, while simultaneously being both part of the patriotic effort and set apart from the usual military ethics. This structure occupies a specific position in terms of verisimilitude. While the game itself attempts the usual level of photorealism (as much a contemporary technology would allow), its relationship to accepted social and cultural "reality" is just as important.

It is, on the one hand, a culturally accepted truism that American soldiers are held up to a higher ethical standard, but it is simultaneously understood that sometimes war requires unethical behavior, which is where the mercenary narrative (and John Mullins) might come in. Sometimes, however, events on the battlefield outstrip our cultural productions. The 2007 massacre in Baghdad's Nisour Square by four Blackwater "contractors" might provide the extreme case of the ethically dubious, yet pragmatically useful mercenary as portrayed in the game. "A jury in Federal District Court found that the deaths of 17 Iraqis in the shooting, which began when a convoy of the guards suddenly began firing in a crowded intersection, was not a battlefield tragedy, but the result of a criminal act" (Apuzzo). In this case, the actions taken by actors within the employ of the U.S. government did something that was revealed to be putatively against the most deeply held and normative values of American culture. Not only was the act seen as atrocious, but it gives proof that in some ways, U.S. military action is not as ethical as many would like to believe. But it also proves that the cynical view implied in *Soldier of Fortune* and, in fact most mercenary narratives, which is that the government is not willing to own some of the actions of mercenaries, but is certainly willing to pay someone else to execute them. The fact that the current American wars are being prosecuted with more non-military personnel than any previous military engagement gives this issue more currency.[5]

Also, because we cynically seem to accept that there are moments when the government must do things we find morally reprehensible (but just don't want to know about), *Soldier of Fortune* is more realistic from that perspective than the information we are given by our government, which again blurs the lines the between the real and its representation. The player is thus (at least narratively) allowed to take part in the endeavor of war in ways and at a level, not just beyond the ordinary citizen, but beyond that of the ordinary soldier. The decisions a player makes within the game are informed by knowledge about what the government is doing in the war that is specifically hidden from the public view in the real world. Because the game is interactive, players are forced to make moral decisions that impact the outcome of the game, and are thus moral agents within the fictive universe of the game. But, because the game validates cultural presumptions we have about the way a war is prosecuted and references recent history, the result is that the game comes to be a kind of historical artifact of the war, which helps rescript the very history it attempts to reflect.

While the "small group fighting against all odds" structure enhances the player's gameplay experience in the game, "real world" descriptions of the "War on Terror" cast the American military in terms of the difficulty of the task and heroism of its troops, rather than the overwhelming size of the force. The rhetoric of evil also allows for the kinds of apocalyptic scenarios which substantiate the level of force or violence used in battle, as well as casting the enemy, and sometimes the innocent victims, as indistinguishable from the evildoers and thus apt cannon fodder (let's not forget the slogan of "shock and awe" with which the Bush administration began the Iraq War in 2003). Games that adopt this view offer players virtual participation in the "war of our generation." The playing experience for these games is advertised as an entrance into the real world of military violence, as if the games themselves were a part of the war effort:

> Enter the world of a soldier-for-hire, a deadly killer who journeys across the globe's most dangerous, political hotspots—from a speeding freight train in Africa to Iraqi oil refineries to Russian chemical plants. Take on 30 deadly missions in a race against time that could determine the fate of the world [*Soldier of Fortune* box].

The promise to the players is to simulate these conditions so they can experience them realistically. The killing involved in the game rivals anything that happens in the *Grand Theft Auto* games, but the rationale and justifications for military violence seem, here, to extend to the represented violence in the game. It is as if social critics of war-based games buy into the idea that this genre of game somehow contributes to the war effort, and therefore what would be abhorrent actions in other genres are seen as tolerable here.

This impulse has not abated even as the industry has matured into a more respected and sophisticated form over the past fifteen years. *Medal of Honor: Warfighter* is a more recent iteration of this type of game which, at least rhetorically, maintains this configuration. Commonsense Media (a religiously conservative website and spin-off from "Focus on the Family" that reviews video games for morally questionable content) warns parents:

> *Warfighter* is a gritty military shooter that depicts modern warfare with unflinching visual realism. Enemies spurt blood, grunt, and sprawl in believable ways when shot, and melee combat scenes show foes getting stabbed in the torso and having their necks snapped. One early mission has players play as a terrorist carrying out training activities against wooden targets, but the rest of the time they're in the roles of honest, noble soldiers doing their best to defend the world from terrorist plots [*Warfighter* review].

This warning raises significant points for us on a number of fronts: first, it seems to focus much more on the graphic representation and not as much content represented; it is the photorealism of the images of spurting blood and snapping necks more than the moral implications of players committing these acts that seems to deserve comment. On the other hand, the warnings about the terrorist training, which seems graphically milder than the other actions described, is based entirely on the symbolic identity of the player. From a religious perspective, for a Christian, we might think that the idea of snapping someone's neck would be the problem and not so much whose neck we are snapping. On the one hand, parents must be warned that their kids can take on the roles of terrorists even if it is "against wooden targets," but the graphic violence performed to protect "freedom" is excused because of its symbolic meaning. We can see a real life manifestation of this sentiment in debates about torture, in which despite significant evidence against its effectiveness, some continue to support torture "if it will lead to information of terrorist plots." In defense of the violence in the game, the review reminds parents that when players engage in combat against their foes (causing them to spurt blood, have their necks snapped, or get stabbed) it is done in the role of "noble soldiers doing their best to defend the world from terrorist plots." So that even in the digital space of video games the "cause of Freedom" is an ennobling pursuit, even if you have to break a few virtual necks to get it.

If we look at the verbs used to describe these actions, we notice that even in the warning the subjective position is eliminated. All these verbs are rendered in the passive voice; the adjectives too help to take a protective posture toward the mission if not the actions of the game. The graphic depiction of violence is described as "gritty," "unflinching visual realism." The same care that is taken to talk about the imaginary war in the context of a video game is also taken when describing any American military action. It is as if representing an American war effort creates a sacred force field within the oft-maligned simulated space of a video game. While some violent video games are denounced as evil for the graphic violence they simulate, war games like these seem to provoke little controversy from that quarter. The understanding of violence as evil depends much more on the justification for the violence than the level of violence or the detail of its graphic representation. Games which uphold contemporary rhetorical stances can be very violent indeed, without coming under attack, but games which seem to transgress the normative rhetorical positions of the culture are often identified as a corruptive force in the culture. If we look at similar descriptions of games like the *Grand Theft Auto* franchise, we find that not only is the subjective position emphasized, but the effect of that subjective position has extension into the real world.

Evil in the Machine

There is, as we have been discussing, an inherent and often assumed tension between mass media and American religion; a tension that is often exploited by both religious and commercial interests to further their own agendas. The public discourse surrounding definitional notions of evil takes place within the tension between these forces. Culture makers often use religious criticisms of their products as a selling point as they market products as transgressive; religious critics often use specific cultural products to help frame larger arguments about the breakdown of moral values. Despite their relatively recent origin, as cultural products video games have already garnered a considerable amount of criticism from both cultural conservatives and more liberal critics, who view these games as negative influences that contribute to the decline of morality and values in American society.

From Columbine to the Newtown school shootings and other similar atrocities, social critics have afterward lined up to hold violent video games, particularly games like *Doom* and *Grand Theft Auto*, responsible for the perceived increase in aggressive behavior among school-aged children.[6] In 2003 Senator Joseph Lieberman claimed (without any evidence) these games are "part of a toxic culture of violence that is enveloping our children, that is helping to desensitize them" (qtd. in Lemos). The incidence of violence among teenagers is often linked to the rise of "realism" and represented violence in video games. This corrosive effect represents a link between video games and evil. Violent games represent an evil threat (so this idea goes) because they can corrupt America's youth into becoming evildoers; but, paradoxically the games engage a system of values that is consistent and even normative within the culture. Violent video games often enact the simple equation of good versus evil deployed within the rhetoric of evil for evil's sake, particularly in times of crisis; this is largely true of war-themed games, but holds true even for the most "depraved" games such as *Grand Theft Auto* and *Manhunt*. So, in actuality, they do not blur the lines between right and wrong, as Leiberman claims, but work to draw that line more clearly.

In June 2003, in Jasper, Alabama, after teenager Devin Moore, who had been arrested in a stolen car, killed three police officers in a police station and escaped by stealing a patrol car, famed anti violent video games crusader Jack Thompson filed suit on behalf of the families of the murdered police officers against WalMart, Gamestop, Sony, and Rockstar Games. The suit alleged that these companies were complicit in Moore's crimes because they had helped "train" him. Thompson reportedly told the *Tuscaloosa News*, "what has happened in Alabama is that four companies participated in the training of Devin … to kill three men" (McCormack). There is an inherent problem with this type of reasoning. While one may argue that there may be a connection between playing graphically violent video games and a certain kind of moral turpitude, or maybe even violent tendencies, it is very difficult to imagine that playing these games constitutes *training* in any real way.[7]

This type of reasoning points to a conflation between represented realism and experiential reality. The idea that movements experienced on a TV screen, performed by an animated figure, and carried out by the player through the manipulation of some buttons on a controller would translate seamlessly into the ability to wrest a real gun away from a real policeman and shoot him and two others while making a daring escape in a stolen police car participates in an ontology of sympathetic magic, in which what happens in the game happens in real life. If this were the case, the lawmen of Jasper would have been better served spending a few hours a day playing *Grand Theft Auto* in lieu of actual police training.

In a way, this particular aspect of the criticism of video games is more complicated today as a consequence of recent advances in technology. Many real world actions (surgeries, air strikes, commando raids) are coordinated and even performed remotely through digital technology in a way that renders them indistinguishable from video games. It is important to remember that the controls for these "real-world" applications are roughly the same as those of a video game, while shooting a real policeman requires the transfer of training from, say, hitting X on a controller to squeezing the trigger of a real gun. The escalation of the use of unmanned drone strikes in the past ten years demonstrates the ways in which video game "training" of this sort has had a real world consequence, one which has become increasingly more important to the war on terror. "Remotely piloted aircraft 'have changed the game on the battlefield with their persistence and ability to both build situational awareness and close the kill chain,' said Gen. Herbert "Hawk" Carlisle, head of Air Combat Command" (Chatterjee).

In the case of drone warfare, there is strange upending of the relationship between representation and reality. For the drone pilots flying missions from

Creech Air Force Base in Nevada, their work consists of actions that are identical to a video game. They are described as "new techno-warriors [who] commute to work like any office employees and sit in front of computer screens wielding joysticks, playing what most people would consider a glorified video game" (Chatterjee). In fact, simulation is one of the oldest genres of video games and one of earliest to be adapted into actual training; and, of course, today there are a remarkable number and variety of drone simulation games, in which a civilian may play at being one of these "new techno-warriors" and replicate these actions exactly.

This transaction feels like the closing of circuit: the simulation in the game is a direct representation of something that is itself a representation. In the case of these airmen, flying missions has increasingly had real life consequences, as a number of them have "come forward to claim that the horrors of war, seen up close on video screens, day in, day out, are inducing an unprecedented, long-distance version of post-traumatic stress syndrome (PTSD)" (Chatterjee). It is significant that in this case real violence experienced only virtually through the mediated space of a video screen has had real psychological effect on the pilots; whereas, it is unlikely that the same would be true of a player of drone simulation game. That one group of people would "play" as entertainment, what others suffer psychological damage to do as a duty to their country—first, seems like the promise of the war themed video game, but more significantly for our purposes—helps us to understand the complexities of the real in the twenty first century.

When we turn to questions of morality, video games negotiate ideas of evil in ways that are problematic: drones strikes are a necessary part of the war on terror and are thus often seen as morally acceptable; video games that simulate that experience are granted a similar standing. Just as there is a simulacrum created in terms of the ontology of the game as opposed to the real, the same structure exists in the moral dimensions of this relationship. The moral rules of the culture apply to the actions taken in the game, even when the game insists on its transgressive nature.

In connection to notions of morality, these relationships reveal interesting contradictory elements in the popular culture. On the one hand, in seeking financial restitution from the game developers and retailers instead of the individual responsible for the "evil" acts, like those of Devin Moore, critics "blame the game," as an attempt to externalize evil. They want to believe that the average American teenager is incapable of such actions, and thus an external force must be made responsible for creating the monster that he has become. Simultaneously, this response engages in a kind of domestication. Once again it becomes unnecessary to examine what this kind of evil may reveal about each of us, or how this kind of evil functions in society at large. But, ultimately "the game," as a part of the culture, refuses to be externalized.

On the other hand, the experiences of drone pilots, as opposed to those who just simulate being drone pilots, have a "real" link to events in the world and a real stake, and yet the players share a kind of immunity from moral criticism. Video games participate in the meaning-making system of the culture, within which they create, parody, reflect, challenge, embrace, and transgress its most widespread attitudes. Because they are fully embedded in the culture, they cannot be made part of an external evil and they cannot break their cultural moorings and transgress the operant moral structure. Games like *Grand Theft Auto* are marketed specifically as violently transgressive of cultural norms. They exist in tension, but never completely break away from normative religious and social mores.

Really Real

As we have just said, along with the usual rhetoric about the corruption and decline of moral values being wrought by mass media's influence on American youth, video games are particularly targeted for two reasons: their interactive nature coupled with their increasingly sophisticated and "realistic" graphics. This combination sets up interesting questions about mimesis, and representation. Since it is the graphic nature of the represented violence which so concerns critics, it stands to reason that this representation must be in some way characterized by a special relationship to the *real*, a heretofore unachieved verisimilitude, complicated even more with new advances in so-called "virtual reality" games and technologies. In comparing the mimetic qualities of violent video games to that of violent films, there is no question that the movies have a clear advantage in terms of their visual representation of reality. In fact, one could say that many video game attempt to simulate (not a real world, but) filmic or cinematic reality and, in this way, they approach Baudrillard's condition of the simulacrum. The real itself becomes part of this "weightless" system, as in the example of drone pilots, who witness their own actions at a mediated remove from their actual effect. The actuality of their experiences inserts itself into their conscience despite this mediation, but here there is a blurring of the real and the represented that seems to invert the usual underlying relationship representation and reality.

On what level is video game representation "realistic," when not actual, and therefore able to engage players whose actions are *not* projected into the real world? Is it only the sense that their actions have real consequence in the world that causes the "real" pilots to suffer PTSD, or is there something in the interactive representation of video games that so capture the actual experience that even the side effects of the real experience are present?

This question particularly has spurred a wave of studies on the effects of violent gameplay on the social aggressiveness of players. According to David Walsh, the president of the National Institute on Media and the Family, "This [violent] segment of games keeps getting more realistic, and they keep pushing the envelope. The problem is that these games are the ones that are particularly popular with kids, particularly teenagers" (firstamendmentcenter.org). The issue seems to be inherently linked to the level of detail in the graphics. The violence itself, for example, as depicted by the graphics of the '70s hit game *Space Invaders*, in which chunky, pixilated monsters were destroyed by the player with a gun that shot rays of light, does not seem to be the issue; and few organized groups ever question the effects of the violence involved in games like cops and robbers or cowboys and Indians played with realistic cap-guns in the *actual* three-dimensional world, games which might have been much better training grounds for the actions of Devin Moore attributed to the influence of the video games. Where, then, do we locate the notion of realism?

Games have become conventionally realistic on a different level as well: contemporary technology allows current political stances and their broad popular expression to exist almost concurrently, so that the news headlines and the latest X-box or Playstation game seem to be on the same page. In the development of recent video games we see two simultaneous trends; video games are beginning to exhibit a kind of hyperreality, graphics and rendering that not only approach the verisimilitude of cinematography, but move beyond it. At the same time, gameplay is much more focused on contemporary issues than it ever was before, and new games often strive for a narrative that contemporizes the action of the game. Because these games tend to focus their attention on the already formulated equation of evil, they are not as closely scrutinized as socially transgressive games. *Fugitive Hunter: War on Terror* (a post 9/11 game release) received low grades from game reviewers at the time, but little attention from the likes of Lieberman, and other critics of video game violence.

Fugitive Hunter featured a series of engagements with "terrorists," another game that culminates in a fistfight with bin Laden. In his review of the game, GameSpot associate editor Brad Shoemaker then wrote:

> There's just not much you can say in *Fugitive Hunter's* defense. It's a short game with bland mechanics, repetitive levels, and almost zero replay value, and that's not even taking into account the total absurdity of getting into a fistfight with Osama bin Laden [Gamespot.com].

He described *Fugitive Hunter*, just as a game, as being "merely bad," but added,

> as a piece of exploitative shlock, it's downright appalling. How much can you really say about a game that features Osama bin Laden as the last boss? This game fed on a nation's grief and outrage and ultimately proved itself to be no more than jingoistic garbage [Gamespot.com].

This "jingoistic garbage" represents the "evildoers" rhetoric taken to its logical conclusion. Bush's "dead or alive" comment regarding the capture of Osama bin Laden comes right out of a cowboy western, where the final scene often *is* a fistfight with the bad guy in the black hat. Games like *Fugitive Hunter* attempt to cash in on the wave of xenophobia and vitriol spurred by the rhetorical response to the attacks. It is entirely reasonable to expect a nation having suffered such an attack and having been given such an uncomplicated explanation would react by showcasing its patriotism and asserting its superiority in the literal face of evil.

In a different context, a month before the Supreme Court decision on gay marriage, a game titled *Kill the Faggot*, developed by a "California developer, skateboarder, and Christian shoe promoter named Randall Herman, launched for public consumption early Monday morning before being pulled from the Greenlight service hours later" (*ars technica*). The game is essentially a "stand and shoot" first person where a player targets caricature versions of gay characters. Players score when they shoot the "gay character" (identifiable, basically by their colorful dress); the game awards bonus points for shooting a transgendered person, and deducts points for shooting a straight person. When players successfully hit a target, the game calls out a series of homophobic invectives, like "you killed that faggot," "straight pride," and "transgender kill." (Interestingly, this last one uses a more politically correct term, rather than a slur). Other games in the same category, such as *Border Patrol* (first appeared in 2002, but has made several appearances since) and *Ethnic Cleansing* (distributed by Resistance Records, producers of white supremacist heavy metal), employ more or less the same structure; a hated group is simultaneously depicted as Other and then violently attacked.

It is reasonable to argue that the bad quality and low circulation of these games renders them insignificant in the broader culture; but, it is the very fact of their poor quality and low cost that makes them remarkable in the context of political discourse, notions of evil and American religion. *Kill the Faggot* originally appeared in the very popular online gaming site Steam, through a project called "greenlight," which is meant to give independent game developers an outlet. The game spent no more two hours on that site before it was taken down by administrators due to complaints from the community. The developer and "Christian shoe designer," Randall Herman claims the game makes a statement about "political correctness," which has become one of the code terms for supposed liberal overreach in recent political rhetoric. The argument might go something like: political correctness makes it impossible to continue to say hateful things of groups, about whom we have traditionally said hateful things, and is therefore ruining America, and impinging on our first amendment rights.

These "cheap" games also might raise a different issue about the questions of verisimilitude that seems to be a part of our discussions about rescriptions of the sacred. The low quality of these games inherently offers a less "realistic," less immersive experience. We could say that the low production values might make the line between actual and the virtual more evident; that because we could never mistake these games for the real or even the cinematic real, they have a less compelling connection to actual violence in the real world. Of these three games, *Ethnic Cleansing* comes closest to a full narrative game, but the characters are chunky and the architecture boxy. The story is: "the race war began yesterday, it's up to you keep the minorities from taking over." The people you kill are African-Americans, Mexicans and Jews. The game itself is very thinly veiled neo–Nazi propaganda. The game is photorealistic in the way that video games at the beginning of the *GTA* series were. What is provocative about the game is that the developers have decided to use the medium to deliver their message in a direct way. What they reveal on the screen in the game is not a fiction to them any more than what the makers of the *Left Behind* think about the rapture. Presenting it audio-visually through the medium of video games enhances rather takes away from their purposes.

The cinematic and televisual graphic seems to insinuate itself into our consciousness in ways that go beyond all other forms of representation; images projected onto a screen become hyperreal and more and more the lines between the real and the represented are blurred. In the popular imagination, projected images have become more influential than any other representational media. As in Catherine MacKinnon's argument, discussed in Chapter 3, in reference to pornography, representation *is reality*. As with pornography in the public sphere, there is something unseemly in the human interaction with video games that is viewed as inherently detrimental. Their relatively recent development as a media form may have something to do with this perception, but somehow, video games, particularly ones that depict violence, have an air of illegitimacy in the public consciousness. For example, *JFK Reloaded*, a game in which a player reconstructs various scenarios for the John F. Kennedy assassination, was released to "universal condemnation" and prompted then Senator Joseph Lieberman to say, "the fact that the assassination of President Kennedy, which broke our hearts and altered our history, could become the subject of a video game from which people are making money is just outrageous, it is despicable, it's unbelievable" (firstamendmentcenter.org). Yet, there have been dozens of books, movies, documentaries and television shows on the assassination and the various conspiracy theories related to it; all of which were ostensibly made for profit and escaped this kind of criticism.

It is difficult to determine the nature of the objections to the game, and these statements seem like rationalizations for an instinctual discomfort with the subject in the form of a *game*. Comments like Lieberman's signal a relationship of the gaming world to the popular culture and a feeling that there is an inherent trivialization of narrative in its conversion to a video game. It seems, however, paradoxical that these games are simultaneously trivial, deeply disturbing, and capable of training an average teenager into an assassin. Either they are "play" and are not to be taken seriously, or they are "real" and deserve serious attention. On some level the ludic aspects of the games might be responsible for the perception of so many that these games might be dangerous training grounds or inappropriate media for serious consideration or commentary on historical events. At the same time, the last ten years have seen a significant shift in academics, artists, students, and college curriculums taking the making, playing, and studying of video games more seriously. A recent critically acclaimed game seems to take the challenge of representing serious and personal subjects to its most extreme. *That Dragon Cancer* is a video game based on the experience of Ryan and Amy and their son Joel who was diagnosed with Atypical Teratoid Rhabdoid Tumor and died after many recurrences. The game has been read not as Lieberman read the Kennedy game, but more as a father's poignant tribute, which re-enacts the last years of his five-year-old son's life, as the boy dies of brain cancer. This game may signal the maturation of the form or perhaps of our attitudes toward it, since it can undertake such serious and personal subjects.

In this sense video games could serve as postmodern interactive morality plays that *toy with* the idea of the real by offering a cultural space where ethical and philosophical issues can be expressed and worked out. This is not a new idea; in medieval Europe the notion of ludae or plays served a didactic function that culminated with the Corpus Christi Cycles, where the plays served to teach a mostly illiterate populace their role in the Christian cosmological scheme. The plays, as might be expected, did not always follow strict Church dogma. The plays were instructive of the major precepts of Christian theology, but not without some controversy. Not only were they resisted by proto-Protestant Lollards and Wycliffites for their "trivialization" of Christian dogma, but matters of representation also became significant when human players/actors took on roles of God, Christ or Satan. A story is told of an actor playing the role of the devil who neglected to take off his costume, and on the way home scared his neighbors half to death.[8] The arguments made by John Wycliff in the fourteenth century and later by the Puritans against the plays are related to this sense of false reality and echo Plato's reservations about poetry (or drama). Today these arguments have been taken up in relation to interactive representations of reality, though film representation is sufficiently long standing to bypass such scrutiny.

The basic question seems to be how to treat a sensitive issue in a "game" or if it even is appropriate to do so, but part of this question is the relationship between representation and reality and ultimately how representation might affect reality, or how that which is represented might become real. These issues are reflected by the Devin Moore case. Jack Thompson's argument seems to be that the graphic representation and interactive function of the violence in *Grand Theft Auto III* and *Vice City* spilled over into the real world and effectuated a reality through its agent, Devin Moore. But, in some cases the "game" becomes even more intimately connected to actions in the real world and some cases where actions in the real word are performed and mediated through a game-like interface, as in the use of drones in military actions. The complications involved in comparisons between games and the "real world" apply as much to what we think of the physical world as much as the cultural word. According to Salen and Zimmerman, "The wider our cultural frame grows in defining game as culture, the more their artificiality begins to unravel.... They are not isolated from their environment, but are intrinsically part of it" (572). Video games are now so much more a part of the culture that they have certainly widened their cultural frames, such that they participate in the cultural negotiations that help shape the moral landscape of the culture. The ubiquity of video games and digital images might also be seen as part of a cultural shift away from words (or even the Word). While religion, especially Christianity, has been rooted in the book and the written word since the Renaissance, the twenty first century is one which, as Katherine Hayles writes, "Graphics, animation, design, video, and sound" become part of our "quest for meaning" (4).

If games can play a role in the development and understanding of a society whose moral compass is determined by simple equations and geopolitical ambitions, they may also contribute to defining more complex popular religious positions within the culture. Putatively "evil" games like *Grand Theft Auto* reinforce Christian values even as they attempt to transgress cultural and religious norms, while war-based games, like *Soldier of Fortune* and *Fugitive Hunter*—in focusing their attention on cartoonish Islamic villains—help to reify the notion of evil as established through political rhetoric in response to external attacks. Games like *Fallout 3*, attempt to recreate a post-apocalyptic moral "standard." Through the interaction of the real and the ludic, these games create spaces within which popular opinion can be organized and shaped along the lines of the rhetorical stance adopted by political leaders (the link between Bush and the Christian movements, for example, assured a certain level of portability between his stance and religious groups, but also to representations of the Iraq war in video games of the post 9/11 period). Video games therefore create a space within which popular culture exerts significant force on popular religion and vice versa. This factor becomes even more prevalent, as we shall see, when games are produced from within the fundamentalist Christian movement itself.

Fallout, Manhunt *and* Left Behind

In this next section, our aim is to interrogate connections between ideas about morality through an analysis and comparison of three games: *Left Behind: Eternal Forces* (the video game version of the evangelical novel series), *Manhunt* and *Fallout*. We will trace how socio-cultural ideas about morality are simultaneously articulated and resisted in these very different games, sometimes simultaneously and often inadvertently. The intentions of these games are quite different in relation to issues of morality and representation; nonetheless, each engages with the concepts from its own particular position. Depending on design and marketing strategy, the games make diverging statements relative to notions of morality, realism, and representation, but among violent video games, each one takes a position within the spectrum. While the creators of *Left Behind: Eternal Forces* see the game as a realignment of American values which reintegrates scriptural teaching and belief into the broader culture, *Manhunt* attempts to transgress those same values by creating a space of chaotic turmoil within which normative socio-cultural rules do not apply. In *Manhunt*, a game described by its own producers as exploring "the depths of human depravity in a vicious, sadistic tale of urban horror," we expect to see a complete violation of Christian morality, but actually, it can be seen as failing to break these cultural moorings. *Fallout* is a post-apocalyptic series, which represents the mood of a world destroyed by war, best exemplified by its opening narrative: "War never changes. The Romans waged war to gather slaves and wealth. Spain built an empire from its lust for gold and territory. Hitler shaped a battered Germany into an economic superpower. But war never changes." While each of these games, for its own purposes, creates a universe determined by a moral system shaped by contemporary values, directly in reaction to them, in each case, they attempt to escape the magnetic pull of culture but come up short and are thus always in conversation with it, always in tension.

Let's start with *Manhunt*. As the game begins, the player's avatar is James Earl Cash, a death row inmate, who is lethally injected in the first cut scene of the backstory. As it turns out, he is not *actually* put to death, but, in fact, "recruited" to be the "star" of a series of snuff films, in which he is hunted through derelict neighborhoods by several gangs. The instruction manual for the game is made to look like a snuff film catalogue from "Valiant Video Enterprises," with the various levels of the game representing "scenes" from the films directed by Lionel Starkweather. The first level of play, "Born Again," introduces us to gameplay and is described in the manual this way:

> ... we find Cash in the abandoned section of Carcer City, where the streets are patrolled by a gang (the Hoods), who have been hired by Starkweather to hunt Cash down. It's a night of kill or be killed for the delight of the director.... Starkweather [*Manhunt* manual].

The manual itself is a study in simulation, which raises some of the same questions about representation and reality that we see with war games. In this case, rather than legitimizing the efforts of the player in a noble cause, the game attempts to make the player complicit in a forbidden act. Remarkably, both intentions attempt to make the players' experience more "realistic" through the manipulation of their extra-ludic and extra-diegetic elements, like the catalogue/manual. In the manual/snuff film catalog, the different levels of the game are described as if they were individual snuff films, with instructions for how to order the films. The entire package with the box and manual represents an impossible object; for, it is a rather dubious item even for someone who produces snuff films to create. The catalog is meant to be an extension of the virtual space created on the screen to an object in the real world. The catalog is like "evidence" (a tangible memento from a created world) of the "reality" of the events in which the player will partake.

Many games participate in this kind of simulacrum, which again raises the question of the division between the "actual" and "virtual" spaces. The liminal space between the actual and the virtual is part of how video games, like much recent popular culture, are implicitly engaged in a project of redefining concepts such as religion and sacred. As Rachel Wagner suggests, "the question of where we situate the 'virtual' in relationship to the 'sacred' and the 'profane' exposes the indeterminacy in our own understanding of what religion even is, and how we can know it when we see it." Wagner refers to several incidents where real churches such as Manchester Cathedral in England charged Sony with "virtual desecration" for staging a shootout in a virtual version of the church. The cathedral even released its "Sacred Digital Guidelines," which included provisions that game designers "respect our sacred spaces as places of prayer, worship, peace learning and heritage," and "do not assume that sacred space interiors are copyright free" (Campbell and Grieve 5). Does this mean that the church sees its virtual doppelganger as somehow an extension of its own sacred space? In defending the virtual representation of their sacred space as somehow inherently connected to the "real" sacred, these churches seem to claim an extension of the sacred space into the virtual. The slipperiness of this issue connects back to the intent of war games, whose violence despite its graphic nature is excused because the "noble cause of Freedom" is somehow seen as having extension into the virtual space of the game or in the Devin Moore case where "virtual training" is transferred *mutatis mutandis* into the actual world.

Manhunt establishes rules that are meant to be transgressive, but almost simultaneously become interconnected with the normative. The simulation of the manual is meant precisely to bridge this gap between the virtual and the actual to create a narrative world in which the actions presented in the game are both abhorrent and "believable." The object of the game is to remain alive, while killing gang members (hunters), all the while Starkweather coaches Cash through an earpiece toward more and more gruesome killing. "C'mon, I want GORE," he screams as you hide in the shadows waiting to sever the next victim's head with a machete. Or he whispers, "This is making dull viewing," if you have not moved for a while. You progress in the game from having only your fists as weapons to a glass shard to eventually a chainsaw and guns. But, the most effective way to work through the levels of the game is to hide in the shadows and "execute" your victims when they do not expect it; bonus points are awarded for the more gruesome executions. The victims begin as the absolute bottom of society, giving an apparent moral rationalization for their slaughter.

The second-level baddies are made up of a gang which calls itself "The Skinz." They are a cobbled together combination of neo–Nazis or skinheads, who wear signs vaguely reminiscent of swastikas, and spout racist and homophobic slurs. While you hide in the shadows waiting to kill Skinz, you hear their constant ranting; most of them keep to the expected homophobic, racist and misogynist banter, but in some cases they have a persistent Christian theme. As the Skinz hunt for Cash, they utter biblically inspired phrases:

> Embrace your salvation and prostrate yourself before the Lord./We are here to save you, to show you the kingdom of the Lord./The Lord sees all./I will remove your serpent's skin./And Cain said unto the Lord, "My punishment is greater than I can bear" [*Manhunt*, level 2 "Born Again"].

The game's apparent attitude toward these characters gives these statements an ironic tone. The game seems to be suggesting that something about the nature of these beliefs ties them to a racist ideology. The Skinz also participate in the kind of jingoistic patriotism that is logically connectable to a literal interpretation of the rhetorical posture of evil as tangible or actual. "This is a good American method of justice," shouts one of the Skinz as they chase Cash wielding baseball bats, or "the real deal, asshole, one hundred percent American," as they converge on him.

These characters represent the worst stereotypical elements of American culture. They seem ignorant, stupid, and morally bankrupt. By showing them as both patriotic and religious, the game engages in stereotyping at the same time it transgresses the normative. On some level, this equation must be part of the cultural rankling that makes this game appear so corrosive to religious conservatives. Yet, there is something in casting these characters as fodder for the homicidal mill that creates a kind of moralist justification. These characters are not everyday citizens out for a stroll only to be murdered in cold blood. *Manhunt* participates in a system of right and wrong/good and evil that is entirely within the norm. While it attempts to transgress the religious-ethical system of culture with its violence and gore, it ultimately reifies the very cultural norms it attempts to transgress.

All of the gangs that hunt Cash are seen as somehow deserving of the punishment meted them. The player, then, can be seen as an agent of a crisis-driven retributive force that engages a somewhat divine justice in order to set things right. In each case, Cash is operating, first of all, in self-defense and secondly against the sort of human garbage that should not expect to survive judgment day. Unlike the war games' positioning of opponents as enemies of America, automatically making them justifiable targets, this game makes a specific argument for the circumstances of these characters and their deserved annihilation. As such, it engages much more thoroughly in the economy of justice for perceived evil. There is something to be said about a game that expects its convict anti-hero to represent the moral high ground; the player's role is situated clearly within bounds of normative morality. There is, however, a complex narrative event that is taking place here, as the player assumes some of Cash's morality while investing him with some of his or her own morality. Unlike the characters whom the player is to execute, the player is not only not in danger of taking immoral action, s/he is, in fact, called upon to make very serious moral decisions. This game thus forces its players to engage in a series of complicated moral puzzles, which continually test and ultimately frustrate attempts to locate evil as a stable and concrete concept.

Cash's agency, in fact, is central to an analysis of this game from a moral perspective. As we will see, when we discuss a fundamentalist Christian game, free will becomes an issue in explaining moral choices within the universe of gaming. The narrative of the game (of any game) restricts the possible choices made by the character/player, but some games allow the possibility of several moral choices while others do not. In *Manhunt*, the player is restricted, in some sense, to making only the better moral choices; that is, each action Cash takes is rationally and morally pre-scripted by the narrative. But, in each case, a morally sound argument can be made for the action. Although Cash must engage in violent, and in some cases, gruesome killing, he acts first and foremost out of self-defense. He is placed in the subjective position of victim within the story of the game and struggles to escape these circumstances. His antagonists are all coded as in some way deserving of their fate.

A rationale can be made for the moral propriety of each of Cash's choices. Ultimately, the message of this "transgressive" game upholds the moral norms of the culture. In the end, the corruptive force (Starkweather) is revealed for what he is, and those who have suffered are seen as deserving of their fate. From his fallen state Cash, and thereby the player, are redeemed within the overall arc of the narrative. The game re-inscribes the moral compass of most American religion and most action movies; the evil and the unjust are punished, those who have been the agents of that punishment are rewarded and allowed to go free. The game never completely escapes the bounds of a peculiar yet recognizable moral convention within which evil is recognized as the product of a human agent whose purpose in doing evil depends upon an unanalyzable external motivation or lack of integration into the culture. Like most villains, Starkweather has financial and material gain from his evil deeds, but the motivation for the acts goes well beyond pure materialism.

The player, however, occupies a relatively stable moral space firmly within bounds of popular religious ethical systems. The evil represented by Starkweather remains a concretized and unproblematic force throughout. The player's role in the narrative supports a non-complicated relationship with this force. The player's position as a narrativized agent, however, guarantees a certain level of moral involvement with the fictive world of the game. In progressing through the game, the player functions as a fully realized moral agent.

While *Manhunt* insists upon its depraved immoral gameworld, its reinforcement of normative cultural rules establishes its place firmly within the culture. Ultimately, neither Cash nor the player can escape the bounds of social order or moral action. The more the game struggles to break these bounds, the more entangled it becomes within them. The fact that Cash has been sentenced to death and, therefore, must have been convicted of a brutal crime creates the possibility for redemption. In killing Lionel Starkweather in the final scene, both Cash and the player exact a level of justice. In the process of the game, Cash is increasingly represented as victim of Starkweather rather than as a brutal killer, even though he is continually performing brutal killings. The evil force within the game, however, is not Cash, since evil is always the Other.

Virtual Armageddon

Cash and the player, by association, are bound to a set of moral principles and must employ those principles from a personal position in relation to an overwhelming evil. The first-person perspective guarantees a certain level of identification with the plight of the character and insures that the violence remains consequential. The opposite is true for *Left Behind: Eternal Forces*, which was released in October 2006 and lives on in a free online version. This game represents the evangelical movement's entrance into the world of violent video games. In the game, the player has an overhead view and is not actually a part of the story. A player moves forces around a map, builds necessary buildings (camps, banks, clinics, churches), makes spiritual or physical war against non-believers (including Jews and Muslims), and creates new converts to the post-apocalyptic fold. Despite the massive popularity of the books that the game was based on, it was immediately taken to task by liberal Christian groups even in advance of its release for promoting intolerance. On the other hand, *Left Behind* author Jerry Jenkins writes that the game is

> beautifully rendered, clearly carries our message (indeed, we have already heard of one young man who has become a believer through playing it), ... and is no more violent than the Lone Ranger or Roy Rogers episodes I grew up watching. Unlike typical video games that show buckets of blood and flying body parts, victims shot in our game fall in a puff of smoke [Left Behind.com].

Jenkins, however, focuses only on the representational aspects of rendering and such, but not on the abstract violence of, say, forced conversion.

The game is based on the doomsday scenario detailed in the *Left Behind* book series, the Rapture. As is often pointed out, the premise for the Rapture actually has little direct scriptural support.[9] The whole plot possibly evolves out of the nineteenth-century-vision of a Scottish teenager, Mary Macdonald, and was popularized in nineteenth-century America by Cyrus I. Scofield, whose *Scofield Study Bible* remains the most popular reference Bible in the United States. Scofield and others are responsible for developing a system of biblical interpretation known as dispensationalism. According to this theory, biblical ages can be sectioned off into seven "dispensations," each with its own theme. Armageddon is the last dispensation and begins with the Rapture of God's people, followed by seven years of "Tribulation," and then the return of Jesus Christ for a millennial reign on Earth. Once he returns there will be a great war between the armies of Jesus and the Antichrist on the plains of Maggido in Israel.

In this end-time scenario, when "God's people" are taken up (or raptured) bodily to heaven they leave behind those who are not "saved." The game makes clear assumptions about those who have and have not been saved. For example, in the training sessions before the actual game begins there is a character who has returned to New York after being on a mission in Africa, where all of the missionaries have been raptured. The game thus implies that missionaries are "saved." The game begins with only some characters under the control of the player. Through the recruiting efforts of these characters, the player builds forces to counteract the evil of the Antichrist, Nicholae Carpathia. In perhaps the game and the books' most subtle move, the army of the Antichrist is called the Global Community Peacekeepers, a not-so-veiled allusion to the United Nations—which some in the evangelical community reads as a sign of the apocalypse—while the "good guys" are known as the Tribulation Forces. The goal of the game is to spread the "Truth" of the rapture and ultimately defeat the forces of the Antichrist.

While *Left Behind: Eternal Forces* does not contain anywhere near as much representational violence as *Manhunt*, it may, in the end be read as more transgressive of cultural norms. The position the player occupies does not allow him/her to be a moral agent:

> You do not personally participate in the action; you *command* your *units* to perform tasks by giving orders via the game interface. You can order them where to go and what to do whenever you wish. (*Left Behind: Eternal Forces* Manual 9; emphasis added)

The "real people" that are recruited into the cause have no real moral choices either. The game is populated with people, all of whom have a back story. "Each person is an individual—with a name, and a background making them unique—there are no faceless masses here" (*Eternal Forces* manual 23). However, these unique individuals do not have a choice when you *command* them. Once an individual is recruited, he or she will answer every command with a positive platitude; when you command a "friend" to walk across the street they will respond with something like, "Praise the Lord," and immediately begin to move. Ironically and surprisingly, the only possible position from which to play the game is the God-view, which makes it impossible to become a moral agent within the game; every move a player makes bears an uncomplicated connection to spreading the gospel of "Truth." This uncomplicated relationship to an action becomes more morally suspect as one engages in both spiritual and physical warfare against the forces of the Antichrist.

In its structure, the game resembles the rhetorical deployment of evil as a concrete construct, whose boundaries are plainly drawn and seen. The Tribulation Forces could be seen as the U.S. forces in the War on Terror. It is a simple matter to identify those who are evil and their motivation for doing evil. Again, they are evil because they are against us, because they resist our truth and values, because they stand in the way of Freedom. This freedom, however, is not expressed through individual choices made by the characters, who are, of course, denied this possibility. The characters respond in prescribed ways without thought.

The extreme anti-intellectual bias of much fundamentalism is in clear view in this game. Suggestively, training for different positions in the Tribulation Forces takes place in appropriate locations; if you want to train a "friend" to be a medic, you send him to a clinic, hospital or trauma center; a recruiter is trained at a Mission Training Center, but for the Global Peacekeeper Forces (the bad guys), professions as unlikely as Rock Star/Pop Star, Pretender, and Gang Boss are all trained at "college." We can perhaps assume that all those who went to college, having lost their faith, have now become easy prey to the immoral temptations of the Antichrist. If this is the case, the game makes certain assumptions about the value of "secular" education and moral vulnerability represented by intellectual pursuit.

Casting doubt on the academy is clearly an intentional move on the part of the game developers, just like the overt sexism of a game in which "individual" women can only be trained for two possible occupations; women can be musicians or nurses, but cannot be builders, recruiters, or soldiers. The game makes a very clear choice in reinscribing old patriarchal roles for women and men as a way of representing what might be described as family values. The game deliberately proposes that the source of much evil in society comes from colleges and mistaken gender roles; it inadvertently argues for dogged social ignorance.

Left Behind: Eternal Forces also perhaps inadvertently presents intolerance as a kind of virtue—those who are not Christian (more specifically, fundamentalist and apocalyptic Christians) are depicted as at best misguided and at worst downright evil. They are in need of conversion: "You're not simply trying to 'win,' you're literally changing the world around you with each person who hears the truth" (*Eternal Forces* 25). And indeed "hearing the truth" is all that is required; one might expect that conversion might occur through a process, perhaps even a dialogue, but what really happens in the game to signify a conversion is that a character is spoken to silently by a recruiter until a glowing light appears. At this point, the new recruit becomes a servile automaton who will follow any commands issued by the player without question (except for those times when they are stuck behind a lamppost because of the game's bad AI).

The very conditions of society within the world of the game become problematic because, of course, by definition those who are left to lead the Tribulation Forces are those who were not as strong in their faith, perhaps not as morally upright as those who were among "the believers in Christ of the Earth" who have been extracted away in the rapture. While the game proposes (as do the books) that the "Truth" of what has happened is a stable sign, this fact might make us doubt the assertions of those who now claim to know what the "Truth" is. The lesson of *Left Behind: Eternal Forces* seems to be that evil is a simple dichotomous thing that can be overcome with sudden pulses of prayer.

Good, Neutral or Evil

In the end, *Left Behind: Eternal Forces*, the game which insists on the individual uniqueness of each of its represented characters ("no faceless masses here"), categorizes people into only three possible moral conditions: good, neutral or evil. While the game does indeed provide a backstory for each character, complete with "spiritual history," this feature is accessed by the player through a pull-down menu, which renders those histories ancillary to the main focus of the game. One can certainly read all of the individual stories, written in the stilted prose of the novels, but it is only determining which of these three categories characters belong to that is important to gameplay. Thus the game casts the conflict between good and evil in clear and stark terms; those who are neutral to the obvious truth are only waiting to be convinced, not by reasoned argument but by a flash of light. As we discussed in Chapter 2, the characteristic American conversion experience occurs instantly. Those who are evil have been deceived by "Pretenders," most likely trained at college, and must either be converted or dealt with through violence.

Attempting to give the characters fully rounded lives within the universe of the game, while providing only three possible moral positions, reveals a fundamentalist worldview. It is a view that echoes the Manichean world described by Edward Said in which two forces clash relentlessly against each other in an uncomplicated structure within which truth, virtue, and value are univocal possessions of one ideological position and all other thoughts, ideas, and beliefs are on the other side, the side of evil. Evil here is defined, like George Bush's rhetorical terms, as a clear and unambiguous mission to be taken up by "good folks." Evil ultimately serves as a militaristic emblem for the defeat of which the forces of good are obliged to muster an army. But the evil the game developers want to portray in the game is a real evil, a war against evil which they are fighting and for which they want to recruit the player.

The game developers, as do the authors of the novels, claim a scriptural basis for the events described under the umbrella term of the "Rapture." The main scriptural source for this belief is in the Book of Revelation where the time of tribulation is described. However, the application as used in these works presumes an interpretation of the text of Revelation—like that suggested by the Scofield Bible—that is simply impossible given the structure of that text. Revelation is a notoriously difficult text, which reads much more like dream vision than prophecy. But in both the game and novel versions, *Left Behind* makes an unambiguous construct of the events to come. They then present these "facts" not as interpretations of scripture, but as a new kind of scripture. By presenting them in video game form, Left Behind Games hopes to access the broad didactic range of gameplay. They hope to counteract the "evil" of other violent video games that do not present the same "positive" message.

In so doing, the game engages with a rhetorical organization that places evil as a distinct and palpable construct with clear boundaries and a simple binary structure, and moreover would seem to argue for some slippage between the fictive world and the real. The actions in the game are not just a representation of the real thing, but are on some level The Real. The arguments for why the interactivity of video games presents a moral problem is paradoxically confirmed and denied. The argument might seem to be that while violent video games like *Manhunt* or *Grand Theft Auto* use their power of hyperrealism for immoral desensitizing evil, this game is using it for "good." Just as with war-themed games which serve to inculcate a sense of patriotism and righteous justice on the players, *Eternal Forces* helps to do exactly what the players' goals are in the game: disseminate the "truth" to more lost souls and save the world from evil.

Left Behind: Eternal Forces transmutes religious interpretation into a sociopolitical action plan. The game thus represents a rescription; it, like the eponymous novel series, becomes an instrument of American evangelism that recapitulates much of the rhetorical framework that places the United States as the ultimate arbiter of justice and goodness in the world by virtue of its exceptionalism and its strict adherence to an Evangelical teaching. As we have seen, this is a common condition of American religious experience; forms of popular cultural productions instantiate new creeds, new belief systems, and ultimately become conflated with the sacred until they themselves become consecrated texts and their ideas become interchangeable and indistinguishable from their predecessors.

Truly Virtual, Virtually True

While *Eternal Forces* attempts to instill a specific morality driven its own eschatological theories, the game series *Fallout*[10] (we will focus on *Fallout 3* specifically) is an apocalyptic scenario based on post-nuclear war. In a sense, the *Fallout* series has much in common with the *Left Behind* game, in that they both involve an apocalyptic vision of the future. The apocalypse itself has become an important trope in much popular culture production, from religiously prophesied destruction to the ravages of zombies on the human psyche, eschatological themes provide a popular frame to either express or interrogate notions of the end of human civilization. Games, films, television dramas, documentaries, and scientists all offer various "secular" apocalyptic scenarios, however, we often find them relying on a religious or theological vocabulary to express their narrative. Whether we are talking about religious notions of the end of the world or the ruins left behind by nuclear holocaust, video games provide a more tactile experience, which could be read as providing moral lessons to its players, whether it is about getting saved, saving the culture after the fall of civilization, or accepting the end of the human race.

In *Fallout*, the cause of the apocalypse is war, in this case war against the Chinese, who invade Alaska for its natural resources. In terms of moral compass, this game is quite different from either *Manhunt* or *Left Behind* in that it does not seek to establish a moral position. The game begins with the player's avatar at birth, and we soon begin working on our character. The first few scenes of the game involve the character's childhood: a toddler, a teenager, and eventually, as a young adult the player's avatar takes the "Generalized Occupational Aptitude Test" (GOAT), which helps to determine what skills your character will be first assigned. Everything you do helps to determine who you will become in the game. On some level, the game is a thought experiment based on the questions of nature versus nurture.

As players go up in levels, they continue to add points to areas of their personality. Players can distribute skill points as they see fit: choosing from the morally suspect to righteous traits. There is a Karma scale, and while Karma points can be lost for morally dubious actions, such as stealing, the scale always remains vague and there are some limitations to having "all good" Karma. For example, certain potential alliances are inaccessible if the Karma level is too high. There are also times when what seems to be the most morally correct action results in a disadvantage. In one early encounter, the player discovers a plot against the local sheriff. There is an option to warn the sheriff, who appears to be a good man, about the plot against him. This seems to be the right thing to do, but telling him results in his death. In other words, as in real life, good actions do not necessarily lead to good outcomes.

The game calls upon the player to continually make morally difficult choices; yet it neither rewards nor penalizes those choices based upon simple structure of good and evil. In one later episode, the player is trying to rescue a young man who has left his home where his parents are found dead. He is reported as being held hostage by an "evil" group. When we find where he is being held, we discover that the people holding him are "Vampires," but, what they actually are can probably be best described as blood cannibals. To rescue the young man, the player has two choices: one is to kill every "Vampire" in order to get to him. The other is to talk to them. Option one leads to the unfortunate discovery (after killing more than a dozen people) that the young man was responsible for killing and eating his own parents and had afterward been "rescued" by the Vampires, who while admittedly cannibalistic "never consume of the flesh." (Oh, and, you have to kill the kid too, because he will not be taken alive.) Option two leads to the discovery of the real circumstances of the kid, before killing anyone. Eventually a deal can be brokered with the "Vampires" to return the kid to his sister. The game does not reward this outcome except with good Karma (which, again, is of dubious value); in fact, as heartbreaking as option one is, choosing it gets you all the ammo and goods of those you kill, and would be the more profitable option for the player.

Like television shows such as *The Walking Dead* or *The Leftovers*, one of the ways the game attempts to show a broader moral spectrum is how it presents religion within its universe. In the game, as you explore the "waste-lands" of Washington, D.C., you encounter a number of strange and some-times ghastly religious beliefs. In Megaton, one of the first "towns" we come to, we find the "Children of Atom." This group worships the still live and unexploded nuclear bomb sticking up out of the ground in the center of town. As one walks through town, Cromwell, the leader of the Children of Atom, can be seen and heard preaching while standing in irradiated water. He shouts things like: "Give your bodies to Atom, my friends. Release yourself to his power, feel his Glow and be divided." The Church of the Children of Atom has a dispensationalist view as they believe that the power of atom is the power to initiate the great division. The great division is not unlike the rapture. The children of atom will be "divided" and their atoms will create new worlds. Much later in the game, after the player has helped provide puri-fied water throughout the wasteland, a splinter group will form that is putting radiation back into the water and calling it holy.

These religious groups can be understood as misguided, but are gener-ally not evil. There are genuinely evil groups in the game; not the least of which are the slavers. One mission requires the player to rescue a young boy who has been taken by slavers; there are a few options for accomplishing this. The most satisfying (though considerably more difficult) is to infiltrate the slavers barracks and then kill every one of them before finding the boy and getting him back to his group. As with the mission to save the young man from the vampires, there are different less violent options, like talking to the slavers; however, this option causes the player to have to do a mission for the slavers. This mission involves hunting down an escaped slave and placing a shock collar around his neck allowing the slavers to control him. Again, there is not much reward for either of these options; but even while the expenditure of ammo and health make the first option a losing proposition, what we know of the slavers makes this option the most attrac-tive.

In the end, the game does not force or push you to make the morally correct decision. As in real life, making difficult moral decisions often results in a disadvantage for moral agents. The moral lesson of *Fallout 3* is that there are many times when you will need to make difficult moral choices and you can choose to make "good" or "bad" choices and they will have varying degrees of success. In this sense, the game approaches a unique form of moral realism. The notion of a score as a motivating factor has been to some extent expanded to realistic complexity. You can amass a great deal of wealth (in the form of bottle caps, the game's main currency), but it would be hard to describe that as the object of the game. One could perhaps play for speed, getting through the many intricate missions as quickly as possible, but after the release of the much anticipated *Fallout 4*, players were instead proudly bragging, not about what level they had reached, but how many hours they had spent in the game's world.

The rules of the game create an open moral environment, so that rather than focusing on any one message the player is immersed in a complex moral universe, which does in fact function to a limited extent as "the real" moral universe. Rather than presenting the player with the spiritual histories of random characters in pull down menu, the player builds relationships with certain characters by force of continued interaction. There are merchants the player deals with continuously, trading goods and bottle caps for services, and people you have saved or interacted with in other ways. All of these interaction help to shape a morally complex world.

Game Over

More than just morality, though, looking closely at these games and the reactions to them, points to cultural shifts in defining what a religion is, in thinking about finitude and endings, and the role of preserving cultural memory. As we have already outlined, because of their position in the culture, video games, as a form of cultural production, represent a significant site to interrogate some of the basic tenets of American culture regarding moral and religious issues. As video games, virtual reality, artificial intelligence, and digital technology change how we think about texts, about narrative, about place, and about scripture, each become more reproducible or alterable, rendering place and text as less material and less unique, if not less "sacred." They function sometimes to reiterate popular beliefs and convenient political stances, but they can create genuinely complex moral tests, and they are often read by moral conservatives for the role they play in boosting already existent pockets of transgressive behaviors such as violence and a-normative sexual practices. Like film, advertising, and television, they work to render explicit ideas, sentiments and prejudices always at work under the surface of the culture. As the views of conservative Christians begin to be digitized into the arena of video gameplay, this category of cultural product becomes even more representative of American identity. Conservatives may continue to rail against the effects of these games and the "moral decay" to which they are said to contribute, but they will remain a crossroads at which philosophical positions, political rhetoric, jingoistic patriotism and religious and social mores meet and get played out, discussed and reflected back to society.

The history of Western religions is full of debates over doctrine and practice revolving around intersecting issues of body and text and the resulting tension over a belief in the "real." Perhaps the most important point we have made in this chapter claims a new kind of blurring between real and virtual; at the same time that video games have become more "realistic," actual lived reality often looks more like a video game. Both fighter planes in video games and drones being deployed and controlled at a distance appear as digitized dots on a screen. Surgeons operate on actual patients thousands of miles away using screens and tools reminiscent of video games. Churches exist and function online, as well as in virtual worlds like *Second Life*. Many Americans date, watch television, work, worship, play, and read scripture through the same electronic device. What we see throughout all of these examples is a changing tension that is in many ways not that different from debates over the nature of Christ, the explanation of the eucharist, or the coherence of the Qur'an.

As was demonstrated throughout the nineteenth and twentieth centuries, and as we continue to see in the twenty first, science is often a major force behind theological change, and, within the popular imagination, is often seen as oppositional to religious faith. Recent innovation in digital, genetic, biotechnological, and cybernetic science have led to increased anxieties about the clear boundaries of the human body, and have initiated a new sense of uncertainty about our bodily presence which has deep significance in our religious beliefs and practices. In video games, but also through social media, we create online bodiless 'avatars' through which we experience much of the world; the concept of gender is no longer fixed, either psychologically or physically; reproduction can occur outside of sexual activity; eyes, limbs, and organs are replaced with increasing ease; and the ubiquity of smart phones and portable devices has partially replaced or augmented memory.

The human body—a traditional guarantor of certainty ("if I can feel it, it is real")—is now imagined in multiple ways that push at the boundaries of material reality. Religious rituals and practices are almost always associated with the body, but what happens when the rituals include virtual altars and online pilgrimages to Mecca? But although a body-less context such as the internet or a video game provides new opportunities for creating religious identities, their construction is still a social process. What has changed, however, is that many of these spaces are virtual. These spaces can be Christian or Wiccan chat rooms, ornate digital mosques, or English cathedrals swarming with aliens. Sacred spaces and texts, too, have long been defined by physical demarcation; a space is said to be sacred because it offers separation from the outside world, a Torah or Qur'an is treated differently from an ordinary object or book. But, again, what happens when that space or text is accessed through a laptop or an iPhone? When they are juxtaposed with music, TV shows, pornography, and shopping lists?

There is, of course, strong resistance in both traditional and new forms of worship toward accepting this new digital world. Bret McCrackle, evangelical author of a book on "hipster Christianity," writes "When it comes to church, we don't want cool as much as we want real" (*WSJ*, Aug. 13, 2010). What this statement does not acknowledge, however, is that the concept of the "real" is a fluid one, socially constructed by technology as well as religion, and that our new virtual world has changed what the "real" even is. What this means within the world of religious beliefs and practices is that a centuries old negotiation between body and soul and between real and imagined is being once again worked out through forms of public discourse. Video games, virtual reality, and online communities are practices of creating meaning and narrative that are on the forefront of changes and shifts in how we understand the terms through which we define the very act of being human and religious.

Epilogue
The Practice of Rescripting

Rethinking religion as a form of cultural work, the study of lived religion directs attention to institutions and person, texts and rituals, practice and theology, things and ideas—all as media of making and unmaking worlds.

—Robert Orsi

We in here talking about practice. I mean, listen, we're talking about practice, not a game, not a game, not a game, we talking about practice. Not a game.

—Allen Iverson, Press Conference, May 7, 2002

In the epilogue to the first edition, we addressed the so-called "new atheism" and its role in popular culture and popular religion. As polls indicate, various identifications with forms of atheism and unbelief were and are still an important subject in the early twenty-first century. Shortly after our book came out, President Obama's first inaugural address mentioned—for the first time—unbelievers along with the obligatory religious references, and, as we have pointed out, the number of Americans who do not identify as belonging to any religious group continues to rise.

But while we acknowledged that the importance of this popular "atheistic literary wave" (Van Biema 50), we also characterized and criticized many of their positions on religion as "limited" or as "monolithic and simplified." Many texts of popular culture, we argued, offer a more nuanced and sophisticated way of processing religious ideas. One idea we developed throughout the book and in the epilogue was what we called a "contradictory and double movement in the idea of the divine" (204). In other words, texts of popular culture—unlike either fundamentalist dogma or absolute atheism—offered a way of thinking about the tension between a determinate God of unity and a God of uncertainty and impossibility, or the tension between desire, doubt, and certitude in a divine force. In a sense, the cultural products we examined had a necessarily more complex and nuanced relationship to these tensions, than either a fundamentalist atheism or Christianity. What has changed, and what we have tried to add to this edition is not that these contradictions have ceased to be, but how they have worked on and shifted the essence of popular culture and popular religion. These contradictions and tensions are still major themes in this second edition, but, as we said in the introduction, part of understanding shifts in both religious scholarship and popular understandings of religion involves a current shift away from a focus on doctrine to a focus on "lived religion."

In a thought experiment, Graham Harvey argues that if we indeed define Christianity as a "belief in God," then—since no other religion defines itself this way—either "Christianity is the only religion, or it is not a religion at all" (43). His point is that if we are to consider the concept of religion as connecting some commonality between Christianity and Judaism, Islam, Buddhism and other religions, we have to move outside of the fundamental vocabulary of "belief," belief in," and "faith" and think instead of what people *do*.

Thinkers such as philosopher Peter Sloterdijk or religious studies scholar Russell McCutcheon have gone so far as to suggest versions of replacing the word or concept of "religion" with some version of "practice." The term or category of "religion" itself—according to Russell McCutcheon—"has no explanatory value whatsoever" (23). McCutcheon encourages a purely social definition of religion, not the "internal" definition that terms like faith and belief suggest. McCutcheon claims to have "no interest in what religion *really* is … instead, my interest has everything to do with *how* and *why* human communities divide up, classify, and ontologize their *ad hoc* social worlds in particular ways" (xi). For Sloterdijk, there is no such thing as religion, it is a modern invention that describes what is better seen as practices of human self-fashioning, some retaining a continuity with past practices more than others. Modernity, according to him, has developed this "practicing life" and in the process has blurred the lines between traditionally "spiritual" practices and the various activities of modern life.

But how do ideas of social or "lived" religion or practice, apply to the ideas of "rescripting"—an essentially text-based concept or metaphor—as we have developed them in this book? Paradoxically, our metaphor is grounded in the aftermath of Gutenberg's invention and its influence on religious practices of the reformation era. Today, as we see a radical shift toward the digital world, "icons" have again become important in the religious habits of believers. Our metaphor is not so much anachronistic as it is an extension—through an almost vestigial trace—of the idea of logos. Whether the "Word" is spoken or written down is cognitively significant to the individual and has an epistemological effect on culture.

Popular culture not only rescripts how we think, and read, and believe. It also reframes the practices of engaging with what we think of as religious, scriptural, or theological. One way—in some ways the only way—to see just how communities perform these actions that we then call religious, is to look at the texts of popular culture and observe how humans interact with them. For example, the traditionally religious questions of what it means to die are explored through watching *Buffy the Vampire Slayer*, *True Blood*, and *The Walking Dead*, but also through writing fan fiction about these shows or dressing as your favorite zombie for Comic Con. Death is also explored in games, like *Fallout*, in which "a life" is lived through game practices. Though the player may "die" many times, they are always returned to the moment just before "death," to continue the one overarching life. At the end, the life of a player—through recounting of their exploits—is memorialized as the game credits roll. Popular and religious practices of death and memorialization were juxtaposed when fans brought flowers to Paisley Park to commemorate Prince's death, or had an all-night all-Prince dance party in the streets of Brooklyn or in a Minneapolis club. Each of these actions—a combination of bodily practices, social interaction, ritual, imaginative narrative, and philosophy—as much as receiving last rites or sitting Shiva, continues to reframe how we imagine ourselves in this world and what happens outside the borders of what we can know.

While popular religion may reify, simplify or abridge concepts like death, when juxtaposed with popular culture they reveal complexities and nuances not often acknowledged within public religious discourse. Whether one believes that the Bible is the word of God or not, the "book" and the "work" are still determinate and determining concepts of closure. It is these concepts that popular culture and its complicated symbiotic and antagonistic relationships to popular religion can serve to destabilize and to open up. The texts of popular culture, then, perform the rescripting that we have been describing, through the repetition of viewers, players, and fans who return again and again to practice what Robert Orsi calls the "making and unmaking of meaning" that we find in the lived practice of rescripting and which has become, in many ways, the modern popular religious experience. But, it is also a bilateral process, as religious practices will simultaneously continue to inform, reshape, and rewrite the products of popular culture.

Chapter Notes

Chapter 1

1. For example, Emil Durkheim and Mircea Eliade are major figures in the traditional study of religion that stress the separation of the sacred and the profane as a defining characteristic.

2. Patrick Allitt, for example, introduces his *Religion in America Since 1945: A History* by citing four general paradoxes: A simultaneously highly religious and highly secular environment, an unprecedented level of Christian wealth whose inspirational figure, Jesus, clearly spoke out against both riches and planning for the future, a technologically forward looking religious movement that claims a nostalgia for a golden past, and an intensely conflicted religious ideology about the most basic questions of the nature of life (xii).

3. Philosopher Hent de Vries makes this connection between miracles and special effects, claiming that in the modern world the "miracle" and the "special effect" may resemble each other formally and phenomenologically (23); the juxtaposition of the two, in both films like *Star Wars* and contemporary religious ritual, is part of the complex relationship popular religion has with the role of magic.

4. As a side note, further increasing the complexity and irony of the situation, at the same time that sports columnists were chastising Ward—often, like Berkow, through quoting the Bible—the front pages of New York papers were running articles about Pope John Paul visiting the Syrian President Bashar al-Assad, who was making even more crude statements blaming Jews for the murder of Christ, and extending the blame to modern Jews. The Pope chose not to jeopardize his visit by making any kind of a strong condemnation, and the New York papers, for the most part, chose not to criticize the Pope for his silence.

5. See, for two contrasting examples, Karen Armstrong's introduction to *The Battle for God* or Jacques Derrida's essay "Faith and Knowledge: The Two Sources of 'Religion' at the Limits of Reason Alone."

6. In *Serving the Word*, Vincent Crapanzano makes the claim that "Literalism in the United States is far more widespread than most realize or are even prepared to accept" (xvii). The book discusses the literalism of conservative evangelicalism, legal originalism, and the religious right as a "system of interpretation" (xxi).

7. What has been almost lost in the history, however, is O'Connor's original statement about the reason for her actions—a statement haunting in its foreshadowing of later events.

> It's not the man, obviously—it's the office and the symbol of the organization that he represents.... In Ireland we see our people are manifesting the highest incidence in Europe of child abuse. This is a direct result of the fact that they're not in contact with their history as Irish people and the fact that in the schools, the priests have been beating the shit out of the children for years and sexually abusing them.

Chapter 2

1. See, for example, Nathan Hatch, R. Laurence Moore, Harold Bloom, and Jon Butler.

2. Several places have claimed to be the birthplace of baseball. The most familiar and romantic is Cooperstown, New York, the

home of the Baseball Hall of Fame. The more probable is Hoboken, New Jersey.

3. There are, of course, many interesting studies outlining differences in the culture of Japanese baseball and American baseball.

4. It is significant to note here that ESPN initially refused to mention or cover fantasy sports, but now—realizing that it is a major interest for their viewing audience—they run special episodes dedicated to players of fantasy sports.

Chapter 3

1. What is interesting in the "War on Christmas" is that the arguments that are presented tend to ignore the tensions that exists (or should exist) between unchecked capitalism and one of the central messages of Christ. "It is easier for a camel to pass through the eye of a needle than to for a rich man to enter the kingdom of heaven" (Mathew 19:24) would seem to stand in contradiction to the promise of capitalism and consumer culture. Of course this tension between wealth and piety is not a new one in Christianity and goes back to at least the Middle Ages.

2. For example, Pastor Ted Haggard, the founder of the wildly successful New Life Church in Colorado Springs, advocates what he calls a "free market" approach to the divine in an attempt to "harness the forces of free-market capitalism into our ministry" (Sharlet 47). Ironically, Haggard's November 2006 revelation that he had paid a male prostitute for sex generated some interesting questions about the desire and the forbidden.

3. See, for example, *Desiring God*, by Charles Winquist.

4. The American Child Pageant Association online claims the industry is worth approximately $55 billion a year.

5. The six-year-old beauty queen and daughter of John and Patsy Ramsey was found dead in her Boulder, Colorado, home on Christmas Day.

Chapter 4

1. Most famously was the uproar over the use of the song for a Pepsi advertisement that was almost immediately pulled from circulation. What is most interesting is that it was the video that incited the controversy—the ad, which just featured Madonna performing the song, was only deemed offensive after the video changed the meaning of the song.

2. "Michael Brown rapped about violence, smoking weed, making big money, and having sex with 'hos,'" O'Reilly wrote. "That does not automatically mean he was a thug. Far worse, it shows that he was not all that different from so many other young men who are stewing in a pernicious culture that glorifies violence and misogyny."

3. As Robert Orsi points out, the American religious community's protest of the video also reflects a cultural animosity to the popular religious strains of Italian Catholicism: statues coming to life and bleeding, stigmata, and the blurring of sexuality with worship (225).

4. Saint Martin de Porres, an important saint within the Hispanic and Spanish Catholic church, was a Dominican Friar in the early 17th century who was born of a Spanish noble father and a black slave mother. He challenged racial barriers within the church and is today often presented as an obviously racially mixed or black icon.

5. Kanye West's 2016 *The Life of Pablo* included updating beats, tweaking lyrics, and altering the track list for weeks following the album's "release."

Chapter 5

1. Reported in most major news outlets (including Peggy Noonan in *The Wall Street Journal*) in December of 2003, this story was later denied by official Vatican spokesmen including Archbishop Stanislaw Dziwisz, who had been initially identified as the source.

2. The reason for this chronological discrepancy may be that John, by placing the Crucifixion of Jesus on the day of Passover preparation, allows him to be symbolically linked to the Passover lambs that were also slaughtered that day in preparation for the meal.

3. The 1999 "Sensation" exhibit at the Brooklyn Museum, which included the Ofili painting, drew ire from then Mayor Rudolph Giuliani, who attempted to close the exhibit down on the basis of anti-Catholic charges.

4. For a detailed discussion of this aspect of the film see Timothy Beal's "They Know Not What They Watch" in Beal, ed., *Mel Gibson's Bible*.

Chapter 6

1. These kinds of acknowledgment of fans and fan activities within the content material

of the show have become more and more common, perhaps best represented in a show like *Supernatural* in which episodes have been based on the characters' visit to a fan convention devoted to the show itself.

2. The shift in fan identity as seen by marketers transcends traditional market demographics. Comic Con attendees or fans of *Game of Thrones* are now more usefully grouped by interest than by age, race, education or other markers. "Demographics are a hangover from mass marketing which is increasingly becoming less effective with the change in technology, culture, and connectedness." A much better measure says Karl Long (creative strategist interested in human behavior, games, technology, design, and more) at Quora.com, is psychographics, which groups potential users not by large categories like age, race, or social class, but by shared interests, behavior, etc.

3. For example, in writing about *The Walking Dead*, a scholar may find useful information and analysis in one of the many published collections of scholarly essays, a piece in the entertainment blog The A.V. Club, or on a fan run site such as *The Walking Dead Wiki*. More importantly, these formerly separate discursive worlds now more commonly draw on each other and even feature some of the same writers.

4. An October 2015 article in *The Atlantic* titled "The Rise of Buffy Studies" accurately points to the continued production of critical writing about *Buffy* and also demonstrated several misconceptions still common in mainstream media. The article recognized the hundreds of scholarly books and articles as well as the academic journal *Slayage* and the conference organized by the Whedon Studies Association. The article, however, while offering a recognition to what had long been known by both fans and scholars, revealed a fundamental misunderstanding by claiming that the scholarly interest in the show "points to the growing belief that TV shows deserve to be studied as literature." This claim has several problems which any serious television watcher or media studies college freshman would instantly recognize. "Literature," with a capital "L" should no longer be seen as inherently more valuable or "deserving" of study than any other type of text; and, even more importantly, to study a TV show "as" literature, is a misguided approach to studying television. While shows like *Buffy* can certainly

be studied through familiar literary approaches such as theme, irony, symbol, and ambiguity, to do so without taking into account the specific television aspects of camera angle, music, acting, episodic structure, advertising, DVD extras, and fan communities is a limiting and reductive approach. *The Atlantic* was correct, however, in pointing to the massive amount of critical writing about *Buffy* that continues to be produced and consumed, and it is also the show that arguably has produced the most commentary on its relationship to religion—from fans to critics to philosophers to theologians.

5. See Jack Miles, for example, in *God: A Biography*.

6. Sources include Janet Reiss's book *What Would Buffy Do* and Reid B. Locklin's *"Buffy the Vampire Slayer* and the Domestic Church" in *Slayage* 6, or, in a more popular vein, websites like Pastor Steve's Buffy Page.

7. For further discussion of the theological implications of this line, see Gregory Erickson's "'Religion Freaky: Or a Bunch of Men Who Died?' The (A)theology of Buffy" in *Slayage* 14.

8. A typical fan dismissal of Season Six complains that "the writing was off and not as good and you can not just send all the characters into the dumps, especially Buffy herself, and expect it to be interesting to watch every week. To add fuel to the fire, the villains were geeks? Maybe in another show that might be funny but it didn't fit here... Spike and Buffy beating the crap out of each other and then having sex. Sorry, not interesting in the least" (NetFlix review).

9. And, in fact, for many fans of the show, the 2000-year-old vampire Godric is a strong Christ-like figure who turns from evil to good and sacrifices himself in an episode entitled "I Will Rise Up" (2.9).

Chapter 7

1. For a discussion of this facet of the philosophical view of "evil," see Susan Neiman's *Evil: An Alternative Philosophical History*.

2. In Bertrand Russell's *History of Western Philosophy*, for example, there are more index entries for Egypt than evil.

3. There go the ships,
and Leviathan that you formed to sport in it.
These all look to you
To give them their food in due season. (Psalm 104:27)

You broke the heads of the dragons in the waters
You yourself crushed the heads of Leviathan. (Psalm 74: 13–14)

4. The Satan in the book of Job, for example, is not the figure of pure evil that later Christians made him out to be, but is instead portrayed as an "adversary" and is not the opposite of God, but appears to be a member of his royal court.

5. Even the Catholic Church has not escaped this cycle of popular folk tales and folk religion. Their 16th century document, the *Malleus Maleficarum*, written as a professional manual for witch and demon hunters, was based on popular anecdotes of the realm of the demonic. Recent church history shows an increase in the number of official church exorcists in the last 30 years, arguably a result of stories of popular culture and the concerns of popular religion.

6. Fundamentalist Christians often object to being called "religious" or calling their belief a "religion" because of the implication that there are other ways of believing and worshipping.

7. These Christians see classical early 20th century Pentecostalism as the first wave of the Spirit, the charismatic movement in mainline churches as the second, and themselves as the third.

Chapter 8

1. In a study of Christian gamers that examined several groups that identified as evangelical Christian as well as "hardcore" gamers, Shanny Luft concludes that "Christian gamers do not recoil from brutal depictions of violence in games" but that "when Christian gamers play mainstream, violent games, they often make choices within those games that avoid content they feel compromises their religious values, particularly having to do with vulgar language and sexually suggestive content" (160–162).

2. News-based computer games have been produced by multiple online sites. In May 2007, for example an Australian-based game developer produced a video game of the Virginia Tech massacre less than a month after its occurrence.

3. In an interview with *NBC Nightly News* on October 16, 2001, Graham made this statement: "We're not attacking Islam but Islam has attacked us. The God of Islam is not the same God. He's not the son of God of the Christian or Judeo-Christian faith. It's a different God, and I believe it [Islam] is a very evil and wicked religion."

4. This was a game which, incidentally, was planned before the second Iraq War, but was held back from release until after reaction to the September attacks had died down.

5. In fact, according to a Congressional Research Service report on the Department of Defense's use of military contractors, "As of March 2013, there were approximately 108,000 DOD contractor personnel in Afghanistan, representing 62 percent of the total force. Of this total, there were nearly 18,000 private security contractors, compared to 65,700 U.S. troops. Over the last six fiscal years, DOD obligations for contracts performed in the Iraq and Afghanistan areas of operation were approximately $160 billion and exceeded total contract obligations of any other U.S. federal" (Schwartz and Church).

6. To give just one example, after the Virginia Tech shooting in May 2007, the news reports focused on video games as possible motivation for Cho Seung Hui's rampage. When it turned out that Cho did not in fact play video games, the news media turned to popular music, which also did not serve as motivation.

7. Ubisoft, the developer of the *Tom Clancy: Splinter Cell Series* and other "strategic war" video game titles, has signed a contract with the CIA to produce spy-training video games with the "War on Terror" particularly in mind. A number of studies have been done to analyze the effect of violent video games on players' aggressiveness. However, none of the studies have shown a clear causal relationship between playing violent games and violent behavior.

8. *One Hundryd Merrie English Tayles*, 1478.

9. While there are some very vague references in both Revelation and Daniel about this feature of the apocalypse, most of the argument comes from the interpretative work of John Nelson Darby and Cyrus Scofield.

10. Now owned by Bethesda Softworks, the original game (*Fallout: A Post Nuclear Role Playing Game*) was an open world role-playing video game developed and published by Interplay Entertainment in 1997.

Works Cited

Adler, Amy. "Inverting the First Amendment." *University of Pennsylvania Law Review* 149.4 (2001): 921–1002.

Allen, John L. "Pope Likes Gibson's New Film, the Passion." *The National Catholic Reporter.* http://nationalcatholicreporter.org/update/bn121703.htm. 17 December 2003.

Allitt, Patrick. *Religion in America Since 1945: A History.* New York: Columbia University Press, 2003.

Anderson, Wendy Love. "Prophecy Girl and the Powers That Be: The Philosophy of Religion in the Buffyverse." South 212–226.

Angel. Television Series. Created by Joss Whedon. 1999–2004.

Angell, Roger. *The Summer Game.* New York: Viking, 1972.

Applying Anthropology: An Introductory Reader. Ed. Podelefsky, Aaron, and Peter J. Brown. Mountain View: Mayfield, 1997.

Apuzzo, Matt. "Blackwater Guards Found Guilty in 2007 Iraq Killings." *The New York Times.* 22 October 2014.

Arac, Jonathan, and University of Illinois at Chicago. Institute for the Humanities. *After Foucault: Humanistic Knowledge, Postmodern Challenges.* New Brunswick: Rutgers University Press, 1988.

Armstrong, Karen. *The Battle for God.* New York: Alfred A. Knopf, 2000.

Associated Press. "The Evolution of Matisyahu from Orthodox Jewish Rapper from NYC to Clean-Shaven Middle Eastern Influenced Songster Living in LA." *Daily Mail.* 16 July 2012.

Bacchiocchi, Samuele. "Mel Gibson's Film on the Passion of Christ." *Come2Jesus.* www.come2jesus.com.au/Melgibson.htm.

Badiou, Alain. *Being and Event.* Trans. Oliver Feltham. London: Continuum, 2005.

Baigent, Michael. *The Jesus Papers: Exposing the Greatest Cover-Up in History.* San Francisco: HarperSanFrancisco, 2006.

Baigent, Michael, Richard Leigh, and Henry Lincoln. *Holy Blood, Holy Grail.* New York: Delacorte, 2005.

Barton, Bruce. *The Man Nobody Knows.* New York: Collier, 1987.

Basham, Don. *Deliver Us from Evil.* Washington Depot, CT: Chosen, 1972.

Battlestar Galactica. Television Series. Created by Ronald D. Moore. 2004–9.

Baudrillard, Jean. *Simulations.* New York: Semiotexte, 1983.

Baxter, Karla (Connie Weber Menger). *My Saturnian Lover.* New York: Vantage, 1958.

Beal, Timothy K. *Religion and Its Monsters.* New York: Routledge, 2002.

_____. "Romancing the 'Code.'" *The Chronicle of Higher Education.* 9 June 2006, B14–5.

Beal, Timothy K., and Tod Linafelt. *Mel Gibson's Bible: Religion, Popular Culture, and the Passion of the Christ.* Chicago: University of Chicago Press, 2006.

Bedazzled. Film. Dir. Harold Ramis, 2000.

Ben-Ami, Joshua. "*South Park* and the Economy." Unpublished seminar paper.

Berkow, Ira. "Countering the Terms of Hatred." *The New York Times.* 24 April 2004: D1.

Bernstein, Richard J. *Radical Evil: A Philosophical Interrogation.* Cambridge, UK; Malden, MA: Polity, 2002.

Bignell, Jonathan. *An Introduction to Television Studies.* London; New York: Routledge, 2004.

Bishop, Kyle W. "Battling Monsters and Becoming Monstrous: Human Devolution in the *Walking Dead.*" *Levina and Diem—My T.,* 73–86.

Bloom, Harold. *The American Religion: The Emergence of the Post-Christian Nation.* New York: Riverhead, 2000.

Boyer, Paul S. *When Time Shall Be No More: Prophecy Belief in Modern American Culture.* Cambridge, MA: Belknap Press of Harvard University Press, 1992.

Braudy, Leo, and Marshall Cohen, eds. *Film Theory and Criticism: Introductory Readings.* New York: Oxford University Press, 1999.

Broaddus, Maurice. Review of *Buffy the Vampire Slayer.* 26 January 2004. www.HollywoodJesus.com.

Broussard, Chris. "Comments by 2 Knicks Called Anti-Semitic." *New York Times.* 21 April 2001: D4.

Brown, Dan. *The Da Vinci Code.* New York: Doubleday, 2004.

Brown, Raymond Edward. *The Death of the Messiah: From Gethsemane to the Grave: A Commentary on the Passion Narratives in the Four Gospels.* New York: Doubleday, 1994.

Buffy the Vampire Slayer. Television Series. Created by Joss Whedon. 1997–2003.

Bull, Malcolm, and Keith Lockhart. *Seeking a Sanctuary.* Bloomington: Indiana University Press, 2006.

Butler, Jon. *Awash in a Sea of Faith: Christianizing the American People.* Cambridge, MA: Harvard University Press, 1990.

Campbell, Heidi. *When Religion Meets New Media.* Longdon: Routledge, 2010.

Campbell, Heidi A., and Gregory Price Grieve. *Playing with Religion in Digital Games.* Bloomington: Indiana University Press, 2014.

Caputo, John D. *The Prayers and Tears of Jacques Derrida: Religion Without Religion.* Bloomington: Indiana University Press, 1997.

Caputo, John D., Mark Dooley, and Michael J. Scanlon, eds. *Questioning God.* Bloomington: Indiana University Press, 2001.

Card, Claudia. *The Atrocity Paradigm: A Theory of Evil.* New York: Oxford University Press, 2002.

Chatterjee, Pratap. "A Chilling New Post-Traumatic Stress Disorder: Why Drone Pilots Are Quitting in Record Numbers." *Salon.* 6 March 2015.

Chester, Gail, Julienne Dickey, and Campaign for Press and Broadcasting Freedom. *Feminism and Censorship: The Current Debate.* Garden City Park, NY: Prism, 1988.

Clark, Lynn Schofield. *From Angels to Aliens: Teenagers, the Media, and the Supernatural.* New York: Oxford University Press, 2003.

Cloud, David. "Mel Gibson's Film the *Passion of the Christ.*" *Fundamentalist Baptist Church Information Service.* www.wayoflife.org/fbns/melgibson-thepassion.html.

Cobb, Kelton. *The Blackwell Guide to Theology and Popular Culture.* Malden, MA: Blackwell, 2005.

Cohen, Jeffrey Jerome. *Monster Theory: Reading Culture.* Minneapolis: University of Minnesota Press, 1996.

Conkin, Paul Keith. *American Originals: Homemade Varieties of Christianity*. Chapel Hill: University of North Carolina Press, 1997.

Coover, Robert. *The Universal Baseball Association, Inc., J. Henry Waugh, Prop.* New York: Random House, 1968.

Coviello, Peter. "Is There God After Prince?" *Los Angeles Review of Books*. 22 April 2016.

Cox, Harvey Gallagher. *Fire from Heaven: The Rise of Pentecostal Spirituality and the Reshaping of Religion in the Twenty-First Century*. Reading, MA: Addison-Wesley, 1995.

Crapanzano, Vincent. *Serving the Word: Literalism in America from the Pulpit to the Bench*. New York: New Press/W.W. Norton, 2000.

Critical Studies in Television. www.criticalstudiesintelevision.com.

Crossan, John Dominic. *The Birth of Christianity: Discovering What Happened in the Years Immediately After the Execution of Jesus*. San Francisco: HarperSanFrancisco, 1998.

Daschke, Dereck, and W. Michael Ashcraft. *New Religious Movements: A Documentary Reader*. New York: New York University Press, 2005.

Davidson, Mark. "Is the Media to Blame for Child Sex Victims?" *USA Today Magazine* (Society for the Advancement of Education). September (1997).

Dawkins, Richard. *The God Delusion*. Boston: Houghton Mifflin, 2006.

DeLillo, Don. *Underworld*. New York: Scribner, 1997.

Dennett, Daniel Clement. *Breaking the Spell: Religion as a Natural Phenomenon*. New York: Viking, 2006.

Derrida, Jacques. "Faith and Knowledge: The Two Sources of 'Religion' at the Limits of Reason Alone." Derrida and Vattimo 1–78.

Derrida, Jacques, and Gianni Vattimo, eds. *Religion*. Stanford: Stanford University, 1996.

De Vries, Hent. "In Media Res: Global Religion, Public Spheres, and the Task of Contemporary Comparative Religious Studies." De Vries and Weber, 3–42.

_____. *Philosophy and the Turn to Religion*. Baltimore: Johns Hopkins University Press, 1999.

De Vries, Hent, and Samuel Weber. *Religion and Media*. Stanford, CA: Stanford University Press, 2001.

Dogma. Film. Dir. Kevin Smith. 1999.

Donadio, Rachel. "A Pope's Beatification Stirs Excitement and Dissension." *The New York Times*. 29 April 2009.

Duggan, Lisa. "Censorship in the Name of Feminism." *Feminism and Censorship: The Current Debate*. Eds. Gail Chester and Julienne Dickey. Garden City Park, NY: Prism, 1988.

Dunbar, Virgil, and Richard Bennett. "The 'Passion of Christ': Mel Gibson's Vivid Deception." Berenbeacon.com.

During, Simon. *Cultural Studies: A Critical Introduction*. London: Routledge, 2005.

Dworkin, Andrea. *Pornography: Men Possessing Women*. New York: E.P. Dutton, 1989.

Eagleton, Terry. *After Theory*. New York: Basic, 2003.

Eck, Diana L. *A New Religious America: How a "Christian Country" Has Become the World's Most Religiously Diverse Nation*. San Francisco: HarperSanFrancisco, 2001.

Edwards, Jonathan: "Sinners in the Hands of an Angry God." Warner 325–346.

Ehrman, Bart D. *Truth and Fiction in* The Da Vinci Code: *A Historian Reveals What We Really Know About Jesus, Mary Magdalene, and Constantine*. New York: Oxford University Press, 2004.

Elliot, Lisa. "Transcendental Television? A Discussion of Joan of Arcadia." *Journal of Media and Religion* 4.1: 1–12.

Erickson, Gregory. "'Religion Freaky' or a 'Bunch of Men Who Died?': The (A)Theology of *Buffy.*" *Slayage: The Online International Journal of Buffy Studies* (13/14), Fall 2004.

Falsani, Cathleen. "Prosperity Gospel." *Washington Post.* January 2010.

Farrer, Austin. *A Rebirth of Images: The Making of St. John's Apocalypse.* Boston: Beacon, reprinted 1963.

Faulkner, Anne Shaw. "Does Jazz Put the Sin in Syncopation?" Walser *Keeping Time* 32–36.

Feldman, Jamie. "Here's the Sad Truth About Calvin Klein's Outrage-Provoking Upskirt Ad." *Huffingtonpost.com* 17 May 2016.

Firstamendmentcenter.org. "Groups Decry Sex, Violence in Video Games." 28 November 2004

Fish, Stanley. "One University Under God?" *The Chronicle of Higher Education.* 7 January 2005.

_____. "Stepping on Jesus." *The New York Times.* 15 April 2013.

Fitzgerald, Francis. "Holy Toledo: Ohio's Gubernatorial Race Tests the Power of the Christian Right." *New Yorker* 2006: 27–32.

Fletcher, Angus. *Allegory: The Theory of a Symbolic Mode.* Ithaca, NY: Cornell University Press, 1964.

Folsom, Ed. *Walt Whitman's Native Representations.* Cambridge, England; New York: Cambridge University Press, 1994.

Forbes, Bruce David, and Jeffrey H. Mahan. *Religion and Popular Culture in America.* Rev. ed. Berkeley: University of California Press, 2005.

Foucault, Michel. *The Order of Things: An Archaeology of the Human Sciences.* New York: Vintage, 1973.

Fox, Richard W. *Jesus in America: Personal Savior, Cultural Hero, National Obsession.* San Francisco: HarperCollins, 2004.

Freccero, Carla. "Our Lady of MTV: Madonna's 'Like a Prayer.'" *Boundary* 19.2 (1992): 163–83.

Fredriksen, Paula. "No Pain, No Gain?" Beal and Linafelt 91–98.

French, Rose. "Classroom Yoga Exercises Prompt Parent Concerns in Cobb." *Atlanta Journal-Constitution.* 21 March 2016.

Freud, Sigmund. "The Uncanny." In *The Standard Edition of the Complete Psychological Works of Sigmund Freud.* London: Hogarth, 1955.

Frye, Northrop. *The Great Code: The Bible and Literature.* New York: Harcourt Brace Jovanovich, 1982.

Geertz, Clifford. *The Interpretation of Cultures: Selected Essays.* New York: Basic, 1973.

Giamatti, A. Bartlett, and Kenneth S. Robson. *A Great and Glorious Game: Baseball Writings of A. Bartlett Giamatti.* Chapel Hill, NC: Algonquin, 1998.

Giles, David. *Illusions of Immortality: A Psychology of Fame and Celebrity.* New York: St. Martin's, 1999.

Gilmour, Michael J. *Call Me the Seeker: Listening to Religion in Popular Music.* New York: Continuum, 2005.

Goldstein, Warren Jay. *Playing for Keeps: A History of Early Baseball.* Ithaca: Cornell University Press, 1989.

Goodlad, Lauren M. E., Lilya Kaganovsky, and Robert A. Rushing, eds. *Mad Men, Mad World: Sex, Politics, Style, and the 1960s.* Durham, NC: Duke University Press, 2013.

Gospel of Thomas. Trans. Thomas O. Lambdin. The Gnostic Society Library. The Nag Hammadi Library. www.gnosis.org.

Gottlieb, Anthony. "Christopher Hitchings Takes on God." *New Yorker.* 21 May 2007: 77–80.

Graeber, David. "Rebel Without a God." *In These Times.* 12 December 1998.

Graham, Billy. *Till Armageddon: A Perspective on Suffering.* Waco, TX: Word, 1981.

Graham, Elaine L. *Representations of the Post/Human: Monsters, Aliens, and Others in Popular Culture*. New Brunswick, NJ: Rutgers University Press, 2002.

Greeley, Andrew M. *God in Popular Culture*. Chicago: Thomas More, 1988.

_____. "Like a Catholic: Madonna's Challenge to Her Church." *Sacred Music of the Secular City: From Blues to Rap*. Durham, NC: Duke University Press, 1992. 244–249.

Green, Leslie. "Pornographies." *Journal of Political Philosophy* 8.1 (2000): 27–48.

Greenberg, David. "Nixon and the Jews. Again." www.Slate.com. 12 March 2002.

Griffin, Susan. *Pornography and Silence: Culture's Revenge Against Nature*. New York: Harper & Row, 1981.

Hall, David W. "The Holiness of God." www.apocalypsesoon.org/xfile-35.html.

Handelman, Susan A. *The Slayers of Moses: The Emergence of Rabbinic Interpretation in Modern Literary Theory*. Albany: State University of New York Press, 1982.

Harris, Sam. *The End of Faith: Religion, Terror, and the Future of Reason*. New York: W.W. Norton, 2004.

_____. *Letter to a Christian Nation*. New York: Knopf, 2006.

Hart, Kevin. "'Absolute Interruption': On Faith." Caputo, Dooley and Scanlon 186–208.

Hartman, Geoffrey H., and Sanford Budick. *Midrash and Literature*. New Haven, CT: Yale University Press, 1986.

Hatch, Nathan O. *The Democratization of American Christianity*. New Haven: Yale University Press, 1989.

Hayles, N. Katherine. *How We Think: Digital Media and Contemporary Technogenesis*. Chicago: University of Chicago Press, 2012.

Heartney, Eleanor. "Pornography." *Art Journal* 50.4, Censorship II (1991): 16–9.

Hedstrom, Matthew. "Why Millennials Are Leaving Religion and Embracing Spirituality." https://news.virginia.edu.

Hentoff, Nat. *Jazz Times* 12 (2004): 134.

Herberg, Will. *Protestant, Catholic, Jew: An Essay in American Religious Sociology*. Garden City, NY: Doubleday, 1955.

Hills, Matt. *Fan Cultures*. New York: Routledge, 2002.

Hoeckner, Berthold. *Programming the Absolute: Nineteenth-Century German Music and the Hermeneutics of the Moment*. Princeton, NJ: Princeton University Press, 2002.

Hoover, Stewart. *Religion in the Media Age*. New York: Routledge. 2006.

Hornaday, Ann. "The Rise of Christian Movies for the Rest of Us." *Washington Post*. 12 March 2016.

Hughes, Debbie. "Spiritual Warfare in the Third Wave Movement." www.vaxxine.com.

Hulsether, Mark D. "Like a Sermon: Popular Religion in Madonna Videos." Forbes and Mahan 75–97.

Hutchinson, Paul. *The New Leviathan*. Chicago, New York: Willett, Clark, 1946.

Institoris, Heinrich, and Jakob Sprenger. *The Malleus Maleficarum of Heinrich Kramer and James Sprenger*. New York: Dover, 1971.

Introvigne, Massino, Templeton Lecture in Harvard. www.cesnur.orgr.org/2001/buffy.

"Is God Dead?" *Time Magazine*. 8 April 1966.

Jackman, Jesse. "A Low Blow: Utah's New Anti-Pornography Law Hits Below the Belt." HuffPost Politics. 22 April 2016. www.huffingtonpost.com/jesse-jackman/utahs-new-antiporn-law.

James, William. *The Varieties of Religious Experience: A Study in Human Nature*. [1902] New Hyde Park, NY: University, 1963.

Jenkins, Henry. *Fans, Bloggers, and Gamers: Media Consumers in a Digital Age*. New York: New York University Press, 2006.

_____, Mizuko Ito, and Danah Boyd. *Participatory Culture in a Networked Era*. Cambridge: Polity Press, 2016.

Jenkins, Jerry. "Left Behind Video Game Controversy." Leftbehind.com.

Jindra, Michael. "*Star Trek* Fandom as a Religious Phenomenon." *Sociology of Religion* 55.1, Religious Experience (1994): 27–51.

Joan of Arcadia. Television Series. Created by Barbara Hall. 2003–2005.

Johnson, Daryl. *Right-Wing Resurgence: How a Domestic Terrorist Threat Is Being Ignored*. New York: Rowman & Littlefield, 2012.

Kahn, Ashley. *A Love Supreme: The Story of John Coltrane's Signature Album*. New York: Viking, 2002.

Kearney, Richard. "The God Who May Be." Caputo, Dooley, and Scanlon 153–185.

_____. *The God Who May Be: A Hermeneutics of Religion*. Bloomington: Indiana University Press, 2001.

_____. *Strangers, Gods, and Monsters: Interpreting Otherness*. London: New York: Routledge, 2003.

Kent, Steve L. *The Ultimate History of Video Games: From Pong to Pokémon and Beyond: The Story Behind the Craze That Touched Our Lives and Changed the World*. Roseville, CA: Prima, 2001.

Kimball, Roger. "Sex in the Twilight Zone: Catharine Mackinnon's Crusade." *New Criterion* 12.2 (1993): 11.

Kinsella, W. P. *Shoeless Joe*. Boston: Houghton Mifflin, 1982.

Konigsberg, Eric. "Marcus Camby Has Nobody to Play With." *The New York Times Magazine*. 22 April 2001, Sec. 6, p. 70.

Kuhns, William. *The Electronic Gospel: Religion and Media*. New York: Herder and Herder, 1969.

LaHaye, Tim, and Jenkins, Jerry B. *Left Behind: A Novel of the Earth's Last Days*. Wheaton: Tyndale House, 1995.

The Last Temptation of Christ. Film. Dir. Martin Scorcese, 1988.

"A Leading Figure in the New Apostolic Reformation." *NPR.org. Fresh Air*. 3 October 2011.

Left Behind Game Manual. Carol Stream, IL: Tyndale House, 2006.

Lemos, Robert. "Violent Video Games Under Fire." *Zdnet News*. 1 December 1998. http://news.zdnet.com.

Leo, John. "Selling the Woman-Child." *US News and World Report*. 6 May 1994.

Levina, Marina, and Bui Dien-My T. *Monster Culture in the 21st Century: A Reader*. New York: Bloomsbury Academic, 2013.

Lévinas, Emmanuel. *Ethics and Infinity*. Pittsburgh: Duquesne University Press, 1985.

Lewis, Tanya. "Virtual-Reality Tech Helps Treat PTSD in Soldiers." Livescience.com. 8 August 2014.

Lindsey, Hal. *The Late Great Planet Earth*. Grand Rapids: Zondervan, 1970.

Lipka, Micahael. "A Closer Look at America's Rapidly Growing Religious 'Nones.'" *Pew Research Center*. 13 May 2015.

Lippy, Charles H. *Being Religious, American Style: A History of Popular Religiosity in the United States*. Westport, CT: Greenwood, 1994.

Little Nicky. Film. Dir. Steven Brill, 2000.

Litweiler, Jim. "Marsalis Plays Coltrane, Minus Religious Fervor." *Chicago Sun-Times*. 30 January 2002.

Locklin, Reid B. "*Buffy the Vampire Slayer* and the Domestic Church: Re-Visioning Family and the Common Good." *Slayage: The Online International Journal of Buffy Studies* 6 (2002).

Luft, Shanny. "Hardcore Christian Gamers: How Religion Shapes Evangelical Play." Campbell and Grieve, 154–169.

Lunden, Ingrid. "2015 Ad Spend Rises to $187b, Digital Inches Closer to One Third of It." TechCrunch.com. 20 Jan 2015.

Luo, Michael. "Billy Graham Returns to Find Evangelical Force in New York." *The New York Times*. 21 June 2005: A1.

Lurker, Manfred. *Dictionary of Gods and Goddesses, Devils and Demons.* London: New York: Routledge, 1987.

Lyden, John, and Eric Michael Mazur. *Routledge Companion to Religion and Popular Culture.* London: Routledge, 2015.

Lynch, Gordon. "The Role of Popular Music in the Construction of Alternate Spiritual Identities and Ideologies." *Journal for the Scientific Study of Religion* 45.4 (2006): 481–8.

_____. *Understanding Theology and Popular Culture.* Malden, MA: Blackwell, 2005.

MacMullen, Ramsay. *Paganism in the Roman Empire.* New Haven: Yale University Press, 1981.

Mad Men. Television Series. Created by Matthew Weiner. 2007–15.

MAKD. 6–10 April 2004. www.soulfulspike.com.

Marrati, Paola. "The Catholicism of Cinema: Gilles Deleuze on Image and Belief." De Vries and Weber 227–240.

Martens, Paul. "Metallica and the God That Failed: An Unfinished Tragedy in Three Acts." Gilmour 95–114.

Marty, Martin A. *Modern American Religion, Volume 3: Under God, Indivisible, 1941–1960.* University of Chicago Press, 1999.

Marx, Leo. *The Machine in the Garden: Technology and the Pastoral Ideal in America.* New York: Oxford University Press, 1964.

Maudlin, M.G. "*Christianity Today* Talks to Frank Peretti." *Christianity Today* 33 (15 December 1989): 58–59.

Mazur, Michael Eric, and Kate McCarthy, eds. *God in the Details: American Religion in Popular Culture.* 2d ed. New York: Routledge, 2011.

_____. *God in the Details: American Religion in Popular Culture.* New York: Routledge, first ed., 2001.

McClary, Susan. "Living to Tell: Madonna's Resurrection of the Fleshly." *Genders* No. 7 2.29 (1990): 1–15.

McCormack, Shaun. "Violence in Video Games." Gamershellwww. www.gamershell.com/articles/876.html.

McCracken, Brett. "The Perils of 'Wannabe Cool' Christianity." *Wall Street Journal,* 13 August 2010.

McCutcheon, Russell. *Critics Not Caretakers: Redescribing the Public Study of Religion.* New York: State University of New York, 2001.

McDannell, Colleen. *Material Christianity: Religion and Popular Culture in America.* New Haven: Yale University Press, 1995.

McGimpsey, David. *Imagining Baseball: America's Pastime and Popular Culture.* Bloomington: Indiana University Press, 2000.

McGowan, Tod. "The Obsolescence of Mystery and the Accumulation of Waste in Don Delillo's *Underworld.*" *Critique: Studies in Contemporary Fiction* 46. 2 (January 2005).

McLaughlin, Thomas. *Street Smarts and Critical Theory: Listening to the Vernacular.* Madison: University of Wisconsin Press, 1996.

McMahan, Alison. "Immersion, Engagement, and Presence: A Method for Analyzing 3-D Video Games." Wolf and Perron 67–87.

McNair, Brian. *Mediated Sex: Pornography and Postmodern Culture.* New York: Arnold, 1996.

Medal of Honor: Warfighter Review. Commonsensemedia.com.

Menger, Howard. *From Outer Space to You.* Clarksburg, WV: Saucerian, 1959.

Metz, Christian. "From the *Imaginary Signifier.*" Braudy and Cohen 800–817.

Miles, Jack. "The Art of the *Passion.*" Beal and Linafelt 11–20.

_____. *God: A Biography.* New York: Alfred A. Knopf, 1995.

Miller, J. Hillis. "Theology and Logology in Victorian Literature." *Journal of the American Academy of Religion* 47.2 (1979): 303.

Mizruchi, Susan L. *Religion and Cultural Studies*. Princeton, NJ: Princeton University Press, 2001.

Moore, R. Laurence. *Selling God: American Religion in the Marketplace of Culture*. New York: Oxford University Press, 1994.

Moreman, Christopher. *Zombies Are Us: Essays on the Humanity of the Walking Dead*. Jefferson, NC: McFarland, 2011.

Moslener, Sara. "Don't Act Now! Selling Christian Abstinence in the Religious Marketplace." Mazur and McCarthy, 2d ed. 197–218.

Murphy, Edward F. *The Handbook for Spiritual Warfare*. Nashville, TN: T. Nelson, 1992.

Nancy, Jean-Luc. "The Deconstruction of Christianity." De Vries and Weber 112–130.

Neiman, Susan. *Evil in Modern Thought: An Alternative History of Philosophy*. Princeton, NJ: Princeton University Press, 2002.

Newman, Jay. *Religion vs. Television: Competitors in Cultural Context*. Westport, CT: Praeger, 1996.

Nietzsche, Friedrich Wilhelm. *The Birth of Tragedy*. New York: Oxford University Press, 2000.

Noah. Film. Directed by Darren Aronofsky. 2014.

Nussbaum, Martha C. "Rage and Reason." *New Republic* 217.6/7 (11 August 1997): 36–42.

Oh, God! Film. Dir. Carl Reiner, 1977.

Oh, God! Book II. Film. Dir. Gilbert Cates, 1980.

Once Upon a Time. Television Series. Created by Edward Kitsis and Adam Horowitz. 2011-present.

Opam, Kwami. "*True Blood*: Theme Music, Editing and Entrails." Unpublished seminar paper.

Orsi, Robert A. *The Madonna of 115th Street: Faith and Community in Italian Harlem, 1880–1950*. New Haven: Yale University Press, 1985.

Pagels, Elaine. *The Gnostic Gospels*. New York: Random House, 1979.

_____. *The Origin of Satan*. New York: Random House, 1995.

Pareles, Jon. "Prince, an Artist Who Defied Genre, Is Dead at 57." *The New York Times*. 21 April 2016.

Parkin, David J. *The Anthropology of Evil*. New York: Blackwell, 1985.

Parsley, Rod. *Silent No More*. Lake Mary, FL: Charisma House, 2005.

The Passion of the Christ. Film. Dir. Mel Gibson, 2004.

Peretti, Frank E. *This Present Darkness*. Westchester, IL: Crossway, 1986.

Peterson, Paul C. "Religion in the X-Files." *Journal of Media and Religion* 1.3: 181–96.

Pew Research Center: Religion and Public Life. "Religious Landscape Study." Pew Research Center, 2015.

Peyser, Marc. "God, Mammon, and 'Bibleman,'" *Newsweek*. 15 July 2001.

Phelan, Joseph. "The Look of Mel Gibson's *Passion*." www.artcyclopedia.com/feature-2004-04.

Pierson, David. "Unearthed Remains Found at an MTA Excavation Site Shed Light on a Time Rife with Anti–Chinese Bias." *Los Angeles Times*. 15 March 2006. A1

Pinn, Anthony B. *Noise and Spirit: The Religious and Spiritual Sensibilities of Rap Music*. New York: New York University Press, 2003.

Poniewozik, James. "Streaming TV Isn't Just a New Way to Watch. It's a New Genre." *The New York Times*. 16 December 2015.

Porter, Lewis. *John Coltrane: His Life and Music*. Ann Arbor: University of Michigan Press, 1997.

Powe, L. A. Scot. *American Broadcasting and the First Amendment*. Berkeley: University of California Press, 1987.

Pranger, Burcht. "Images of Iron: Ignatius of Loyola and Joyce." De Vries and Weber 182–197.

Primiano, Leonard Norman. "'I Wanna Do Bad Things With You': Fantasia on Themes of American Religion from the Title Sequence of HBO's *True Blood*." Mazur and McCarthy 2d ed. 41–61.

Pritchard, Andrea, et al. *Alien Discussions: Proceedings of the Abduction Study Conference.* Cambridge, MA: North Cambridge, 1994.

Prothero, Stephen. *American Jesus: How the Son of God Became a National Icon.* New York: Farrar, Straus and Giroux, 2003.

Rabin, Nathan. "Kanye." AV Club, 3 January 2013.

Radano, Ronald Michael. *New Musical Figurations: Anthony Braxton's Cultural Critique.* Chicago: University of Chicago Press, 1993.

Reitter, James. "Religion, Blasphemy, and Tradition." In Moreman. 100–111.

Riess, Jana. *What Would Buffy Do? The Vampire Slayer as Spiritual Guide.* San Francisco: Jossey-Bass, 2004.

Root, Dave. "An Introduction to Spiritual Warfare." *Christian Evangelism, Healing, and Teaching Resources.* 9 July 2005: www.layhands.com.

Russell, Bertrand. *A History of Western Philosophy.* [1945]. New York: Simon & Schuster, 1990.

Sagan, Carl. *The Demon-Haunted World: Science as a Candle in the Dark.* New York: Random House, 1995.

Said, Edward W. "Clash of Ignorance." *The Nation.* 22 October 2001.

_____. "Michel Foucault, 1926–1984." *After Foucault: Humanistic Knowledge, Postmodern Challenges.* Ed. Jonathan Arac. New Brunswick: Rutgers University Press, 1988. 1–12.

Sakal, Gregory J. "No Big Win: Themes of Sacrifice, Salvation and Redemption." South 239–252.

Salen, Katie, and Eric Zimmerman. *Rules of Play: Game Design Fundamentals.* Cambridge, MA: MIT Press, 2004.

Santella, Jim. "Review of Lincoln Center Jazz Orchestra's a *Love Supreme*." February 2005. www.Allaboutjazz.com.

Saul, Scott. *Freedom Is, Freedom Ain't: Jazz and the Making of the Sixties.* Cambridge, MA: Harvard University Press, 2003.

Schaberg, Jane. "Gibson's Mary Magdalene." Beal and Linafelt 69–80.

Schneidau, Herbert N. *Sacred Discontent: The Bible and Western Tradition.* Berkeley: University of California Press, 1977.

Scholem, Gershom Gerhard. *Major Trends in Jewish Mysticism.* Jerusalem: Schocken, 1941.

Schudson, Michael. *Advertising, the Uneasy Persuasion: Its Dubious Impact on American Society.* New York: Basic, 1984.

Schwab, Katharine. "The Rise of Buffy Studies." *The Atlantic.* 1 October 2015.

Schwartz, Moshe, and Jennifer Church. *Congressional Research Service.* "Department of Defense's Use of Contractors to Support Military Operations: Background, Analysis, and Issues for Congress." 17 May 2013.

Schwichtenberg, Cathy. *The Madonna Connection: Representational Politics, Subcultural Identities, and Cultural Theory.* Boulder: Westview, 1993.

Scofield, C. I. *The New Scofield Reference Bible: Holy Bible, Authorized King James Version, with Introductions, Annotations, Subject Chain References, and Such Word Changes in the Text as Will Help the Reader.* New York: Oxford University Press, 1967.

"A Series of Ads for Breast Enlargement Has Been Popping Up on NYC Subway Cars." Reddit.com.

Shakespeare, William. *Titus Andronicus*. In *The Riverside Shakespeare*. Boston: Houghton Mifflin, 1997. 1065–1100.

Sharlet, Jeff. "Soldiers of Christ: Inside America's Most Powerful Megachurch." *Harper's*. May 2005, 41–54.

Shore, Bradd. "Loading the Bases: How Our Tribe Projects Its Own Image into the National Pastime." Podelefsky and Brown 125–126.

Silberstein, Sandra. *War of Words: Language, Politics and 9/11*. New York: Routledge, 2002.

Simon, Merrill. *Jerry Falwell and the Jews*. Middle Village, NY: Jonathan David, 1984.

Skippy, R. "The Door Theologian of the Year." *The Door Magazine* 183 (September/October 2002). www.thedoormagazine.com.

Sloterdijk, Peter. *You Must Change Your Life*. Cambridge: Polity, 2013.

Smith, Joseph. "King Follett Sermon." Warner 584–599.

Smulo, John. "Spiritual Warfare Profiles of Satanism: Are They Misleading?" *Sacred Tribes: Journal of Christian Missions to New Religious Movement* 1.1 (Summer/Fall 2002).

South, James B. *Buffy the Vampire Slayer and Philosophy: Fear and Trembling in Sunnydale*. Chicago: Open Court, 2003.

South Park. Television Series. Created by Trey Parker and Matt Stone. 1997-present.

Star Trek. Television Series. Created by Gene Roddenberry. 1966–1969.

Strieber, Whitley. *Communion: A True Story*. New York: Beech Tree, 1987.

Sunday, Billy. "Food for a Hungry World." Warner 787–793.

Sylvan, Robin. *Traces of the Spirit: The Religious Dimensions of Popular Music*. New York: New York University Press, 2002.

Sweeney, Patrick. "8 Best Guns for the Zombie Apocalypse." *Guns and Ammo*. 15 November 2011.

Taves, Ann. *Fits, Trances, & Visions: Experiencing Religion and Explaining Experience from Wesley to James*. Princeton, NJ: Princeton University Press, 1999.

Taylor, Mark C. *About Religion: Economies of Faith in Virtual Culture*. Chicago: University of Chicago Press, 1999.

_____. *The Moment of Complexity: Emerging Network Culture*. Chicago: University of Chicago Press, 2001.

_____. *Nots*. Chicago: University of Chicago Press, 1993.

Tennant, Agnieszka. "Possessed or Obsessed?" *Christianity Today*. 3 September 2001.

True Blood. Television Series. Created by Alan Ball. 2008–2014.

Unger, Merrill Frederick. *What Demons Can Do to Saints*. Chicago: Moody, 1977.

Van Biema, David. "God vs. Science." *Time Magazine*. 13 November 2006.

Voltaire, Francois. *Candide*. ed. Robert M. Adams. New York: W.W. Norton, 1991.

Wagner, C. Peter. *Warfare Prayer: How to Seek God's Power and Protection in the Battle to Build His Kingdom*. Ventura, CA: Regal, 1992.

Wagner, Rachel. *Godwired: Religion, Ritual and Virtual Reality*. New York: Routledge, 2012.

The Walking Dead. Television Series. Created by Frank Darabont. 2010-present.

Walser, Robert. *Keeping Time: Readings in Jazz History*. New York: Oxford University Press, 1999.

_____. *Running with the Devil: Power, Gender, and Madness in Heavy Metal Music*. Hanover, NH: University Press of New England, 1993.

Ward, Geoffrey C., and Ken Burns. *Baseball: An Illustrated History*. New York: A.A. Knopf, 1994.

Ward, Graham. *The Postmodern God: A Theological Reader*. Los Angeles: Blackwell, 1997.

Ward, Priscilla. "White Beyoncé Haters Don't Get It: 'Formation' Isn't 'Race-Baiting'—but It Is Unapologetically About Race." Salon.com. 11 February 2016.

Warner, Michael, ed. *American Sermons: The Pilgrims to Martin Luther King, Jr.* New York: Library of America, 1999.

Warren, Rick. *The Purpose Driven Life.* Philadelphia, PA: Miniature, 2003.

Watson, April. "Madonna and Child II." From *A Capital Collection: Masterworks from the Corcoran Gallery of Art.* https://www.corcoran.org/collection/highlights.

Wax, Emily. "Hassidic Reggae-Rapper Matisyahu Shaves Beard." *Washington Post.* 12 December 2011.

Weinstein, Deena. *Heavy Metal: A Cultural Sociology.* New York: Lexington, 1991.

Westbrook, Deanne. *Ground Rules: Baseball and Myth.* Urbana and Chicago: University of Illinois Press, 1996.

"What Would Buffy Do?" *Arts and Faith.* 1 January 2007 www.artsandfaith.com.

Wilkinson, Alissa. "*Noah*: After a Flood of Reviews and Controversy, It's Finally Here. So Should You See It?" *Christianity Today.* 27 March 2014.

Williams, Peter W. *Popular Religion in America: Symbolic Change and the Modernization Process in Historical Perspective.* Urbana: University of Illinois Press, 1989.

Williams, Raymond. *Television: Technology and Cultural Form.* New York: Schocken, 1975.

Wills, Garry. *What Jesus Meant.* New York: Viking, 2006.

Wilson, A. N. *Jesus.* New York: W.W. Norton, 1992.

Winnie the Pooh and the Blustery Day. Film. Dir. Wolfgang Reitherman, 1968.

Winquist, Charles E. *Desiring Theology.* Chicago: University of Chicago Press, 1995.

Wolf, Mark J. P. *The Medium of the Video Game.* Austin: University of Texas Press, 2002.

Wolf, Mark J. P., and Bernard Perron. *The Video Game Theory Reader.* New York: Routledge, 2003.

Wright, Stuart A. *Armageddon in Waco: Critical Perspectives on the Branch Davidian Conflict.* Chicago: University of Chicago Press, 1995.

The X-Files. Television Series. Created by Chris Carter, 1993–2002.

Žižek, Slovoj. *An Introduction to Jacques Lacan Through Popular Culture.* Cambridge, MA: MIT Press, 1991.

_____. *On Belief.* New York: Routledge, 2001.

Žižek, Slavoj, and John Milbank. *The Monstrosity of Christ: Paradox or Dialectic?* Cambridge: MIT Press. 2009.

Zoerhof, Josh. "5 Reasons Why You Should Not Play Grand Theft Auto Five." Ridge Point Community Church. www.ridgepoint.org.

Index